Bishop Ignatius Kung Pin-Mei
May 31, 1951, Shanghai

Courtesy of the California Jesuit Archives, Santa Clara, California

IGNATIUS

The Life of Ignatius Cardinal Kung Pin-Mei

✠

Msgr. Stephen M. DiGiovanni, H.E.D.

2013

Printed in the United States of America.

ISBN: 978-1-4895-5066-8

CreateSpace, a DBA of On-Demand Publishing LLC, part of the Amazon group of companies.

Preface

There is a trio of confessors of the Faith who come to my mind, all named Ignatius. The first chronologically is Saint Ignatius of Antioch. A disciple of Saint Peter, he was dragged a prisoner across Asia Minor in the first years of the second century and thrown to the lions in Rome's Colosseum, imitating the earlier martyrdom of Saints Peter and Paul. He wrote a number of letters to the Church in various towns and cities as he passed nearby, and in one, his *Letter to the Smyrnaens*, this disciple of Saint Peter gave the Church founded by Christ the name *Catholic*. The true Church is not one founded by any government or interest group, offering salvation only to a few chosen. The true Church is that founded by Christ on the Apostles, and found everywhere, offering salvation to everyone.

The next is Saint Ignatius of Loyola, the Basque founder of the Society of Jesus, who did all "For the Greater Glory of God", bound by obedience to the Successor of Saint Peter.

Finally, we have Ignatius Kung Pin-Mei, a simple Chinese-born priest and first native-born Bishop of Shanghai, who led his people to bear witness to Christ in the world. For his unflinching loyalty to the Successor of Saint Peter, he endured more than thirty years imprisonment at the hands of the Chinese Communist government.

Throughout, Bishop Kung stood squarely to defend his position that he was a loyal citizen of his homeland. He loved China: he was born in China, grew up in China, and ministered as a priest and bishop in China; and it was in China that he hoped to die and be buried. His life of humble witness was not as an enemy of his homeland, but as a Chinese citizen who was also a faithful Roman Catholic, in communion with the Successor of Saint Peter. His is the same claim as that of other witnesses to Christ throughout the life of the Church: one can be both a faithful Catholic and a faithful citizen. This is his story.

In June, 2005, Bishop William E. Lori, then Bishop of Bridgeport, asked me to begin studying Cardinal Kung's life as well as the canonical documents concerning the process of beatification and canonization. This was in response to numerous requests Bishop Lori had received to begin the process of canonization. This small book is the fruit of my studies, which I offer for two reasons: that the witness and saintly heroism of Cardinal Kung be known, and that those who read this may be moved in charity to pray that the cause for canonization of Ignatius Kung Pin-Mei be opened.

My thanks go to the Cardinal Kung Foundation for the use of their archives. The staff of the Sterling Memorial Library at Yale University offered generous assistance. I am also very grateful to Joseph McAleer (Oxon) who has taken time from his own busy life and literary labors to work as the editor of this monograph.

i

Referring to the Communist persecution of the Catholic Church in Hungary, Bishop Fulton Sheen wrote in 1957, "The West has its Mindszenty, but the East has its Kung. God is glorified in His Saints." Please pray for the opening of his Cause of Canonization, that the third Ignatius may join the saintly ranks of the Church's earlier Confessors of the Faith.

And please pray for China.

– Msgr. Stephen M. DiGiovanni, H.E.D.

Basilica of Saint John the Evangelist
Stamford, Connecticut
June 8, 2013
Feast of the Immaculate Heart of Mary

Youth and Early Education

Ignatius Kung (Gong) Pin-Mei was born to Kung Xin Yuan (1871-1947) and Li Xian Yuing (1878-1958) on August 2, 1901 in Tangmuqiao Village, Chuansha County, Jiangsu Province, China.[1] He was the eldest of four children: two brothers, Kung HaiMei (1902-1951) and Kung SunMei (1910-1991) and one sister, Kung CuiBao (1905-1930). He was baptized soon after his birth in Our Lady of Lourdes Church in Tangmiqiao Village, Pudong, Shanghai, China.[2]

The family name, *Pin-Mei*, means "the character of a flower that blooms in the bitter winter." The Kung Pin-Mei Family is a venerable Catholic family, practicing the Faith for at least five generations at the time of Ignatius' birth.[3] The village was a Catholic village, and nearly everyone was a descendant of the Kung Family. His father's elderly sister, Martha, was a consecrated virgin, and presided over a small village school teaching classical Chinese and the Catholic Catechism. Aunt Martha also played a further role in Ignatius' religious education and spiritual formation. For example, each Saturday she would walk with Ignatius and his younger brother Vincent to their village parish church for confession. The Cardinal credited his vocation to the priesthood to the influence of his Aunt Martha.[4]

A story is told that when Ignatius was six or seven years old, his mother would give him and his siblings a small coin each Saturday, then she would put it away in a small box for safekeeping for them. One day, Ignatius wanted to purchase a small roll of twine so he could join his friends flying kites. His mother not being home, the boy decided to take one of his own coins his mother was safekeeping for him in her room. He fell, scattering the contents of the small box over the floor. When his family came in, they thought Ignatius was stealing money from his mother. Aunt Martha urged him to confess that he was stealing money from his mother as they walked to the parish church for their usual Saturday

---

[1] Bishop Kung's Appeal Letter, 1979: Appendix 12. There are a variety of spellings of the Cardinal's family name in the various contemporary texts used in this brief study: Kung, Gong, Kiong, to mention a few. For clarity sake, I will usually use *Kung* throughout, even in quotations of texts, even if other spellings were originally used.

[2] The parish Church of Our Lady of Lourdes is a large church, not typical of village churches. The church was seriously damaged during the Cultural Revolution. During the 1990's the church was renovated by the Patriotic Association Diocese of Shanghai, assisted by funds from the Archdiocese of New York, solicited by the Patriotic Association Bishop of Shanghai, Jin LuXian. The church is now one of the tourist sites in Shanghai.

[3] *Inside the Vatican*, "Ignatius Kung Pin-Mei, 'A Noble Son of China'", January 2001. Margaret Chu, a niece of Ignatius Kung, recalled that Kung's grandmother dedicated him to God when he was born, saying "I hope he can become a priest."

[4] *Soul Magazine, An Interview: Cardinal Ignatius Kung of Shanghai –The Persecution Continues in China*, July-August 1993, p. 19.

confession. But, Ignatius stood his ground that he would not confess the sin of stealing because he was not stealing his mother's money, he was simply taking his own money that his mother was holding in safekeeping for him. Despite his aunt's insistence, Ignatius continued to profess that he was innocent of the sin of stealing. Even as a young man, Ignatius had a clear sense of right and wrong, and would not yield under pressure to relinquish his innocence. Cardinal Kung related this story to his nephew, Joseph Kung, years later.

Ignatius' aunt also provided him at home with the equivalent of his first five years of primary school education. He continued his classical Chinese education at the village school, studying the Four Books (*The Great Learning*, *The Doctrine of the Mean*, *The Analects*, and *The Book of Mencius*), and the Five Classics (The Confucian Canon, comprising the *Book of Changes*, *The Book of Odes*, *The Book of History*, *The Book of Rites*, and *The Spring Annals* and *The Autumn Annals*). A Marist brother provided the young Ignatius with his instructions for his First Confession and First Holy Communion. He received the Sacrament of Confirmation at the customary age of eight or nine years. The precise dates of his reception of the sacraments are difficult to ascertain since all parish records have been destroyed.

When 12 years old, he attended Dayi Primary School, a Catholic school. After one year, he transferred to the Xuhui College (St. Ignatius High School) in Shanghai. [5] Part of this educational program was the memorization of the 300 Poems of the Tang Dynasty. [6]

The study of European languages was emphasized in the high school, especially French. A section of Shanghai was known as the French Settlement District, and French was an important language of business and politics in the city. Ignatius therefore studied French during his first year; then changed to the study of Latin, since he was seriously considering enrolling in the local seminary to study for the priesthood. As Cardinal Kung recalled years later, "I am grateful to both

---

[5] Bishop Ignatius Kung, May 1979, Appeal Document submitted to the Beijing People Supreme Court. This was written in prison, as he indicated in the first page, "I have been jailed for reform for 24 years and two months for the time being." The complete text in English translation can be found in Appendix 12, which also provides details of his early life and priestly ministry.

[6] Joseph Kung, "Information on Cardinal Kung", July 2, 2012. The Cardinal's prodigious memory allowed him to recite the poems even when 90 years old. Likewise, the pain of his long 32.5 year imprisonment in solitary confinement was lightened by his writing and reciting by heart the entire Ordinary and Canon of the Latin Tridentine Mass. When the guards confiscated his writings, he would start anew, if he laid his hands on some paper. He finally acquired a small note book [3" x 4"], in which he could write the entire Canon of the Mass. Three months prior to his release, Bishop Kung was sent to a military hospital, so he could recover his health prior to release. He succeeded in hiding the notebook in his clothing, which he finally brought with him to Stamford.

the Marists and the Jesuits who taught me the knowledge of God and inspired me to pursue the priesthood." [7]

Years earlier, as was the ancient Chinese custom, Ignatius was engaged to be married at a very young age. The arranged engagement was taken very seriously as a sign of the union of two families. However, as Ignatius' thoughts of the priesthood matured, he found it necessary to break off the engagement, which had been widely publicized. The girl's family was highly insulted, but Ignatius explained to the girl that he felt it to be God's will that he should become a priest. The young man told her that if he did not follow God's call, God would be displeased by his refusal, and, if his betrothed did not accept this, God might be displeased with her, as well. The girl's family continued to protest, accusing Ignatius of duplicity, using the priesthood as an excuse to break off the engagement.

Seminary Formation, Ordination, and Priestly Ministry

Following graduation from high school in 1920, Ignatius decided to pursue a priestly vocation and entered Xujiahui Seminary. The seminary was then administered by French Jesuit priests, in whose charge the Shanghai missions had been assigned by the Church's missionary Congregation *de Propaganda Fide*. His course of studies of philosophy, theology, and canon law, would have included the papal social teachings as part of the common intellectual fare offered in seminaries around the world.

His seminary studies were not without difficulty. In fact, as his course of studies concluded, some members of the faculty raised questions about Ignatius' suitability for ordination to the priesthood. Three charges were brought against the young man as the officials of the Diocese of Shanghai considered his petition for Holy Orders: the marriage engagement of his brother; his possession of an expensive camera; and his cigarette smoking.

The first charge concerning his life as a seminarian involved Ignatius' "interference" in his brother's engagement to be married. Ignatius explained that he was the eldest brother, with a responsibility to guide and protect his siblings. His family had arranged a marriage for his brother, as they had for Ignatius, when still a child. As his brother approached graduation, he decided against marrying a girl he neither knew nor loved. Ignatius intervened with the girl's family to explain his brother's situation, and the matter ended amicably. Ignatius respectfully

---

[7] *Soul Magazine, An Interview with Cardinal Kung*, p. 19.

pointed out to the seminary faculty that he was not interfering, but simply exercising his familial responsibility to help his brother in a difficult circumstance.

The second charge concerned Ignatius' possession of an expensive photographic camera, contrary to seminary rules concerning poverty and simplicity of life. Ignatius explained his brother had given it to him soon after his return to Shanghai after graduating from the Sorbonne in Paris. His brother had purchased a newer camera and decided to give the old one to Ignatius, who was very willing to give it back if the seminary faculty demanded.

The final charge concerned Ignatius' smoking of cigarettes during his two years of parish internship. While the rules prohibited seminarians from smoking while at the seminary, there were no rules concerning smoking at the parishes. His pastor had given him permission to smoke, so Ignatius had taken advantage of the permission.

Following the successful completion of his seminary studies and formation, Ignatius was ordained a priest on May 28, 1930.

Father Kung was assigned to the mission at Gaoqiao, Fenxian for various apostolic works from 1934-1936. He successively held the posts of headmaster and director at various primary and middle schools. These were Yaochan Primary School in the village called Nanqiao; ZhenXin Middle School and Guanqi Middle School, both in Songjiang. He then returned to Yaochan Primary School in Nanqiao, remaining until August 1937. He taught Latin at Guanqi in Songjiang, which was a newly founded Jesuit school serving as a preparatory school for Aurora University in Shanghai. [8] He was headmaster of Guanqi when the school was destroyed in the summer of 1937, following the opening of hostilities in the Sino-Japanese War, and the subsequent bombing of the main building and auditorium of the college during a Japanese air raid. [9]

In anticipation of the dangers of war, Father Kung evacuated the school, saving many student lives. It proved necessary to transport wounded civilians and military personnel by ambulance along with a corps of young doctors and medical students, some as young as 16 years of age, to the University of Aurora. There a military field hospital was set up, but lasted only a few months, when it was completely destroyed as a result of the Japanese bombardment. In the midst of the bombing, as walls of the hospital collapsed around him, Father Kung directed the workers in their efforts to rescue the wounded. Following the bombing, Father Kung was ordered to organize the moving of the wounded to the railroad station for transport to the Province of Chekiang. Father Kung and others worked

---

[8] Stamford July 7, 2012, e-mail from Joseph Kung to Monsignor DiGiovanni, Basilica of Saint John Archives. See also Appendix 12.

[9] n.p. n.d. Father George Germain, S.J. to Joseph Kung, p. 1, Cardinal Kung Foundation Archives. Father Germain was the Chancellor of the Diocese of Shanghai under Bishop Kung.

tirelessly to accomplish this, after which he returned with Father George Germain, S.J. to Shanghai.

Father Kung was immediately assigned as the headmaster of the Aurora College Preparatory School in Shanghai [Avenue Dubail], which assignment coincided with the Japanese military occupation of China until August 1945, where he continued to work until 1946. When he arrived in 1937, the Aurora College Preparatory School enrollment totaled only a few hundred students. By the end of his tenure in 1946, the number had risen to nearly 1,000 students. This was the fruit of Father Kung's administration, marked by clear rules of discipline, which transformed the school, so that it was renowned as one of the best in Shanghai. [10]

In 1946, Father Kung was transferred to his new post as headmaster of Gonzaga High School in Shanghai, and Pastor of Saint Louis Gonzaga Parish, where he remained until 1949. Two Jesuit priests who worked with Father Kung recalled his priestly ministry during these years in Shanghai:

> His work among the youth, before his elevation to the episcopate, had already revealed in him the qualities that the persecution would put into full light: perfect loyalty, candor, uprightness, and, at the same time, a great simplicity in his rapport with the world. In action, he was sure in his decisions with a strength of character far from common. In all circumstances, he would act with flexibility, but was never weak and would never tolerate prejudices. He was the enemy of those compromises that are shameful surrenders and concessions that so confuse people of good will in their relationships with the Communists.
>
> Steadfast without pretensions, his whole person breathed a simple and sweet goodness. He never put on airs; and he would do everything with a certain deliberation, the whole world sensing that it was with an exceptionally profound awareness of the gravity and responsibility of his work.
>
> Each day a hidden smile made him blush. When he couldn't help it, he would become playful and spirited, and he would never fail to be pleasantly mischievous. [11]

Following the Japanese occupation of Shanghai, China was in a pitiable state, as was most of Asia and Europe following the termination of hostilities during World War II. This was exacerbated by civil war, followed by the slow

---

[10] Ibid., p. 2.

[11] *Mission Bulletin*, Vol. VIII, January, 1956, No. 1, Jean Lefeuvre, S.J. and Yves Raguin, S.J., *La Geste de Mgr. Kiung et de Son Eglise*, p. 24.

armed progress of the Communist People's Liberation Army through the country. One result was an almost daily inflation of prices for commodities of daily life, especially from mid-1948 through the Communist takeover in 1949, when "the paper money literally became paper", with no value. During these months of hardship, because the school teaching staff and personnel were paid modest salaries, life was even more difficult.

> Father Kung persuaded some richer parents to pay the total annual tuition in a lump sum instead of monthly. He then used the money to purchase foreign currency. Each month he was able to pay the staff with the equivalent amount, taking the inflation into consideration without suffering the decrease of the money value. In this case, the staff were able to maintain a reasonable standard of living. [12]

Father George Germain, S.J., a co-worker with Father Kung, who later served as his Chancellor in the Diocese of Shanghai, recalled that

> A tireless worker, Father Kung gave his heart and soul to his work. His only recreation was half an hour each day devoted to Chinese gymnastics, which exercises he continued even after he became bishop. Because of these daily exercises, he was never seriously ill, even though he was not a robust man. [13]

During the years 1947-1949, Father Kung also served as a consultor of the Diocese of Shanghai, which was territorially large and administratively hampered by the erection of the Dioceses of Haimen and Nanjing, which had divided it in half. Because of the flourishing state of the Church in Shanghai, it was decided to divide the territory itself to form two new dioceses of Shanghai and Soochow, in the territory south of Yangtze River, and two new apostolic prefectures of Haizhou and Yanzhou north of the Yangtze River. By 1948, there were 3,276,282 Catholics in China, served by 2,676 Chinese and 3,015 foreign priests, 632 Chinese and 475 foreign religious brothers, 5,112 Chinese and 2, 351 foreign religious sisters, with 216 Catholic hospitals, 254 Catholic orphanages and 4,446 Catholics schools of various grades and levels. [14]

---

[12] Stamford, July 3, 2012, e-mail from Joseph Kung to Monsignor DiGiovanni, Basilica of Saint John Archives. Cardinal Kung's nephew recalled the words of a Mr. Wong who had been one of the school's teachers during this period, and who visited the Cardinal in Stamford, Connecticut.

[13] Fr. Germain to Joseph Kung, Cardinal Kung Archives, p. 2.

[14] Hubert Jedin, Konrad Repgen, John Dolan [eds], *The Church in the Modern Age*, New York, 1981, p. 754.

The First Native Son

On May 24, 1949, the People's Liberation Army entered Shanghai and, with only a few shots fired, "liberated" China's largest city. A few days later, on June 9, 1949, a native son, Father Ignatius Kung Pin-Mei, was appointed the first Bishop of Soochow.

Father Thomas Phillips, S.J., Rector of Christ the King Church, recalled the new bishop as "a gentle, charming and absolutely fearless man, in his early forties", when appointed.[15] Once the Communists assumed control, they issued daily regulations about every aspect of life. Fearful of governmental interference, the Apostolic Internuncio wanted to consecrate Father Kung as soon as possible after his appointment to the Diocese of Soochow. But Father Kung asked for a postponement. As Father Germain recalled years later,

> Father Kung was a rather modest person, who never thought he would become a bishop. He was rather upset when he learned he was to become a bishop and he prepared for his consecration by going on a thirty day retreat, at which time he studied the writings of St. Ignatius while at Xujiahui.[16]

Father Kung asked that the consecration be delayed until October 7th because as, Father Kung insisted, "without the help of Our Lady of the Rosary, I will not be able to serve as bishop under the Communist regime." [17] He was ordained a bishop on October 7, 1949, the Feast of Our Lady of the Rosary, by the Apostolic Internuncio to China, Archbishop Anthony Riberi, assisted by Bishops Simon Zhu Kai-min, S.J., and James Edward Walsh, M.M., in the Jesuit church of Saint Ignatius Loyola in Xujiahui.[18]

During the Mass, the new bishop spoke to those gathered. His remarks read like a catalogue of those priests who formed him in the Christian life, his priestly ministry, and, now for the episcopate. Many in the cathedral that day would share public humiliation, suffering and imprisonment, bearing witness to Christ and His Catholic Church with the young Bishop. He then called attention to the courage of the Holy Father, Pope Pius XII, who created the new Diocese of Soochow and named Father Kung its first bishop to continue preaching the Gospel in the very face of the Chinese Communist onslaught:

---

[15] Kurt Becker, *I met a Traveler, The Triumph of Father Phillips*, New York, 1958, p. 24.

[16] Fr. Germain to Joseph Kung, Cardinal Kung Archives, p. 2. Xujiahui was the town in which the Jesuit seminary was located.

[17] Stamford, August 25, 2012, Joseph Kung to Msgr. Stephen DiGiovanni, Basilica Archives.

[18] October 7, the Feast of the Holy Rosary, commemorated the Christian victory over Islamic forces at the naval Battle of Lepanto on October 7, 1571. The victory was termed miraculous and credited to Our Lady's intercession, as the Christian troops prayed the Rosary before and during the battle.

民國三十四年十一月七日

The Kung Pin-Mei Family, January 7, 1945

Back row, standing from left with scarf:
- Young Ji Guo (A nephew of the Cardinal).
- Kung Ming Rong (Baby held in her mother's arm. Niece of the Cardinal).
- Mrs. Kung Sun Mei (Sister-in-law of the Cardinal).
- Attorney Kung Sun Mei (Second younger brother of the Cardinal).
- Father Kung Pin Mei (later Bishop, then Cardinal Kung).
- Dr. Vincent Kung Hai Mei (First younger brother of the Cardinal).
- Mrs. Theresa Kung Hai Mei (Sister-in-law of the Cardinal. Joseph Kung's mother).
- Theresa Kung Ming Tso (A niece of the Cardinal. Joseph Kung's elder sister.)

Middle row, from left:
- Joseph Kung Ming Sun (Standing. A nephew of the Cardinal. Joseph Kung's brother).
- Margaret Kung Ming Ren (Standing. A niece of the Cardinal. Joseph Kung's sister).
- Mrs. Kung Xin Yuan (Sitting. Mother of the Cardinal. Joseph Kung's grandmother).
- Mr. Kung Xin Yuan (Sitting. Father of the Cardinal. Joseph Kung's grandfather).
- Mr. Li Ren Xin (Sitting. An uncle of the Cardinal).
- Joseph Kung Ming Chuan (Standing. A nephew of the Cardinal).

Front row: five children standing:
- Kung Ming Ai (A niece of the Cardinal).
- Kung Ming Wang (A nephew of the Cardinal).
- Margarita Kung Ming Xin (A niece of the Cardinal. Joseph Kung's sister).
- Michael Kung Ming Nee (A nephew of the Cardinal. Joseph Kung's brother).
- Peter Kung Ming Zhi (A nephew of the Cardinal. Joseph Kung's brother).

Courtesy of the Cardinal Kung Foundation

> I thank the Holy Father above all for his confidence in me. Better than anyone else, he knows our situation. Despite this, he has created a new diocese. Is this not a palpable proof of his paternal confidence? Yet, it is he who holds the rudder of this new ship, and, as if repeating Christ's order, "Put out into the deep", and I confidently respond, "At Your word, I will lower the nets." [19]

Knowing the situation, and aware of the dangers as the Communists grew in power, Bishop Kung was faced with important decisions immediately upon taking the reins of the new Diocese of Soochow:

> Did he have to collaborate with the regime, and along with that decision, would he have to enter into discussions with those civil authorities bent upon the destruction of the Church?
>
> The great merit of Monsignor Kung[20] was to lead the way by taking a conciliatory attitude in dialogue, while remaining uncompromising with respect to the fundamental principles of Christianity. Yet, he always understood that the goal of the Communists was never clearly or openly discussed, but couched in sneaky, self-protectionist terms. He never refused to dialogue by means of an intermediary. But he sought a peaceful co-existence of the Catholic Church with the Communists, hoping to find a middle ground that would permit Catholics to demonstrate their patriotism without adhering to atheistic Marxism. But the Communists were never able to admit such distinctions that would allow the possibility for Catholics to act without violating their consciences, and finally refused to deal with any group too faithful to their Church.
>
> Monsignor Kung wanted peace more than anything else, but he always refused to agree to public statements or unclear and troublesome statements, which could not be understood or justified except by petty phrases or subtle distinctions. In spite of all the good will he showed, he could never agree to the concessions demanded. This was not a lack of flexibility on the bishop's part; for him it was a question of the lack of clarity by the Communists, and about the needs of the souls in his care.[21]

---

[19] Bishop Kung's complete remarks can be found in Appendix 1.

[20] At this time Bishops were often addressed as "Monsignor."

[21] *Mission Bulletin*, Vol. VIII, January, 1956, No. 1, Lefeuvre and Raguin, op.cit., p. 26.

Bishop of Shanghai

On July 15, 1950, Bishop Kung was transferred to become the first Chinese Bishop of Shanghai and Apostolic Administrator of Soochow and Nanking. The Jesuits had administered Shanghai during the interregnum, and now turned over the reins of government to their new Bishop and to the Diocesan clergy.

Young and enthusiastic, the first native-born Bishop of Shanghai began his episcopal ministry in a whirlwind of activity: Masses, devotions, meetings, and all the other normal Episcopal administrative duties related to the governing of a diocese. Even during the periods of trial and active persecution, the Bishop continued to perform the usual episcopal duties, administering the sacraments, supporting priests and religious, and guiding his flock.

The consecration of the first native son as the ordinary of a new diocese, and his transfer as the first Chinese-born ordinary of the largest city in the country, was the latest in a series of developments of the Church in China: the first native-born Catholic bishops in China were ordained in 1926 by Pope Pius XI;[22] in 1939, the Congregation *de Propaganda Fide* issued new directives concerning Chinese rites in the Roman liturgy; by 1946, Pope Pius XII recognized the development of the Church in China by establishing the Chinese hierarchy with 20 ecclesiastical provinces, naming Archbishop Thomas Tien Ken-sin, SVD the first Chinese Cardinal, and raising Peking to a cardinalatial see; and on November 24, 1946, the Pope beatified 29 martyred Chinese priests, religious and laypersons who died during the Boxer Rebellion in 1900.

The Catholic Church in China had not merely survived the Japanese occupation of World War II, it was growing and experiencing a great spiritual renewal, beginning with the defeat and expulsion of Japanese military forces from China. The establishment of the Catholic Central Bureau and the growth of spiritual movements such as the Legion of Mary and catechetical groups on university campuses, both under the direction of the Jesuits, reached out into society to convert their countrymen. "They drew their greatest strength from the life of the Church, a true Christian resurgence, taking with it the entire [Chinese] society."[23]

The Church, therefore, was on a trajectory for battle with the growing Communist party.

---

[22] Bishops Aloysius Chen Guo-di, OFM, Odoric Cheng He-de, OFM, Joseph Hu Ruo-shan, CM, Melchior Sun De-zhen, CM, Philip Zhao Huai-yi, Simon Zhu Kai-min, S.J.

[23] Jean Lefeuvre, *Shanghai: Les Enfants dans la Ville*, Tournai 1962, p. 67. Lefeuvre was a Jesuit seminarian in Shanghai during these events.

Bishop Ignatius Kung's first blessing following his episcopal blessing,
St. Ignatius Cathedral, Shanghai, October 7, 1949

At right, Bishop Ignatius Kung,
the first native Bishop of Shanghai, August 13, 1950.

上海龔品梅

龔品梅天主榮任上海教區
首任國籍主教紀念
一九五〇年八月十五日

These were dangerous times, and the Communist government quickly began expelling foreign missionaries, especially foreign-born Catholic priests, religious brothers and religious sisters. Any who remained were incarcerated, as were many native clergy. Bishop Kung warned his priests at a retreat,

> You must not have any more illusions about our situation. . . You have to face prison and death head on. This is your destiny. It was prepared for you because Almighty God loves you. What is there to be afraid of?" [24]

The government crackdown on the Catholic Church was more virulent than against any other religious institution. The guiding government principle was the same in their relationship with all religions: the destruction of all religious institutions, but the methods varied. Eventually, the government planned to destroy all religion by subjecting them to state control. Because the Catholic Church was the most highly organized of "foreign" religious institutions, and because it was structurally dependent upon a foreign "ruler", the pope, it was targeted more viciously than any others. It was also the largest Christian religion with more than 3,000,000 Catholics throughout the country.

The Catholic Church and Communism

The Chinese Communist Party knew exactly the stance the Catholic Church would take in its regard. There was a century-long history of papal condemnations of Communism by the time the Communists were victorious in China, beginning with Blessed Pope Pius IX in 1846, who wrote,

> To this goal also tends the unspeakable doctrine of Communism, as it is called, a doctrine most opposed to the very natural law. For if this doctrine were accepted, the complete destruction of everyone's laws, government, property, and even of human society itself would follow. [25]

He continued in more heated terms just three years later:

> The final goal shared by these teachings, whether of Communism or Socialism, even if approached differently, is to excite by continuous disturbances workers and others, especially those of the lower class, whom they have deceived by their lies and deluded by the promise of a happier condition. They are preparing them for plundering, stealing, and usurpation first the Church's and then everyone's

---

[24] *America*, July 29, 1995, George M. Anderson, S.J., *Witnessing for the Faith in China's Prisons*, p. 17.
[25] Blessed Pope Pius IX: *Qui Pluribus*, 16, November 9, 1846; *Quanta Cura*, 4, December 8, 1846.

property. After this they will profane all law, human and divine, to destroy divine worship and to subvert the entire ordering of civil societies. [26]

Pope Leo XIII continued to condemn socialism and Communism in two encyclicals, the first in 1878, specifically about the dangers of socialism. [27]

It was Pope Pius XI who provided the clearest and most stringent condemnation of Communism prior to the Communist takeover in China. His encyclical letter *Casti Connubii* on Christian marriage of December 31, 1930 referenced the works by Pope Leo XIII, reminding the world that Communism was a threat even to the family. But, it was in *Quadragesimo Anno* of May 15, 1931, written on the fortieth anniversary of Pope Leo XIII's landmark encyclical *Rerum Novarum* on capital and labor, that provided the most complete condemnation to date:

> Communism teaches and seeks two objectives: unrelenting class warfare and absolute extermination of private ownership. Not secretly or by hidden methods does it do this, but publicly, openly, and by employing every and all means, even the most violent. To achieve these objectives there is nothing which it does not dare, nothing for which it has respect or reverence; and when it has come to power, it is incredible and portent-like in its cruelty and inhumanity. The horrible slaughter and destruction through which it has laid waste vast regions of eastern Europe and Asia are the evidence; how much an enemy and how openly hostile it is to Holy Church and to God Himself is, alas, too well proved by facts and fully known to all. Although We, therefore, deem it superfluous to warn upright and faithful children of the Church regarding the impious and iniquitous character of Communism, yet We cannot without deep sorrow contemplate the heedlessness of those who apparently make light of these impending dangers, and with sluggish inertia allow the widespread propagation of doctrine which seeks by violence and slaughter to destroy society altogether. All the more gravely to be condemned is the folly of those who neglect to remove or change the conditions that inflame the minds of peoples, and pave the way for the overthrow and destruction of society. [28]

One year later, he continued his alarm to the world about Communism as the enemy of religion:

---

[26] Blessed Pope Pius IX *Nostis et Nobiscum*, 18, December 8, 1849.

[27] Pope Leo XIII *Quod Apostolici Muneris*, December 28, 1878; *Diuturnum*, 23, June 29, 1881.

[28] Pope Pius XI, *Quadragesimo Anno*, 112, May 15, 1931.

Furthermore—and this may be called the most perilous of all these evils—the enemies of all order, whether they be called Communists or by some other name, exaggerating the very grave straits of the economic crisis, in this great perturbation of morals, with extreme audacity, direct all their efforts to one end, seeking to cast away every bridle from their necks, and breaking the bonds of all law both human and divine, wage an atrocious war against all religion and against God himself; in this it is their purpose to uproot utterly all knowledge and sense of religion from the minds of men, even from the tenderest age, for they know well that if once the Divine law and knowledge were blotted out from the minds of men there would now be nothing that they could not arrogate to themselves. And thus we now see with our own eyes—what we have not read of as happening anywhere before—impious men, agitated by unspeakable fury, shamelessly lifting up a banner against God and against all religion throughout the whole world.[29]

On March 19, 1937 Pius XI issued *Divini Redemptoris*, an encyclical on atheistic Communism, which developed the ideas first mentioned in his *Caritate Christi compulsi*. In this work, the Holy Father described the methodology already proven effective by Russian Communism, which would be employed in China less than twenty years after its publication:

In the beginning Communism showed itself for what it was in all its perversity; but very soon it realized that it was thus alienating the people. It has therefore changed its tactics, and strives to entice the multitudes by trickery of various forms, hiding its real designs behind ideas that in themselves are good and attractive. Thus, aware of the universal desire for peace, the leaders of Communism pretend to be the most zealous promoters and propagandists in the movement for world amity. Yet at the same time they stir up a class-warfare that causes rivers of blood to flow, and, realizing that their system offers no internal guarantee of peace, they have recourse to unlimited armaments. Under various names that do not suggest Communism, they establish organizations and periodicals with the sole purpose of carrying their ideals into quarters otherwise inaccessible. They try perfidiously to worm their way even into professedly Catholic and religious organizations. Again, without receding an inch from their subversive principles, they invite Catholics to collaborate with them in the realm of so-called humanitarianism and charity; and at times even make proposals that

---

[29] Pope Pius XI, *Caritate Christi Compulsi*, 4, May 3, 1932. This is his encyclical on the Sacred Heart of Jesus.

are in perfect harmony with the Christian spirit and the doctrine of the Church. Elsewhere they carry their hypocrisy so far as to encourage the belief that Communism, in countries where faith and culture are more strongly entrenched, will assume another and much milder form. It will not interfere with the practice of religion. It will respect liberty of conscience. There are some even who refer to certain changes recently introduced into soviet legislation as a proof that Communism is about to abandon its program of war against God. [30]

In one of his most important works, Pope Pius XII penned a strongly worded warning to the world about Communism, issued less than two months before Father Ignatius Kung was ordained a bishop on October 7, 1949. The Pope wrote:

> If anyone examines the state of affairs outside the Christian fold, he will easily discover the principal trends that not a few learned men are following. Some . . . support the monistic and pantheistic opinion that the world is in continued evolution. Communists gladly subscribed to this opinion so that, when the souls of men have been deprived of every idea of a personal God, they may the more efficaciously defend and propagate their dialectical materialism. [31]

Even on the more popular level, the 1917 apparitions of the Blessed Mother at Fatima, Portugal provided evidence for Catholics that Communism was a scourge to all humankind and a threat to God-fearing people everywhere. And the Communists in China as elsewhere fully understood this fierce opposition of the Catholic Church to the party's progress. Another popular note in Catholic culture in China was the memory of Chinese government martyrdom of Catholics during the Boxer Rebellion at the turn of the twentieth century, still living memory in the post-war years.

The Church in China was acutely aware of the threat to its Chinese missions and institutions, even before the Chinese Communists came to power. Bishop James E. Walsh wrote his Maryknoll superiors in late 1948,

> It is possible to live and work under the Commies for a time, even though it is certain that they will scotch or kill us in the end (that is, once their power is in a place is really established and consolidated).

---

[30] Pope Pius XI, *Divini Redemptoris*, 57, March 19, 1937. The full Encyclical can be read in Appendix 2. Pope Pius XI issued numerous papal statements and encyclicals condemning the various government sponsored persecutions of the Church at this time in the Soviet Union, Mexico, and Spain. In a few years, he would likewise be the only world voice condemning Hitler and Mussolini as they began their persecutions of the Church, of the Jews, and of other groups and institutions.
[31] Pope Pius XII, *Humani Generis*, 5, August 12, 1950.

. . . Nobody has any illusions about Red determination to eliminate all religion. [32]

Chinese Communism and the Catholic Church

Knowing the difficulties faced in attempts to eradicate religious life faced by the Communist Party in Russia following the 1917 revolution, the Chinese Communist Party decided to exercise patience. On September 29, 1949, the Feast of the Archangels, the Communist Party put into effect its Common Program during the First Plenary Session of the Chinese People's Political Consultative Conference.[33] The document was worded to reassure all groups of Chinese that they had a united interest, represented and defended by the Communist Party. The violent intention and program prepared by the party that would remake China is neither mentioned nor hinted at in the Common Program. The Church might feel secure by the reassurance of freedoms for legitimate religious institutions, yet the party's insistence upon its sole authority to define legitimacy gave it unlimited powers, which the Church would soon feel.

The most immediate results of the implementation of this program, specifically regarding the Catholic Church, would be the party's religious policy, which included the closure of churches and brutal treatment of priests throughout China; exceptionally heavy taxation of Catholic Church property; the takeover of all educational institutions; and the formation of the young. The policy against foreigners and the Catholic Church became more intensely applied after June 25, 1950, when North Korean troops crossed the 38th parallel into South Korea, and even following the entry of more than 300,000 Chinese across the border to assist North Korea during the first weeks of October. Soon after, the government established the *Resist America, Aid Korea* movement, giving further emphasis to the potential dangers of foreigners in China, especially Americans and French, now at war with China's ally, Korea. The bulk of the Catholic foreign missionaries came from France and the United States. Now their efforts became increasingly suspect. They were labeled "imperialists", wrapped in a cloak of religion, and public government-backed demonstrations against them and the pope became more common and virulent. The government demanded a choice be made by Chinese Catholics: loyalty to the nation or to the foreign-based Catholic Church. Chinese could not be Catholics.

---

[32] Shanghai, November 22, 1948, Bishop James E. Walsh to Father General, MMA, Walsh Papers, Cardinal Kung Archives.
[33] Mariani, Paul, *Church Militant, Bishop Kung and Catholic Resistance in Communist Shanghai*, Cambridge, MA, 2011, p 31ff.

All three aspects of party policy would come to be defined by the formula of "The Three-Self Movement", as revealed in a secret government document, *Instructions on Questions Concerning Catholic and Protestant Churches*, drawn up in Shanghai as guidelines that summer. It gives a clear picture of the Catholic Church, with a membership of 3,000,000 throughout China, ministered by 12,000 priests, and the Protestant groups, with a membership of 700,000 persons. The document begins, "Marxists are absolute atheists. We believe that religion is an impediment to the people's awakening." [34] Patriotism would be the key to slowly build confidence and trust among Chinese Catholics, without mentioning the universal Catholic Church. "We will lead and support patriots within the church and we will unite the majority of the believers to fight against the minority who are linking up with imperialists", as stated in the *Instructions*. Once the majority of Chinese Catholics had been won over, then could the party rebuild a Chinese church, based upon self-governing, self-propagating and self-financing of a purely Chinese church, fully controlled by and at the service of the Chinese Communist Party, freed from foreign control, personnel or financing.

Many Protestant groups eventually signed on, with some resistance by Evangelical groups. But the authors of the *Instructions* knew there would be difficulties with one specific religious institution in China:

> But in the powerful Catholic Church now we do not have such a movement [the Three-Self Movement]. We hope that the local government will pay attention to the patriotic Catholics and unite them at a proper time to launch such a movement." [35]

Bishop Kung's Plan: The First Pastoral Letter

The appointment by the Holy Father of the first Chinese Bishop of Soochow took some of the sting from the Communist charge that the Catholic Church was a foreign institution. Now, the response of the Church in China was formulated by Bishop Kung with his clergy, and with the Jesuits, both native-born and foreign.

The Bishop outlined this in his first pastoral letter barely two months after his episcopal consecration and installation as the first native-born Bishop of Soochow.[36] However, as Bishop of China's newest diocese, and later when transferred to be the Bishop of China's largest city, Shanghai, and Apostolic Administrator of Soochow and Nanking, Bishop Kung "was intimidating to the

---

[34] Quoted in Mariani, *Church Militant*, p. 39.
[35] Ibid., p. 42.
[36] Bishop Kung's Pastoral Letter of October 7, 1950 can be found in Appendix 3.

Communists, and he knew that his position could protect him only for a time." [37] His policy was one of conciliation with the government on indifferent matters, but of refusal to compromise on the essential tenets and principles of the Catholic faith and practice. [38]

> His clear attitude towards the communists was decisive. He never spoke of anything other than that the fidelity of the Church of Shanghai was the sum total and fruit of thousands of other fidelities: the fidelity of all the Chinese priests, the fidelity of nearly all Chinese Christians, of school children and college students, the fidelity of the missionaries, the fidelity of all the religious, both Chinese and foreign. By a special providence, God has given to all a pastor who never failed them. [39]

He first worked to unite the clergy by seeking the cooperation of both regular and secular priests. The other points of emphasis were the spiritual formation of the Catholic youth, and the establishment of the Legion of Mary for the spiritual formation of Catholic families. He entrusted various aspects of his program to prepare Shanghai's Catholics for the upcoming battle to various religious orders best equipped to carry them out.

In his first pastoral letter, Bishop Kung began by thanking all the clergy and Catholic faithful for their strong faith and devotion to the Church. He then called all Catholics to remember the sacrifices of earlier generations of priests, religious sisters and brothers, and lay Catholics:

> We take in hand today the work that cost so much labor. Crushing is our responsibility. Our duty, which is also yours, my very dear Brethren, is to never let perish that which actually constitutes the form of the Church in our diocese, of the works and methods for which She pursues the goal of evangelization. We would consider this to be a grave failure. We would consider as a failure no less grave to leave all these works without progress, simply maintaining them as they are. Without a doubt, the task is arduous, especially under the present circumstances. Still, unity provides us with the necessary strength: with the Grace of God, we can accomplish this by the intimate collaboration of the faithful laity and the clergy. [40]

---

[37] *Mission Bulletin*, Vol. VIII, January, 1956, No. 1, Jean Lefeuvre, S.J. and Yves Raguin, S.J., *La Geste de Mgr. Kiung et de Son Eglise*, p. 25.
[38] *America*, August 11, 1956, Joseph M. C. Kung, *God Help China!*, p. 440.
[39] *Mission Bulletin*, Vol. VIII, January, 1956, No. 1, Lefeuvre and Raguin, op.cit., p. 25.
[40] *China Missionary Bulletin*, Vol. III (IV), February 1951, No. 2, p. 98.

The result was a unified clergy and faithful:

> All had one heart and one soul, without distinction of race or religious habit. So, never could the communists discover anyone with whom they spoke who was in opposition or in disagreement with Monsignor Kung. They could never find dissidents, or very few, so they began personal attacks on the bishop himself. The whole Church of Shanghai was with him. [41]

The Bishop manifested a self-assured firmness based on the benevolence he felt for his flock. Any concession that he might make with the Communist regime was made only if he was assured it would not be harmful to the Church.

> If he refused [to agree with the Communists] it was the entire Church of Shanghai which, with one voice and one gesture expressed its relationship with its leader. It was a time when the Holy Spirit spoke in the hearts of each of the faithful. One had to live in Shanghai during those great years to understand the power of the breath of the Holy Spirit and the light and energy born of that intimate union of the faithful and clergy with their pastor. [42]

Father Thomas Phillips, S.J., Rector of Christ the King Church in Shanghai, proposed that the Chinese priests begin a preaching series in each parish, which would teach the basics of the faith, while strengthening the devotional life of the Catholics throughout Shanghai. Bishop Kung agreed, giving his permission that nightly Benediction of the Most Blessed Sacrament conclude each evening session. Thousands of Catholics attended these sessions, to the frustration of the Communist officials, who sent their own people to man trucks with loudspeakers outside each church, verbally abusing those who entered in an attempt to dissuade them from participating, but without effect. [43]

The youth would be formed by reviving the Marian Sodalities, first established by Jesuit missionaries in the sixteenth century as a means to popularize the *Spiritual Exercises* of Saint Ignatius Loyola. Not only would membership in the sodalities strengthen high school and university age Catholics, they would also be training grounds for young adult Catholics to defend and propagate the Catholic faith, in the very sight of the Communist onslaught.

The Legion of Mary had begun in Ireland on September 7, 1921, the eve of the Feast of the Nativity of Mary, and was introduced in China by an Irish Columban missionary priest, Father Aedan McGrath, in 1937. When Archbishop Anthony Riberi was assigned as Internuncio to China in 1946, the Legion received

---

[41] *Mission Bulletin*, Vol. VIII, January, 1956, No. 1, Lefeuvre and Raguin, *La Geste*, p. 25-26.
[42] Ibid., p. 26.
[43] Becker, *I Met a Traveler*, p. 27-31.

his energetic support and thrived from 1948 through 1951. In China, the mass arrests of Catholic clergy and laity, including Bishop Kung, took place on the same Feast of Our Lady in 1955. Because of this, the Feast held immense significance among the Catholics of Shanghai as the Communist program to destroy the Catholic Church intensified during the subsequent decades. The heart of the Legion is fervent devotion to Our Lady, as a means to come closer to her Divine Son, and to further His saving work. Home visitations, weekly spiritual meetings and an active apostolate are the hallmarks of the Legion.

Archbishop Riberi asked Father McGrath to expand the Legion, and he found his greatest successes at both Aurora Middle School and Aurora University, the heart of the Legion in Shanghai. As the Communist pressure and restrictions of the Church increased, so did the fervent response by the Catholics in Shanghai, and especially by the Legion and Sodality members. As one Legion member recalled, all Catholic China "looked to Shanghai and Shanghai looked to Aurora [University]". [44]

One danger was the obvious non-Chinese origin of the Legion of Mary, the very many foreign-born Catholic priests and religious, including Father McGrath and the Papal Internuncio, who were seen as holding political allegiance to a foreign ruler, the pope. A new native-born Jesuit leadership team was formed to meld the work of the Legion and the Sodalities. Led by Father Beda Chang, S.J., it began offering retreats and weekly catechism study groups for Shanghai's Catholic youth in 1950 with great effect, just as the Chinese Communist Party was working to form the hearts and minds of Chinese youths throughout the country.

The Catholic Students

The Catholic student catechism groups and Legion of Mary formed at Aurora University in Shanghai, studying in *la Faculte des Lettres* in the summer of 1950, were particularly determined and dedicated. They took it upon themselves to pursue one goal: the growth of the Church in China. As threats from the Communists grew, so, too did their dedication. They were not public in their profession of faith, but simply accepted the reality of the danger they were in as believing Catholics in Communist China. They made four promises: each morning, before God, they were willing to accept imprisonment and death; to renounce all relationships for the time being in order to consecrate themselves to the defense of the Church; to adopt a fixed program of spiritual life; and to accept whatever mission might prove useful to the Church, regardless of the danger. [45]

---

[44] Philomena Hsieh, *The Bright Cloud*, Taipei, 2003, p. 32.
[45] Lefeuvre, *Shanghai*, p. 70.

The movement received the blessing and support of Bishop Kung, who "strongly believed that the Catholic youth were the hope and future of the Church". [46] During a rally at Saint Ignatius College on December 8, 1950, hundreds of Catholic students gathered to greet their new bishop. Speaking in the name of all, one student told Bishop Kung that they had been disappointed when he had been named to the Diocese of Soochow. They prayed that God might send him to Shanghai, because "he is one of us", having taught many at Aurora University and at the College of Saint Ignatius and the College of Saint Louis Gonzaga. Now, they expressed their joy that their prayers had been answered:

> When we cried out in our adversity, and we were in need of that balm that strengthens, it is our bishop who will supply it. It is with our bishop that we will find the strength. . .That the Diocese of Shanghai, under the direction of Your Excellency, joyously marches toward our glorious destiny.

Bishop Kung responded, telling the young Catholics of Shanghai,

> We have no need for any Three Self-Movement, because we do not govern ourselves.

> God has entrusted you to my care so that I might guide you. But, in the same way, He has entrusted me to you so that you might sustain me. We all advance together toward the heights of holiness, but our road will not be easy. . . we need strength. One might say to me that I am the one who will give the balm that strengthens. That is not absolutely correct. He who gives it is Jesus. Continuously He pours upon us the balm of His grace. I am but one channel by which that beneficent balm passes coming to you. And the channel that I am, with your help, will never break. Whoever comes needs that balm.

And, turning to the Crucifix, he continued,

> Because I have the responsibility to guide the great Diocese of Shanghai, because the Lord Jesus Himself placed this upon my shoulders, I vow to exhaust all my strength to fulfill my duty. I wish that you, with all your strength, might sustain me. [47]

---

[46] Ibid., p. 400.
[47] Jean Lefeuvre, *Shanghai*, p. 70-71.

Bishop Kung and the Jesuit Ordination Class of May 31, 1951 in Shanghai.

Front row. Left to right:

- [unidentified priest]
- Bishop Kung
- Father Fernand Lacretelle, S.J., Superior of the Jesuit Mission
- Father Charles McCarthy, S.J., Rector and Dean of the theologate at the seminary in Zikawei, Shanghai.

Courtesy of the California Jesuit Archives, Santa Clara, California.

Clarifying Positions

On January 17, 1951, Zhou Enlai, the Premier of the People's Republic of China, met with representatives of the Catholic community, trying to calm their fears that the government might attempt to destroy the Catholic Church in China. He told those gathered that the government understood that Catholics needed "to adhere to Rome in spiritual matters." [48] Likewise, the restrictions on the Church throughout the country were the result of agrarian reform, and religious liberty would be restored once those reforms were realized. Zhou Enlai's soothing comments received great press. But their sincerity was put into question by an article published in a government periodical simultaneously accusing the pope of being "the fascist valet of the Americans." [49] It was clearly established that The Three-Self Movement of the government was to be imposed on the Church, "under the direction of President Mao Tse-Tung", not under the direction of the pope or the Chinese Catholic bishops. [50]

In February, 1951, the Chinese Catholic bishops made public a letter clarifying the Catholic position concerning the government's *Three-Self Movement*, stating that no government could claim to respect the people's rights to freedom of religion by marginalizing the Catholic Church. [51] To clarify and further publicize the authentic Catholic position, the Chinese language secretary to Archbishop Riberi, and a member of the Catholic Central Bureau published *The Church: Holy and Catholic*, stressing the indivisible unity of the Catholic Church and the essential bond with the Holy Father. [52] Father Matthew Chen Zhemin continued giving the authentic Catholic version of the government's Three-Self Movement: self-government, self-support and self-propagation. Fr. Chen Zhemin wrote that, according to canon law, native Chinese bishops would gradually assume control of the Church in China, especially once the number of native-born priests and religious increased; the Catholic Church in China would be self-supporting, since it would accept no funding with foreign political implications; the foreign missionaries would work solely to build up the local Church throughout China, and not for the benefit of any foreign interests.

The official government response was swift and clear. The pamphlet explaining the Catholic Church's position

. . . was issued by the imperialist elements of the Catholic Church, the serious attention and indignation of all quarters have been aroused. It

---

[48] *China Missionary Bulletin*, vol. III (IV), no. 5, May 1951, p. 440.
[49] Lefeuvre, *Shanghai*, p. 48.
[50] Ibid, p. 49.
[51] Ibid, p. 51.
[52] *China Missionary Bulletin*, vol. III (IV), no. 5, May 1951, pp. 384-386.

affords irrevocable proof of the attempt on the part of the imperialist elements of the Catholic Church to sabotage the Chinese Catholic Church's patriotic independence and reformation movement, and of the presence of imperialist elements who try, under the disguise of the clergy, to make use of the Catholic Church as an instrument of aggression for the American-Chiang [Kai Shek] bloc to injure the interests of the Chinese people.[53]

On April 9, 1951, even as this confrontation was unfolding, Pope Pius XII issued his own decision. He excommunicated all bishops named by the Chinese government, who had not been appointed by the Apostolic See, as well as those bishops who were involved in the "consecration" ceremonies of those illegal and illicit bishops.

Bishop Kung's Battle Plan: His Second Pastoral Letter

On April 22, 1951, in the midst of this great turmoil, Bishop Kung issued his second pastoral letter, announcing the consecration of the Diocese of Shanghai to the Immaculate Heart of Mary.[54] At first glance this may appear to be merely a devotional document. But the Bishop understood that authentic Catholic devotion and daily life are one. Consequently, there is much more here than meets the eye, especially when seen in light of his first pastoral letter, reaffirming his loyalty to the Successor of Saint Peter and outlining his pastoral plan for the diocese. Because religion was disdained by the atheistic government, these letters could be overlooked by the Chinese Communists, for there was no apparent value, other than Catholic piety. For this letter dealt with his opening of two Marian Years: one in 1953, dedicated to Our Lady of Fatima, and the second in 1954, dedicated to Our Lady of Lourdes.

At face value, these two pastoral letters were the religious instructions of a bishop to his flock, in which he stated clearly his unbending Creed, expressed to the Catholics of Shanghai. But for those who knew their faith, and had an inkling of the history and content of these Marian apparitions, and the Church teachings involved, they were more. These are Bishop Kung's training instructions for his troops, the Catholics of Shanghai. He drew up the battle plans, and gave them the spiritual weapons for the upcoming battle, at least for those with eyes to see. But these were not battle plans to overthrow the government. They were plans that the Catholic community of Shanghai might not lose their faith during the government persecution and battles. He was preparing them spiritually for the inevitable

---

[53] Ibid., p. 387.
[54] Bishop Kung's Pastoral Letter can be found in Appendix 4.

onslaught by a government whose weapons would include imprisonment, starvation, torture, slave labor and death.

Bishop Kung called the faithful and clergy to spiritually arm themselves under the protection of the Blessed Virgin Mary, while reaffirming their dedication to the Successor of Saint Peter and to the Catholic Church founded by Our Lord. The heart of his troops would be the Catholic family, united by praying the Family Rosary, and daily study-meditations on the Mysteries of the Rosary. The Bishop sought to link the diocese's efforts with those of the various religious orders, especially the Jesuits, publishing his pastoral letter on the Feast of Our Lady Queen of the Society of Jesus.

In this pastoral letter, the Bishop called the attention of the faithful to the role of Mary in the saving work of her Son. She is an example and teacher of virtues, as can be seen in the Mysteries of the Rosary. How does Mary teach us virtuous habits? Above all, by her own example, as seen in Scripture, and through her many apparitions, in particular, at Lourdes, France and at Fatima, Portugal. Drawing upon the love for family so deeply rooted in Chinese society, Bishop Kung then described the strong family bonds between the Catholics of Shanghai with Our Lady:

> A strong affection naturally unites children with their mother. Her greatest gift given to us her children is Jesus, the Son of God, as our eldest brother. That the human family could be glorified by a brother infinitely good and noble, conferring upon us a new dignity and a pledge of divine life and grace on 'the adopted sons and daughters of God', is that they possess them through the merits of Jesus. Mary, Mother of all Christians, watches to prevent discord among her children. She both inspires and defends them, that they be charitable in thought and in word for those members of the family who might be unjustly accused. For if a member is tempted by folly or weakness to leave the family, Mary, as a good Mother, tries to save and call him back.

Mary teaches her children "the language of the family", in the Rosary:

- The *Sign of the Cross* reminds us of Christ the King [which was also the most important parish church in Shanghai], who ransomed us on the Cross, and also that "the worst sufferings can be the prelude of a glorious resurrection."
- The *Creed* expresses the faith the Apostles received "from the lips of Jesus", born witness to by the martyrs who "shed their blood for us in order to hand that faith down to us in its purity and integrity."
- The *Our Father* is Jesus' own prayer. Pope Pius XI [who consecrated the first Chinese bishops in 1926, and condemned

Communist ideology] wrote, "How could the Eternal Father refuse to come to our aid, when we pray using the words of His own Son?"

- The *Hail Mary* reminds us of our Celestial Mother, and by this prayer, "we commend ourselves to our Mother, and through Her to God, with all our needs "now and at the hour of our death."
- The *Glory Be* lifts our hearts to the Blessed Trinity, "and we know that whoever lifts his heart to God lifts also the world around him."

Bishop Kung continued with a rhetorical question: Is the Rosary meaningless repetition of prayers? No, for "to speak like this, one would have no understanding of the language of love, and to be insensible of the language of children." By the daily recitation of the Rosary, following the consecration to the Immaculate Heart of Mary, "we meditate and live the Mysteries of the Rosary, and should feel thrilled to dedicate all our strength to the patronage of Mary our Mother and our Queen."

Pope Pius XII consecrated all humanity to the Immaculate Heart of Mary on December 8, 1942. He realized that each person, each parish must personally consecrate oneself, and renewed his call in his encyclical of May 1, 1948, *Auspicia Quaedam*, 22.

The Consecration of the Diocese of Shanghai to the Immaculate Heart of Mary, was a pious expression of many things: obedience to the Successor of Saint Peter, Pope Pius XII, who had appointed Bishop Kung the first Chinese Bishop of Shanghai; obedience to the call of Our Lady in the 1917 apparitions at Fatima, when she warned the world of the evils of atheistic Communism and of sin; the consecration would be a public act of witness to begin on June 24th, the Solemnity of the Birth of John the Baptist, recalling another witness to Christ who preferred imprisonment and martyrdom by King Herod rather than to deny the Lord. As for past generations of Christ's followers, so now it was the turn of China's Catholics to bear witness to Christ.

As if to assist in the preparation for this consecration, Pope Pius XII issued his encyclical *Evangelii Praecones* on June 2, 1951, on the promotion of Catholic missions around the world. After listing the facts that the number of native born priests, religious and bishops was increasing in many mission countries, so too were the persecutions and the shedding of the blood of martyrs. He then mentioned Korea and China briefly, extolling the people of both countries "who are naturally cultured and honorable and have been renowned from early times for their high standard of civilization." He hoped they might end wars and strife and soon free themselves "from the inimical doctrine which seeks only the things of earth and scorns the things of heaven" and strive for "the genuine good of their people." [55]

To complement the consecration to the Immaculate Heart, Bishop Kung then announced the consecration of all families to the Sacred Heart of Jesus.

A few months later, the bishop announced the first Marian Year to begin on January 1, 1953, with a statue of Our Lady of Fatima making a pilgrimage to all the parishes in the Diocese of Shanghai. On December 8, 1953, Bishop Kung began the second Marian Year of 1954, dedicated to Our Lady of Lourdes, as part of the Marian Year announced for the entire Church by the pope. Shanghai's Marian Year began in the Church of Our Lady of the Immaculate Conception, the oldest church in the diocese. The centerpiece of this second Marian Year was a statue of Our Lady of Lourdes. During each year, a statue of Our Lady of Fatima in 1953 and Our Lady of Lourdes in 1954, would be the focal point in parishes for the Round-the-Clock Rosaries to be recited by the faithful, who would also receive catechetical preaching and Benediction of the Blessed Sacrament during each parish visitation throughout the two Marian years.

The Bishop's decision to emphasize the 1858 apparitions of Our Lady at Lourdes also had deeper meaning for Bishop Kung and the Catholics of Shanghai, as they faced ever-increasing demands by the Chinese government to break ties with the Pope, and to join the government's version of the Catholic Church. In 1858, when pressed by anti-clerical and hostile local officials of the French government, Saint Bernadette said that the lady in the vision identified herself, saying, "I am The Immaculate Conception".

The December 8, 1854 encyclical *Ineffabilis Deus*, by Blessed Pope Pius IX solemnly defined the Dogma of the Immaculate Conception, but it was also a statement about Papal authority and the nature of the Catholic Church. This is clear when taken into context of the Pope's future efforts to raise a warning against dangerous modern trends and errors, such as Marxism, by his encyclical *Quanta Cura*, accompanying the *Syllabus of Errors*, of December 8, 1864, and his attempt to protect the Church from the pretensions and incursions of modern governments, as seen in the two dogmatic constitutions on the Church, *Dei Filius* and *Pastor Aeternus* of the First Vatican Council, the latter defining Papal Infallibility on July 18, 1870. [56] Blessed Pope Pius IX understood the implacable progress of nation states, growing in military and industrial power and subjecting the rights of the individual to the forces of the market and developing nationalism. His efforts were designed so the Church could remind a world rushing toward self-destruction in wars and revolutions that the individual person, created in the Image

---

[55] *Evangelii Praecones*, 27.
[56] Giacomo Martina, *Pio IX (1851-1866)*, Roma 1986, pp. 275-356; *Pio IX (1867-1878)*, Roma 1990, pp. 110-232.

and Likeness of God was of greater importance than the initiatives and policies of governments or the economic pressures of the marketplace.

Under the heading *En union avec le Saint-Pere* at the end of his article, *L'annee Mariale a Shanghai* in the *Mission Bulletin* of September 1954, the editor expressed his understanding of the true nature of Bishop Kung's actions by quoting Pope Pius XII from his apostolic letter *Sacro Vergente Anno* consecrating Russia to the Immaculate Heart of Mary :

> It is shown to Us that wherever the Most Blessed Virgin Mary Mother of God is venerated, with a sincere and ardent piety, never could one lack the hope of salvation; since, while men strive, being wicked and powerful, to uproot religion and the Christian virtues from the hearts of their brethren,

> . . . If Mary opposes them, the gates of Hell will not prevail. She is the most clement and all powerful Mother of God and our Mother. Never has it been known to be said that whoever had recourse to Her, never felt her support and all powerful protection. Continue, then, to pray with devotion, with fervent love, to invoke with these words: 'To You only has it been given always to be most holy and most pure, Mother of God. [57]

The consecration of the Diocese of Shanghai to the Immaculate Heart of Mary on June 24, 1951, and the two Marian Years of 1953 and 1954 dedicated to Our Lady of Fatima and Our Lady of Lourdes were important parts of the pastoral plan of Bishop Kung. [58] They were designed to demonstrate to the local Communist government authorities and to the police that the Catholics of Shanghai were devoted and serious, as clearly seen in the popular Catholic reaction to the martyrdom of Father Beda Chang, S.J., and the government's outlawing of the Legion of Mary:

> These strong characteristics, deliberately chosen by this people possessed of a calm and staid temperament, experienced the open joy of children who have nothing to lose. But when the trials took on overwhelming proportions, these characteristics gave to Shanghai's Christianity a certain light buoyancy which more than once shocked their [Communist] adversaries. [59]

---

[57] *Mission Bulletin*, Vol. VI, September 1954, No. 7, p. 611.
[58] *Mission Bulletin*, Vol. VI, September, 1954, p. 609-611: gives a full description of the parish devotions during the 1954 Marian Year.
[59] Lefeuvre, *Shanghai*, p. 70.

The Persecution Intensifies

On February 18, 1951, Pope Pius XII beatified other Chinese martyrs, while the government's insistence upon the implementation of the Three-Self Program intensified. On February 20, 1951, five Catholic priests were invited to attend a meeting with Chinese government officials, Protestant representatives and educators to discuss the role of private schools and universities. A motion was made that all schools and institutions work to propagate the government's Three-Self Program as a manifestation of patriotism. The Catholics refused, and their spokesman, Father Beda Chang, S.J., detailed the objections of the Catholic Church to those assembled. [60] The same day, the government promulgated its *Regulations for the Suppression of Counterrevolutionaries*, which served as China's criminal code for years to come, and was a turning point for the government. Within a few months, mass arrests of Catholic priests and laity began. In Shanghai, among the priests arrested was Father Beda Chang, S.J., who would die in prison in November, and was hailed as a martyr by Shanghai's Catholics, enraged by his death at the hands of the Communist government. [61] Likewise, public executions of Catholics and other "running dogs of imperialists" began in Shanghai at the Shanghai Race Track. The government estimated that 100,000 persons were shot before cheering crowds; non-government sources claimed between 500,000 and 1,000,000 were killed. [62]

At the beginning of 1951, the government established the Religious Affairs Office [later Bureau], which, by the end of the year, had offices in every city and province. It reported directly to the Party Central Committee. [63] In its program to control the Catholic Church for its own political ends, the Communist government finally realized that having their own men in Catholic leadership positions was insufficient to gain control of the Church in China. They needed a validly ordained Catholic bishop to do their bidding, who would help convince Catholics to join the Patriotic Association. Efforts were made by the local Communist government to obtain the cooperation of Bishop Kung, which he refused. [64] Even while Catholics of Shanghai were forcefully reacting to the death of Father Chang and the public executions of Catholics following the implementation of the Regulations against counterrevolutionaries, Bishop Kung along with twenty Catholic priests and

---

[60] Ibid., pp. 77-98.

[61] Becker, *I Met a Traveller*, p. 165. Fr. Chang died in prison on November 11, 1951 and was buried from Saint Ignatius Loyola Church in Shanghai on November 13th, at which Mass Bishop Kung gave the absolution. Bishop Kung had given permission that this Mass and any other funeral Masses for Fr. Chang be offered in red vestments, the color of martyrs.

[62] Mariani, *Church Militant*, pp. 61-62.

[63] Eric O. Hanson, *Catholic Politics in China and Korea*, Maryknoll, N.Y. 1980, p. 69, ft. nt. 5

[64] Ibid., p. 75-76.

laypersons, were invited by the deputy mayor of Shanghai, P'an Han-nien, to attend a meeting on November 29, 1951. This was the first time that the Shanghai government had addressed officially any non-"patriotic" Church authorities. [65] The actual topic was the government's insistence upon the registration of all members of the Legion of Mary with the police. On October 8, 1951 the government had raised the stakes by declaring the Legion of Mary to be a counterrevolutionary organization, a façade for American imperialists. All members were ordered to register with the police. Bishop Kung instructed them not to register, but to remain true to the faith. [66]

At first, the Catholics were quite willing to cooperate with the government, if the government were willing to cooperate with the Church. One of the members of the Legion of Mary, Ms. Ma, a member of the Catholic contingent, asked at the meeting, "Is there no way to find any agreement between us? Couldn't the Legion register with Catholic authorities, for example, instead of with the police?" [67] Then, Bishop Kung spoke to those assembled:

> The Government gives the peoples [sic] freedom of faith and grants its citizens who have a religious belief a right to protect their belief and its practice; it permits them to fulfill their duties as patriots in the integrity of the dogma and moral principles.
>
> As for me, as regards the Catholic Church, I am the Bishop of the two Dioceses of Shanghai and Soochow. As to my Country, I am a [Chinese] citizen who professes the Catholic faith. Today, Mr. Mayor, in your presence and in the presence of these gentlemen and these Christians I give you firm assurance that I shall not abandon my pure and proper stand with regard to the Church and with regard to my country.
>
> As regards the Church, I am a bishop and in conformity with the doctrine and discipline of the Church I am administering the two Dioceses. . . I have never spoken, up to now, contrary to dogma and moral principles and I shall certainly neither say nor do anything contrary to dogma and moral teaching in the future.
>
> As regards my country, I am a citizen who is a Catholic. I was born here, I grew up, and I became old and I shall be buried here. Under the guarantee of the government's *Common Program* I conform myself, on the one hand, to Catholic doctrine and discipline; on the other, I love my country ardently and I shall fulfill my duties as a Catholic citizen. I have a horror for the imperialism that is invading

---

[65] Lefeuvre, *Shanghai*, p. 97.
[66] Hsieh, *The Bright Cloud*, p. 20.
[67] Lefeuvre, *Shanghai*, p. 98.

my country. I have never been used by it and I shall surely not be used by it in the future. [68]

Bishop Kung ended his remarks during the meeting, "There is the Catholic attitude; here is my life." [69] While Shanghai's Mayor agreed that the Legion of Mary did not appear "as reactionary as was first portrayed", nevertheless, China's central government had promulgated a law that members were to be registered. Since the law must be obeyed, he set the deadline for registration as December 15, 1951.

Some members of the Legion of Mary, the clergy and the government sought means to compromise. All prepared for arrests. The students from Aurora University prepared small bundles of clothes they could use in jail, which they kept near the doors of their homes, waiting for the police to arrest them. [70]

They also created a dramatic means to express their undying loyalty to Christ and His Catholic Church. They wrote Bishop Kung, pledging their fidelity:

> We are very young, weak and inexperienced, who, for no reason could lose our way and wander down the wrong path. We have no support other than the vigilance and fortitude of our pastors who guide us. It is they who tell us to go right or to go left; they can dispose of us, and our destiny is in their hands. Since our bishop, Monsignor Kung has been sent as our head, we have daily marched down a sure path in a set direction: we now maintain our *position*: steadfastly and resolutely Catholic, come what may.
>
> And, not long ago, when the government wanted to force us to tell the police how the Legion operated, all our brothers, except three rare exceptions, showed how resolute was their spirit.
>
> We hope that our still fresh blood transcribes on this paper the passionate desire of our hearts. May these drops of our blood, symbol of our union with you, accomplish our union with the redemptive Cross of Christ upon which we desire to remain until the completion of this sacrifice. [71]

And they signed it in their own blood, as if to say clearly " [we] trusted Bishop Kung as our shepherd". [72]

---

[68] *Fides News Service*, February 2, 1952, as quoted in Mariani, pp. 92-93.
[69] *China Missionary Bulletin*, Vol. IV (V), February 1952, p. 141.
[70] Hsieh, *The Bright Cloud*, p. 13.
[71] Quoted in Lefeuvre, *Shanghai*, p. 93.
[72] Hsieh, *The Bright Cloud*, Taipei, 2003, p. 20.

Political Cartoons published in Shanghai in October, 1951,
in a book entitled, *The Vatican, Servant of American Imperialism.*[73]
The Chinese commentary to the right of each cartoon is original; the English translation
was provided by the China Missionary Bulletin.

工作。
國特務機關代表的聯席會議，討論怎樣加強反人民的
一九五〇年二月和十月，梵蒂岡曾兩次舉行敎廷和美

*"In February and October of 1950 the Vatican twice convened meetings between
church officials and representatives of American secret service organizations,
to discuss ways of strengthening the opposition against the people."*

際資本主義反蘇反共反人民陰謀活動的中心之一。
可是骨子裡並非這樣，它的全部歷史說明了它却是國

*"However, it [the Papacy] is not what it appears to be. Its whole history
declares clearly that it is the principal center of the international capitalistic movement
to oppose Russia, Communism and the people."*

---

[73] Reproduced in the *China Missionary Bulletin,* vol. IV (V), Aug-Sept 1952, No. 7, pp. 574-575.

This was quite a tribute to the faith of these young people in Our Lord, His Church, and Bishop Kung following the sufferings of 1951. The Papal Internuncio, Archbishop Anthony Riberi had endured imprisonment, months of painful interrogations and deprivation, and, finally, public humiliation and forcible expulsion by the government along with the vast majority of foreign missionaries. Likewise, all Catholic schools, universities, healthcare and charitable institutions had been confiscated or closed by the Communists. Chinese priests were being arrested, the Legion of Mary was outlawed and public executions of Catholics and others dubbed counterrevolutionaries increased daily.

There was, in the face of these government pressures, a Catholic re-organization of sorts. The Legion of Mary disbanded, reconstituting themselves into catechetical groups based in the parishes. With all Catholic schools and universities closed or confiscated by the government, the parishes would provide the space where the Catholic youth would train a new generation of Catholics, loyal to their Bishop, to the local priests and to the Successor of Saint Peter.[74]

Another New Year arrived, and the Catholic students again wrote their bishop. This time, however, Aurora University and all other Catholic schools were no longer Catholic, having been taken over by the government. Thanking Bishop Kung for his example and leadership, these phrases sounded similar to the strident Communist tracts frequently appearing in the media. Yet, this letter expressed the hopes of young Catholics for 1952, which, in light of the persecution, were not those common to college students:[75]

> The dawn of the year 1952 marks a milestone in the growth of our life.
>
> The last year has passed. Yet how vibrant is that past, how much full of meaning! Although it was a period which cost blood and tears, in our sorrow there is sweetness and hope; in our sacrifices there is love and joy. We now long for the coming of the Cross. We rejoice in the unity of our Holy Church and in its victory. Under your direction, Your Excellency, the Diocese of Shanghai is stirring to noble life. You, Bishop Kung, are our light shining on the darkened road. You, Bishop Kung, are our guide directing our steps along the road through adversity.
>
> In the dire circumstances of this age, Your Excellency has protected the integrity of our faith, and the traditional spirit of the Church. We reverently hail our leader.

---

[74] Mariani, *Church Militant*, p. 95.
[75] *China Missionary Bulletin*, vol. IV (V), March 1952, No. 3, pp. 228-229. The full text of the student letter can be found in Appendix 5.

Echoing sentiments Bishop Kung had expressed in his second pastoral letter, the students continued,

> The struggle requires sacrifices. Victory exacts its price. The safeguarding of our faith demands blood and tears. Although both fight and sacrifices are distressing, our hearts are deeply filled with joy. The three hundred years of persecution of the primitive Church show the comparative minuteness of our own sufferings. In comparison with the intensity of the sufferings of innumerable holy men and women of the past, our own cross seems such a little thing."

They ended their letter, "Your Excellency, Happy New Year! Guide us onward."

Just a few days after the students delivered this pledge of fidelity to Bishop Kung and to the Church, on January 18, 1952, then the Feast of the Chair of Saint Peter, Pope Pius XII issued his apostolic letter "to the bishops, priests and people of China", *Cupimus Imprimis*. [76] The Holy Father began expressing his admiration for the Chinese people and culture.

> In fact, as you well know, the Catholic religion does not contradict any doctrine that is true, to any public or private institution that has a basis in justice, freedom and love. . . it is in no way opposed to the natural character of each people, their particular customs and their culture, but graciously accepts them and willingly adorns them.

> For this reason, we were extremely saddened to know that among you, the Catholic Church is considered, presented, and fought as an enemy of your people. . .

The Holy Father stated that the Church existed only to spread the Gospel, "to promote harmony, to alleviate sufferings, to strengthen the foundations of society", and to that end supplied missionaries, as well as native Chinese priests, religious, bishops and a cardinal. He concluded,

> Throughout the course of many centuries your Church in China had to sustain the fiercest persecutions, and your nation's soil has been empurpled by the holy blood of its martyrs; now, quite appropriately, can those famous words [of Tertullian] be applied to you 'We are become more numerous each time we are cut down; the blood of Christians is the seed of the Church'.

Early in 1952, the Chinese government inaugurated the "Oppose Catholic Reactionaries" movement throughout the country. The press was filled with attacks on all priests: labeling foreign missionaries "wolves in sheep's clothing", while dividing the Chinese priests into two groups: the "running dogs of the

---

[76] The complete text of the Encyclical can be found in Appendix 6.

imperialists", faithful to the pope and to Bishop Kung, or the "Patriotic Catholic priests", who had joined the government Patriotic Association. [77]

Catholics Do Battle

During an audience granted to national mission directors during their annual Roman meeting with officials of the Congregation for the Propagation of the Faith, Pope Pius XII referred to the persecution in China, telling them of the Chinese government's plan to destroy the Church by dividing the priests and people from their bishops, and then expelling or imprisoning the clergy. Using Our Lord's words, the Pope said, "They will smite the shepherd and the sheep of the flock will be scattered [Mt. 26:31]". [78]

On July 12, 1952, Brother Leonard Voegtle (R. Gilbert) was summoned by the police to answer questions. He immediately sought the counsel of Bishop Kung, who had recently visited the College of Joan of Arc to administer Confirmation. The Bishop told him, "Dear Brother, do as the police ask because there is no way over [sic]." Since the Bishop was not against the government, his counsel was merely a suggestion of prudence. Brother Leonard was the Director of Saint Joan of Arc College and worked with the Legion of Mary. Soon after, Brother Leonard was expelled from China with many others. [79]

In an interesting article in the *China Missionary Bulletin* December 1952 number, "A Missionary", as he styled himself, claimed to have been asked by Catholic students to publicize their struggles, after he was expelled from Shanghai and China by the government. One student handed him a short poem, which he quoted,

> My words are not a cry of terror but of exultation. We are not asking for help for we know that our struggle is the united struggle of all the Church. It is the whole Church which is triumphing today, not with mere human victories devoid of the Cross but with the labor, pain and blood of Chinese Christians. Brothers throughout the world! We are proud of our testimony, proud to be the vanguard of your own hopes. [80]

The author reported that it was Bishop Kung, the Jesuit missionaries and religious order clergy and sisters who provided the inspiration for these Catholic

---

[77] *Mission Bulletin*, Vol., VIII, February, 1956, No. 2, p. 144.
[78] *China Missionary Bulletin*, Vol. IV (V), June-July 1952, p. 481.
[79] Lyon, August 16, 1988 Brother Leonard Voegtle to Cardinal Kung, Cardinal Kung Archives.
[80] *China Missionary Bulletin*, Vol. IV (V), December 1952, No. 10, p. 819.

students and for the entire Catholic community in Shanghai. The author concluded observing that

> Communism is outright totalitarian by the invasion and attempted control of the State in every field of human activity, but more so because it seeks to absorb the individual into its ideology, its program and its strategy. Our Catholics in China are meeting Communism with precisely the same totalitarian attitude. [81]

By the summer of 1952, the Chinese born Jesuit priests organized a special preaching series, to be delivered at Saint Ignatius and Saint Peter Churches. Based upon the *Spiritual Exercises* of Saint Ignatius Loyola, they were to prepare the Catholic students and the larger Catholic community of Shanghai for the inevitable. [82]

Likewise that summer, Father George Germain, S.J., former President of Aurora University, was arrested. [83] He was charged with "imperialist espionage activities under the cloak of religion", forced to sign a confession, imprisoned and later expelled from the country. The real reason behind the arrest of Father Germain was the government's methodical chipping away at the public image of Bishop Kung, for Germain was a trusted confidant and collaborator of the Bishop. [84] A young Jesuit novice recalled this very aspect of the government's program written only a few months after Bishop Kung's arrest:

> Because he desired to be authentically a bishop of Jesus Christ, as well as a man and a true Chinese, Monsignor Kung stood as an obstacle that had to be toppled by the functionaries of the government's plan. Why did they wait so long to pull him down? For a reason that we will express, and pardon [as a distortion of the original meaning], as cited in the Bible telling us, 'Because they did not want the death of a sinner, but his conversion" [to Communism].
>
> They [the Communists] wanted Monsignor Kung's complete submission, which could not be had except by the disintegration of his personality. This explains their long and patient waiting, in the hopes of discovering some fault that would permit them to creep into the individual's conscience and shatter it. [85]

---

[81] Ibid., p. 820.

[82] Mariani, *Church Militant*, p. 104.

[83] Becker, *I Met a Traveler*, p. 169. According to Father Phillips, Bishop Kung had granted the privilege to all missionaries in his diocese that, if imprisoned, in order to offer Mass, the imprisoned priest "could have simply made a mental offering of the bread and wine, uttering the words of consecration, and consumed the species", if they could get hold of bread and wine.

[84] Ibid., p. 105.

[85] *Mission Bulletin*, Vol. VIII, January, 1956, No. 1, Lefeuvre and Raguin, *La Geste*, p. 27.

The author used the example of stone cutters, whose goal is to split rocks: they search out a fault in the stone, insert a wooden wedge, pour water on it repeatedly, and patiently wait for the wedge to expand and split the stone. With Bishop Kung, "The Communists were looking for that fault, worked on it, and waited until everything fell apart."

Yet the Bishop and his Catholic community continued as best they could and in a very public manner. On October 4, 1952, at one of his annual Masses of the Holy Ghost in preparation for the opening of the school year, Bishop Kung addressed hundreds of Catholic middle school students. The Mass was offered at the Jesuit Church of Christ the King, by then staffed mainly by Chinese Jesuits, which had become the center for Catholic resistance.

The Mass was briefly described by Father Charles McCarthy, S.J.:

> About 700 youngsters filled the church to overflowing. Bishop Kung presided in the sanctuary; he spoke to the students before the Mass in the former lawn tennis court behind the rectory. It's wonderful to see how solicitous he is for their spiritual welfare, how ready to trouble himself to help them, and how responsive and grateful they are towards him. [86]

The November 1952 number of the *China Missionary Bulletin* contains an interesting article about the Church in Shanghai written by Richard Willier. He wrote that businessmen, diplomats, Catholics and non-Catholics alike, coming from mainland China into Hong Kong reported that

> The Catholic Church in Shanghai is one of the brightest if not the brightest spot in the picture. From the Bishop, down through the priests, sisters, brothers, and lay people, the story runs the same—a strong and unbending faith practiced openly, loyally, and perseveringly in the face of every effort of the Communists, and overcoming every trick and show of force of trained persecutors.

> As the Communists liberated Shanghai, a Chinese bishop took over the leadership of the Church which had always been in foreign hands before. It might well have been argued that it was dangerous to make the change at that crucial moment. However, the choice of His Excellency, Bishop Ignatius Kung, has not only in no way been regretted but rejoiced at for he has shown wisdom, firmness and courage at every new move of the Communists. When called 'on the carpet' as it were, by the Mayor of Shanghai for not cooperating with the Independent Church Movement, he explained simply the schismatic character of the 'new church' and then said firmly, 'There

---

[86] Quoted in Mariani, *Church Militant*, p. 113.

can be no compromise on this question. If you want my life, here it is. Take it.' The Mayor walked out in an embarrassed silence. As each new question arises, the Bishop holds consultation and makes the decision as to the response of Catholics. Before nightfall every Catholic in Shanghai knows what is his or her duty as they face new requirements. [87]

The backbone of the Church in Shanghai, Willier continued, was the clergy, both foreign and native. "In view of the well-formed and zealous native clergy in Shanghai, the foreign clergy has been contented to place the administration of the Church in Chinese hands and itself play the role of counselor and stabilizer." He reported that the Catholic churches in Shanghai were crowded, and quoted one Catholic as having said, 'Before the Communists came, if I had a free afternoon I would go swimming or play tennis. Now, I wouldn't think of missing the Rosary, sermon and Benediction for anything.'" Those Shanghai Catholics who fled to Macao or Hong Kong were surprised that Catholics there were "cooler" in their practice of the faith. Expressing the thoughts of one Shanghai Catholic, "'The time has come when ordinary religious practice and weekly Mass are not enough; it is a question of the salvation or loss of one's immortal soul. Ordinary virtue and prayer will not suffice'." To bolster the Catholics of Shanghai, Bishop Kung composed a traditional eight Chinese character banner, hung in the churches: *Neither Fire nor Sword Can Take Away My Faith in God.* [88]

1953 was dedicated to Our Lady of Fatima, and round-the-clock Rosaries were recited, beginning at midnight on New Year's Eve by Bishop Kung at the Church of Christ the King. Each parish in the Diocese of Shanghai played host to the statue of Our Lady, with a nightly sermon, procession, Rosary and Benediction, oftentimes with Bishop Kung present. On New Year's Eve, along with the already large crowd filling the small church, 1,300 Catholics students joined, the crowds were so large that Benediction had to be celebrated outside the church in the parish garden. [89]

The Catholics students presented spiritual bouquets to the Bishop, and then addressed him through one of the students as their spokesman: [90]

> The splendor of the glorious tears of 1952 still shines on this New Year. We look to 1953 to make us holy; we look to 1953 to be grounded on the tears of holiness. This year will give to the Church a splendid variety of flowers, and it is the love of God that will make

---

[87] *China Missionary Bulletin*, Vol. IV (V), November 1952, No. 9, pp. 727-728.
[88] Bishop Kung's banner in the original Chinese characters can be found in Appendix 7.
[89] *China Missionary Bulletin*, Vol. V (VI), May 1953, No. 5, p. 402.
[90] Ibid., pp. 443-444. The full text of the student letter can be found in Appendix 8.

them bloom; thanks to your care as a good gardener, they will be overflowing with sweet fragrance and life.

We carry the hope of the Church with pride. And you, Monsignor, you are the solid ground in which is rooted this immovable tree of our hope, the solid ground where this immortal tree sends forth its sap. In the Diocese of Shanghai, Monsignor, you are also the sun that gives light and warmth; other than in Rome, the Holy City of our Holy Father the well-beloved Pope, from which comes light and warmth, it is you who transmit these to us here.

Before the darkness that surrounds us, you shine like a star. You guide China towards the Truth, towards Happiness. The Catholic youth of the schools and universities of Shanghai live, work, suffer and carry the Cross of Christ, without weakening, to spread the Divine Truth.

Through the struggles of last year, God has purified us, as one would purify silver, seven times in a crucible. Now our life has left the kingdom of Herod to settle in Nazareth. This life of Nazareth already has a great value, and its grandeur depends upon our willingness to follow along the direction of Your Excellency, which is the will of the Most High.

They concluded,

This is our mission. This is the direction of our efforts for the year 1953.

The glorious battle of 1952 continues to shine on the year just begun. It is sublime to live for battle; but the grandeur of this life depends upon the desires of the Bishop and the Will of God. That Your Excellency may be blessed by the vision of the Heavenly Jerusalem. . . . That the Reign of God may arrive on earth.

Such enthusiasm and unity was not limited to Catholic students, but was found as well among the rest of the Catholic community of Shanghai, and among both the secular and regular clergy, "thanks to the saintly guidance by Bishop Kung and Fr. Lacretelle", and among the Chinese clergy and foreign-born missionaries. [91]

---

[91] Fr. Charles McCarthy, S.J., quoted in Mariani, *Church Militant*, p. 119.

The Government Strikes and Catholics Resist

By June, the local Shanghai government had prepared to move against the Church more forcefully. A dossier entitled "Notification Concerning Attacking and Expelling the Imperialists within the Shanghai Catholic Church" outlined the plan. The document reveals the government's party line that the Catholic Church in Shanghai was being used by imperialists and was obstructing national reform and interests. The first move would be against foreign missionaries, the next against the Chinese clergy. Once the clergy had been expelled, imprisoned, or subdued, the Chinese Catholic laity would be "re-educated", and they would then fell the final blow upon their own Church.

Beginning on June 15, 1953, and lasting nearly three days, hundreds of policemen occupied Christ the King Church. They arrested the American Jesuits, Fathers Thomas Phillips and John Clifford; at Saint Peter's Church, they arrested Father Fernand Lacretelle, S.J. that same night; foreign Vincentian, Maryknoll, and Franciscan missionaries were also arrested. The police also closed the Church of the Immaculate Conception. But the police occupation at the two Jesuit parishes, both vibrant centers of Catholic life, enraged the parishioners and Catholic students whose vehement public protests surprised the police. Throughout the night of June 16th, "the faithful recited the Rosary and made the Stations of the Cross from morning to night." [92] The Catholic stand-off with the police lasted for three days, despite arrivals of police reinforcements with machine guns. The Catholic protestors responded to the police accusations that the churches were "centers of espionage, in which live imperialists and counter-revolutionaries", shouting back that "the People's police had no right to prevent The People from entering their church." And they challenged the police, "Will you disobey the directives of President Mao?", who had repeatedly claimed to protect religion in China. [93]

Brother Kevin Doheny, a Marist Brother who taught at Saint Joan of Arc College in Shanghai since 1937, witnessed the events:

> The people sang with all their heart and soul. Once the Communists told a shopkeeper to put on his radio (directed toward the Church) full blast to drown the noise of the singing but a Catholic neighbor pulled out its wires. The climax was when everybody stood up to sing *Chi Lai* [*Arise*], putting every ounce of energy into that hymn, so much so that I thought it would lift the roof. [94] This is a thought

---

[92] *China Missionary Bulletin*, Vol. V (VI), October 1953, No. 8, p. 697.
[93] Lefeuvre, *Shanghai*, p. 143.
[94] Mr. Ignatius Chu and his wife Margaret Kung Chu were active members of the Legion of Mary in Shanghai during these years. They remembered this hymn and its importance to the Catholic students of

which came to my mind and to the mind of others during the singing: No number of machine guns would prevent these people from proclaiming undying fidelity to the true Catholic Faith. They would have loved nothing more than to have been mown down while proclaiming their fidelity. [95]

Father Jean Lefeuvre, S.J. recalled that it was difficult for anyone not familiar with the situation to appreciate the value of the Catholic reaction to the government's police action beginning on the night of June 15th. He wrote,

This [Catholic protest] strongly impressed the millions of non-Christian inhabitants of the city. This is the only time since the beginning of the Communist regime [in Shanghai] that so prolonged a popular manifestation of this unfolded in clear public view for the sole purpose of rejecting a government action. [96]

Bishop Kung and the Catholics of Shanghai were dedicated to protecting the Church from being subjected to the State. The lines were drawn, and Catholics were not backing down. "Shanghai, the center of resistance to the religious policy of the Communist government gave an example and an inspiration to the whole country, and those who had the courage to push back against this policy now must respond [to the government] for their *crimes*." [97]

The *China Missionary Bulletin* ran a long article in its October, 1953 number, listing all the foreign-born priests and religious sisters and brothers arrested and imprisoned during the police raids in Shanghai during the months of June and July 1953. The *Bulletin* reported that the Catholic youth proposed to follow up these evenings of government terror against the Church by novenas of devotions to the Sacred Heart, "to ask God to forgive the ignorance of the persecutors, to ask the Holy Ghost to guide the Shanghai Diocese, and to ask our Holy Mother to protect priests and Catholics who are suffering for their faith." [98] The *Bulletin* also noted that the emphasis in the government's press had changed regarding the Catholic Church. No longer was there reference made to the Three-Self Program. Now the government was interested in rooting out imperialist influences within the Catholic Church, repeating this in all the media, especially in the July 1953 number of the *Courier Dove*, the government "Catholic" periodical.

Shanghai . They clarified one important point for me: the National Anthem of Communist China is entitled *Chi Lai*. The hymn referred to by Brother Kevin Doheny was the most popular Legion of Mary hymn, "The Love of Jesus", whose first two words were *Chi Lai*, the same as those of the national anthem. The Legion of Mary hymn sung that day by Shanghai's young Catholics was *not* the Chinese national anthem. Both Ignatius Chu and his wife Martha Kung were imprisoned in forced labor camps for 23 years for their roles in the Shanghai Legion of Mary.

[95] *China Missionary Bulletin*, Vol. V (VI), October 1953, No. 8, p. 702.

[96] Lefeuvre, *Shanghai*, p. 150.

[97] *Mission Bulletin*, Vol. VIII, January, 1956, No. 1, p. 84.

[98] *China Missionary Bulletin*, Vol. V (VI), October 1953, No. 8, p. 698.

The Love-Country, Love-Church, Purge-Imperialist Struggle

The government's Consultative Committee of the Shanghai All-Circle Representative Conference met on June 25th, and made the resolution that the public be warned about Catholics:

> Although a serious blow has been dealt to the Imperialist conspiracy of carrying out sabotage through the Catholic Church, yet not all Imperialists and counter-revolutionaries hiding in the Catholic Church have been cleared out. They are using 'ecclesiastical power' in all sorts of ways to prevent Catholics from participating in this love-country, love-church and purge-Imperialist struggle, sabotaging it in various manners. . .[99]

The raids against the Catholics during the summer of 1953 clearly demonstrated to the government that Shanghai Catholics were not easily bullied. It also showed the metal of the Chinese clergy, and the need for the government to fulfill Our Lord's words quoted the summer before by Pope Pius XII: "Strike the shepherd and the sheep will scatter." They now began to move more efficiently against the priests and Bishop.

The *Bulletin* reported that twenty foreign priests, twenty-two Chinese priests and fifteen Chinese religious brothers were placed under house arrest at the Jesuit residence in the Zikawei section of Shanghai on the night of June 15th. They were daily interrogated during the subsequent month. The *Bulletin* continued that,

> There seems to be more pressure on the Chinese priests to force them to confess. One or two of the group of Chinese priests were propositioned to head the [government's] Independent Church. Fr. Wan Kin Wen after 15 days of pressure and [his] 15 days refusal, could not eat or sleep and was almost out of his mind. Fr. Anthony Wang was also another who was worked on by the Communists to become leader of the Independent Church. Two or three other priests in the country have also been invited to fill the post but all refused. On July 18 an emissary from the Reds approached Bishop Kung to ask him to head the Independent Church. He refused. [100]

Because of the strong and prolonged public demonstrations against the government by Catholics, the Mayor of Shanghai decided to appeal to the non-Catholic majority so that the church closures and arrests of priests would appear to have popular support. On June 25th, the Mayor of Shanghai, General Chen Yi,

---

[99] Ibid., p. 700.
[100] Ibid., p. 703.

convened a meeting of the representatives of the people of the city to appeal to the citizens of Shanghai "to actively join in the battle against the imperialist cells of the Catholic Church [the pope, Bishop Kung and the foreign missionaries] and those who are their supporters, their 'running dogs' [Chinese priests and laity]." [101]

In the midst of the arrests of priests and the public Catholic demonstrations, Bishop Kung published his prayer for priests:

> All Powerful and Eternal God, through the merits of Your Son Jesus, and through Your love for Him, I implore You, have pity on the priests of the Holy Church. In spite of their sublime dignity, they are fearful and weak, like all created beings. In Your Infinite mercy, inflame their hearts with the fire of Divine Love. For the sake of Jesus, your Son, bestow grace on the priests and uphold them. Do not let them fall into temptation and tarnish their noble vocation.
>
> O Jesus, we implore You. Look with pity on the priests of the Holy Church: those who are serving You faithfully and proclaiming Your glory; those who are persecuted for tending Your flock; those who are abandoned, weary and sorrowful; those who are lukewarm, confused and who have denied their faith; those who are sick, dying or in Purgatory, Lord Jesus, we entreat You. Listen to our supplication, have pity and console them.
>
> O Jesus, we entrust to You the priests of the whole world: the priests who baptized me, absolved my sins, offered Holy Mass and consecrated the Eucharist to nourish my soul. We entrust to You the priests who instructed me when I was ignorant, gave me strength in my weakness, showed me the Way and the Truth and comforted me in my sorrow and affliction. For all the blessings they obtained for me, I implore You to support them in Your loving kindness.
>
> O Jesus, shelter our priests in Your Sacred Heart. Let them take refuge in Your mercy and love, in this life and to the hour of death. Amen. [102]

Strike the Shepherd, But the Shepherd Stood Firm

The next targets of the summer's terror were Chinese priests and foreign missionaries still in the city who had close ties to Bishop Kung. The evening of

---

[101] *China Missionary Bulletin*, Vol. V (VI), December 1953, No. 10, p. 846.
[102] Cardinal Kung Foundation Archives.

July 8th was another night of church occupation by police and arrests of priests. The two most important parishes of the diocese were targeted that night, the Cathedral of Saint Francis Xavier, and the Church of Saint Joseph in Yangjingbang. Father Nepomucene Fu Hezhou, an official of Bishop Kung's curia, was taken from Saint Joseph Church, and Father George Beauregard, S.J. from the cathedral parish, where Bishop Kung lived and had his office.

Father Beauregard had been told by parishioners who worked at the telephone company that government agents had tapped the Bishop's telephone and that the police were intercepting and reading his mail. [103]

On July 25th, all the remaining Catholic priests in Shanghai were forcibly transported to city hall to meet with the police chief, Hsu Chien-kuo who told them that the government wanted to protect them and free them from oppression by foreigners, and that they desired the collaboration of the patriotic priests, and favored the establishment of a truly Chinese Catholic Church, and that they would be entirely implacable towards those who refused to disassociate themselves from the imperialists and counter-revolutionaries (by which was meant those Chinese priests and laity already arrested). Being generous, the government would give them time to reflect, but their time would be short.[104]

On July 28th, Bishop Kung, accompanied by two of his priests, was brought in to meet personally with the Mayor. He was met by five high officials of the Bureau of Cultural Affairs. The Bishop told the Mayor that he and his priests would continue their practice to refuse giving Holy Communion to members of the Patriotic Church, despite the government's protests. The *China Missionary Bulletin* reported:

> The greatest discretion was maintained on both sides during this meeting.
>
> One can say only that the Bishop of Shanghai was implacable regarding the strictly supernatural work and goals of the Church and explained that far from opposing the government, he and his priests would remain faithful to the essential tenets of their Catholic faith.[105]

A few days later, Catholics from around the city were told by the government that certain tenets of the Catholic faith and of the Church's canon law were the "product of reactionary influence that had to be removed from their religion so that it could be truly purified." Despite the warning, on July 31st, the feast of Saint Ignatius Loyola, and the patronal feast day of Bishop Kung, more

---

[103] Mariani, *Church Militant*, p. 133.
[104] *China Missionary Bulletin*, Vol. V (VI), December 1953, No. 10, p. 847.
[105] Ibid., p. 847.

than 3,000 Catholics attended Mass at the re-opened Cathedral of Saint Ignatius, as a sign of their loyalty and support for their Bishop. [106]

In an article entitled, *Bow to the Courage of Catholics*, the *Mission Bulletin* reported that a foreign businessman who just left Shanghai related that

> . . . when about to leave Shanghai, I stopped at the railway station and took off my hat in a deep bow to the courage of the Shanghai Catholics. They are magnificent! If you knew Shanghai before, you wouldn't know it now. It's rough. No white rice; no white flour; no oil; and someone to watch and report everything you say! But the Catholics, they are the one bright spot left in Shanghai.[107]

1954 Marian Year: Our Lady of Lourdes

As the arrests of priests and expulsion of religious sisters and brothers continued throughout China well into the New Year and beyond, Bishop Kung continued to urge the Catholics of his diocese to greater fervent devotion to Our Lord and His Blessed Mother. He had begun 1953 as a Marian Year under the protection of Our Lady of Fatima, during which round-the clock Rosaries were prayed without interruption day and night, as the statue of Our Lady of Fatima passed through each church. On December 8, 1953, the Feast of the Immaculate Conception, Bishop Kung began a second Marian Year of 1954, this time in union with the entire Universal Church, as proclaimed by Pope Pius XII. During this second Marian Year in the Diocese of Shanghai, a statue of Our Lady of Lourdes visited each parish, and the daily Living Rosary was prayed. There was a strong link between the apparitions at Lourdes and the See of Peter, as Pope Pius XI mentioned in his decree canonizing Saint Bernadette Soubirous:

> What the Sovereign Pontiff defined in Rome through his infallible Magisterium [Pope Pius IX's definition of the Dogma of the Immaculate Conception], the Immaculate Mother of God, blessed among all women, wanted to confirm by her own words, it seems, when shortly afterward she manifested herself by a famous apparition at the grotto of Massabielle.[108]

During Shanghai's Marian Year of 1954, the statue of Our Lady of Lourdes travelled to the parishes of the Diocese, residing in each parish for one month, and a set ceremony and ritual were followed.

---

[106] Ibid, p. 847.

[107] *Mission Bulletin*, Vol. VI, February 1954, No. 2, p. 191.

[108] Pope Pius XI, *De Tutto*, in *Acta Apostolicae Sedis*, 25 (1933), p. 377.

The statue arrived by car and was greeted by assembled clergy and faithful of the parish. In the church sanctuary a magnificent repository was erected, "thanks to the offering for electrical decorations of Chinese letters delicately sculpted, which do not lack for originality and charm." Sick children were brought earlier to await the arrival of their "Mama". The statue was carried on a litter borne by four men. "The priest blesses the statue and then the children, boys and girls, carrying multicolored Chinese lanterns, processing slowly singling loudly the Lourdes and Fatima hymns, melodiously adapted for Chinese." [109] Following the children were delegations of men and women carrying candles, representing the parish societies. As the statue moved into the sanctuary the priest began his sermon and "the people think of their absent loved ones, about their absent priest and friends, imprisoned, waiting to undergo interrogations such as Jesus Himself endured, when He was asked, 'What is Truth?'" The Rosary was then prayed, and the Stations of the Cross, solemn Benediction of the Blessed Sacrament and a novena of prayers offered, including the prayer composed by Bishop Kung:

> Holy Mother, once speaking to Bernadette you said: "I shall make you happy, not in this world, but in the next." Throughout your whole life you followed the way of the Cross which is the unique road leading to Heaven. We do not ask for the happiness of this world, but we ask to imitate your courage to follow the way of the Cross through this world. O Holy Mary of the Immaculate Conception, we ask you to pray for us. Please turn your eyes of mercy towards us, protect us and help us through this world in order that we may enter into the Kingdom of God and enjoy life eternal. Amen. [110]

At mid-month, and again at the end of the month in each parish, a more intense form of these ceremonies was celebrated, culminating in a large procession with the statue around the church. Members of other parishes were encouraged to make pilgrimages to the parish in which the statue of Our Lady was then visiting. Buses were provided in the evenings during each mid-month and end of month processions. Not only did these nightly pilgrimages and parish prayers strengthen the bond of the Catholics of Shanghai, it also provided public demonstrations of the strength of the faith of Shanghai's Catholics, and insinuated that the Catholic Church was interested only in the glory of God and not in politics. The *Mission Bulletin* narrated that during one such pilgrimage in February, as four buses carrying Catholics to one of the local churches in which the statue of Our Lady was visiting:

---

[109] *Mission Bulletin*, Vol. VI, September 1954, No. 7, p. 609.
[110] *Mission Bulletin*, Vol. VI, May, 1954, No. 5, p. 475.

All along the route heads turn to get an eyeful of the four buses passing by in line. "Is it a peace delegation?", ask the curious. No, because the faces are all the same color, and, besides, there is no police at the intersections to stop the traffic. Finally, they realize, hearing this group reciting something unfamiliar to their ears: Catholics, again? Some might even think, "after all that has been done and said against them, they are truly not ordinary people." Arrived at their destination, the neighbors of the church push their noses to their house windows and ask, "What is this? What are they doing!?" [111]

Bishop Kung's initiating the two Marian years was well understood as his means to strengthen the faith of Catholics in Shanghai. The Marian years also were public demonstrations of the strength of that faith to the Communist authorities, and a clear statement that this was a faith very much linked and supported by their communion with the Successor of Saint Peter, whether the government liked that or not.

And the Successor of Saint Peter understood well the reality of the Church in China. In an article in the *Mission Bulletin*, the story of Monsignor Gustave Prevost from the Quebec Foreign Missions was told. On his return to Shanghai following a visit to his family in Canada in late 1949, he visited Rome and had an audience with the Holy Father. After his arrest in 1951, his jailers interpreted his audience with the Pope as proof that he was a spy for the imperialist Pius XII. The *Bulletin* reported the conversation between the missionary and the Pope:

> He [Msgr. Prevost] asked the Holy Father if he should stay in China under the Communists and the Holy Father told him, "The good pastor remains with his sheep." He then asked the Holy Father what he should do if a storm of persecution swept his mission and the Holy Father answered, "*Eritis mihi testes* [you will be witnesses of the faith for me]." [112]

Catholics Persecuted

Bishop Kung continued his duties as Ordinary of the Diocese of Shanghai and Apostolic Administrator of Soochow and Nanking, even with so many of his priests arrested and foreign missionaries expelled. He warned Rome against raising a parish church to the dignity of a minor basilica in the Diocese of Peking.

---

[111] *Mission Bulletin*, Vol. VI, September 1954, No. 7, p. 609-611.
[112] Ibid., p. 688.

The priest authoring the petition was the vicar general of Peking, suspected of sympathies for the "reformed" Church in China, and the parish was in the hands of the Communist clergy. [113] It was an underhanded trick to seek Vatican approval for the government Catholic Church, foiled by Bishop Kung with the help of Father George Germain, S.J.

At the same time, public denunciations of the Church continued in the daily Shanghai press, on billboards, on loudspeakers throughout the city, and in the lobby of the International Hotel, where the government opened its *Exhibition Showing the Crimes of the Capitalist Imperialist Agents*. A ramshackle collection of junk had been hastily gathered and assembled with notes describing the exhibits as "evidence" of Catholic espionage against the People's government. One exhibit was "from a copy of *Life Magazine*, found in the priests' residence, the Reds cut out pictures of models in swim suits and accused the priests of "keeping obscene pictures." [114]

In an attempt to bolster the fidelity of the seminarians to the Holy See, Bishop Kung led the seminarians to the local Shrine of Our Lady of Sheshan to make a vow to remain faithful to the Church. The vow ended, "*Christus vincit, Christus regnat, Christus imperat et cum Christo, mater nostra vincit, mater nostra regnat, mater nostra imperat* (Christ triumphs, Christ reigns, Christ rules and with Christ, our mother triumphs, our mother reigns, our mother rules)." [115]

On May 23, 1954, Bishop Kung ordained two new priests at the pilgrimage church of Zose with 4,000 Catholics in attendance. While Catholic life appeared to return to normal, albeit after mass arrests and expulsions of clergy and religious, the government was still hard at work to undermine the Catholic community. Their means now were to divide the Catholic community from its priests and bishop, and to kidnap the lay leaders.

> It is a persecution that requires that the chain be strong in every link and that it be forged the stronger by the personal holiness of those being tested by fire and reinforced by the prayers and sacrifices of the other members of the Mystical Body of Christ. [116]

The Catholic Central Bureau, or what was left of it, received notifications from the Communist government of the deaths of various imprisoned priests, usually months after each actually died. Since the death of Father Beda Chang, S.J. and the massive and angry response by the Shanghai Catholic community a few years earlier, the government prohibited solemn requiem Masses for any priests who died while in prison. They also prohibited any large public

---

[113] Mariani, *Church Militant*, p. 137.
[114] *Mission Bulletin*, Vol. VIII, February, 1956, No. 2, p. 144.
[115] Mariani, *Church Militant*, p. 138.
[116] *Mission Bulletin*, Vol. VI, October, 1954, No. 8, p. 787.

acknowledgment of the death of these priests, in order to avoid possible international trouble from the few foreign diplomats still accredited to the Chinese government. Bishop Kung's response was that parishes should offer low Masses for the deceased priests, and the celebrant of the Mass would be vested in red vestments, the color of martyrs. Despite these being low Masses, usually offered early in the morning, the churches were usually filled, and it was not uncommon that Bishop Kung and Bishop Walsh would be present, offering the Mass, or presiding at it, or offering the final absolution. [117]

Papal Clarification

On October 7, 1954, the Feast of the Holy Rosary, and the fifth anniversary of the episcopal consecration of Bishop Kung, Pope Pius XII issued his encyclical *Ad Sinarum Gentem*, "On the Supranationality of the Church". [118] Yet it was not made public until he was assured the bishops in China had received copies to be read in all churches and by all those priests in communion with him and still functioning. The encyclical was addressed specifically and by name to the hierarchy, clergy and people of China in communion with the Apostolic See; not to the members of the government's Patriotic Catholic Association. It was, however, meant for everyone to read.

The Pope reminded the Catholic clergy and community of his earlier apostolic letter, *Cupimus Imprimis*, issued "not only to express to you Our sympathy in your afflictions, but also to exhort you paternally to fulfill all the duties of the Christian religion with that resolute fidelity that sometimes demands heroic strength." He continued, bluntly,

> In recent years, however, the conditions of the Catholic Church in your midst have not improved in the least. The accusations and calumnies against the Apostolic See and those who keep themselves faithful to it have increased. The Apostolic Nuncio, who represented Our person among you has been expelled. The snares to deceive those less instructed in the truth have been intensified.

He continued, quoting from his earlier Apostolic Letter that the Chinese government suppressed, never permitting it to be read inside China,

> However, as we wrote to you—'you are opposing with a firm will all forms of insidious attack, whether subtle, hidden, or masked under a false appearance of truth.' We know that these words of Our

---

[117] *Mission Bulletin*, Vol. VI, Dec, 1954, No. 10, p. 984-985.
[118] *Ad Sinarum Gentem*, 1. The Encyclical can be found in Appendix 9.

previous Apostolic Letter were not able to reach you. So We willingly repeat them for you by means of this Encyclical. [2-3]

The Holy Father then addressed the Chinese government's Three-Self Movement, which demanded the Church in China be independent of any foreign contact or support. The Pope warned the priests of China that a national church established by the government was no authentic church, and, once communion with the Successor of Peter was broken, that government creation was no longer Catholic. Certain aspects of the Church could be adapted, such as its finances and certain organizational structures that are by nature transitional in nature, dictated by the culture and times. It must be recalled that the foreign missionaries were not imperialists. They freely left their own home countries to preach the Gospel; that was their only motivation, "they seek only, and desire nothing more than, to illumine your people with the light of Christianity, to teach them Christian customs and to help them with a supernatural charity." [10] Nevertheless, native born Chinese priests and bishops were being provided for the Church in China for well over the past twenty-five years. While the Church could be flexible about certain aspects and practices of the Church, all bishops, priests and faithful remained subject to the Successor of Saint Peter in the areas of faith and morals. This was non-negotiable and immutable. Finally, he addressed the notion that the Church's doctrine in China should be independent of Rome, writing,

> We do not at all deny that the manner of preaching and teaching ought to differ according to place and therefore ought to conform, when possible, to the nature and particular character of the Chinese people, as also to its ancient traditional customs. If this is properly done, certainly greater fruits will be gathered among you.

> But—and it is absurd merely to think of it—by what right can men arbitrarily and diversely in different nations, interpret the Gospel of Jesus Christ? [15-16]

Finally, the Pope addressed by name China's imposed Three Self Movement, or as he termed it "The Three Autonomies", so stressed by the Chinese government and so steadfastly opposed by Bishop Kung, his priests and the faithful of Shanghai. Anyone who preaches or teaches differently from that which the Successor of Peter preaches or teaches, cannot be called Catholic.

> This includes those persons who have adhered to the dangerous principles underlying the movement of the *Three Autonomies*, or to other similar principles.

> The promoters of such movements with greatest cunning seek to deceive the simple or the timid, or to draw them away from the right path. For this purpose they falsely affirm that the only true patriots

are those who adhere to the church thought up by them, that is, to that which has the *Three Autonomies*. But in reality they seek, in a word, to establish finally among you a *national* church, which no longer could be Catholic because it would be the negation of that universality or rather *catholicity* by which the society truly founded by Jesus Christ is above all nations and embraces them one and all. [21-23]

Just a few days later, on November 2, 1954, the Holy Father addressed the cardinals and bishops gathered in Rome for the canonization of Pope Saint Pius X, repudiating those governments and individuals trying to restrict the Church's teachings to liturgy and piety.

> This tendency confines their [Pope's, cardinals' and bishops'] authority, duty and vigilance to precise limits of strictly religious matters, the promulgation of the truths of the Faith, the regulation of practices of piety, the administration of the sacraments of the Church, and the performance of liturgical functions.

He continued,

> They strive to separate the Church from all enterprises and things concerning real life—'the reality of life' as they say—as if this were beyond her power.

> According to divine ordinance, there is indeed a relation between the observance of the law of nature and that road man must follow to tend to his supernatural end. Now, on the road which leads to the supernatural end, the Church is the guide and the guardian of man. This practice was followed by the apostles, and the Church has always observed it and still continues to observe it up to this day, and this not only as a private guide or counselor, but through the order of Our Lord and with His authority.

Being gathered for the canonization of Pope Pius X, the Pope quoted the Saint's 1912 encyclical *Singulari quadam*: "It is absolutely certain that any social problem is first of all moral and religious, and thus must be solved above all according to the principles of moral law and of religion." Pope Pius continued,

> In social matters, there is not only one but many problems, and very grave ones—purely social or political-social—which come into the field of morality, conscience, and the salvation of souls, and which therefore may by no means be considered as beyond the authority and vigilance of the Church. Moreover, even besides social order, many questions arise, not strictly religious, but concerning political affairs of some nation in particular or of nations in general which

come into the moral order, entangle consciences, and very often actually threaten the attainment of the last end.

He then hit a nerve for all governments:

> Such for example is the question of the aim and the limits of civil power; the problem of the relations between the individual and society; the problem of totalitarian states regardless of their principles or origin; the problem of total secularization of the State and of public life; the secularization of schools; the morality of war and its legitimacy or illegitimacy in the conditions of the present time; the problem of the moral links and connections which regulate the mutual relationships of nations and put them under obligation.

> In all this the authority established by God may interfere not only in secret, inside the walls of the temple and the sanctuary, but also in public, and to use the words of Our Lord 'to cry out from the roofs' (Mt 10:27), on the battlefield itself, in the midst of the battle which is fought now between the 'World' and the Kingdom of God, between the prince of this world and the Savior of the world, Christ.[119]

Bishop Kung and his priests read the encyclical about China during their annual end of the year retreat. While maintaining as best they could the day-to-day practices in the parishes and in the diocese, the Bishop and his priests understood that they needed to continue considering the future of the Church when the priests and Bishop of Shanghai would no longer be free to exercise their ministries. It was rumored that Bishop Kung drew up a list of potential candidates as his successor as Bishop of Shanghai after his arrest. A bishop was essential to normative Catholic life because only a bishop could ordain priests, thus assuring the transferal of apostolic charism and the sacramental life of the Church to the next generation of Catholics. In February 1955, before a picture of Our Lady of China, Bishop Kung revealed his *terna* of three possible candidates to a few close and trusted associates. Another version of this states that the Bishop instructed Father Martinez-Balirach, S.J. to send the *terna* to Rome, adding further candidates' names as well. [120]

1955 was to be "a year of special devotion to the Sacred Heart" in the Diocese of Shanghai. Bishop Kung announced this and inaugurated the year during a High Mass followed by 40 Hours Devotion offered at the Church of the Sacred Heart at Honkew. Each parish throughout the Diocese would be scheduled to offer the 40 Hours Devotion throughout the year, along with special prayers for

---

[119] *Acta Apostolicae Sedis*, 46 (1954): *Magnificate Dominum*, pp. 666-677.
[120] Mariani, *Church Militant*, p. 138-139.

peace. [121] The consecration to the Sacred Heart of Jesus was the natural complement to the earlier consecration to the Immaculate Heart of Mary, as a means to strengthen the faithful for their struggles.

Years later, Bishop Kung described the Church's situation in Shanghai:

> The government hoped that by imprisoning the clergy, crushing the Church financially, and isolating the Chinese Church from the Universal Church, it would bring the Catholic Church to its knees. On the contrary, most of the clergy and faithful were ready to take up their crosses to Calvary. Many Catholic faithful followed the great heroic examples of the priests and religious sisters, and chose imprisonment rather than betray their faith. Others bravely took on responsibilities and helped in the many works of the dioceses. When the government failed to crush the Church, it formed the Chinese Catholic Patriotic Association which was meant to replace the Roman Catholic Church.
>
> Those who refused to join the Patriotic Association and remained loyal to the Holy Father were given jail sentences of ten, twenty, thirty or more years. After the jail sentence, it was common for them to be sent to a labor camp. Torture, extreme hard conditions in jail and long hours of hard labor were common for the Roman Catholics. Thousands died as witnesses of Christ. [122]

On April 17, 1955, Pope Pius XII beatified a third group of Chinese martyrs, just as the Chinese government launched a new purge of local and national government figures under the guise of a new nationwide movement to suppress counter-revolutionaries. Because Bishop Kung was one of the few Catholic bishops left relatively free in any large city in China, his telephone was tapped and his mail intercepted, the alleged contents of which were shrieked about in the Communist press that reached new heights of anti-Catholic hysteria. [123] All this was exacerbated by the growing dissatisfaction of the Chinese people with the Communist government. Brother Xavier Coupe, S.J. reported that by 1955,

> The anti-Communist spirit is growing, especially in the country districts. There have been terrible famine conditions during the last month. The people have become embittered by the deceit, the seizure of crops and wealth and the tyranny and now they are

---

[121] *Mission Bulletin*, Vol. VII, April, 1955, p. 350.
[122] *Soul Magazine*, July-August 1993, *An Interview with Cardinal Kung*, p. 18.
[123] *Mission Bulletin*, Vol. VII, November, 1955, No. 9, p. 819.

disillusioned with Communism. They bow their heads but their minds and hearts give no consent to Communism. [124]

The Catholic Church Family

Brother Xavier continued that the Church's response to the government persecution was prayer and courageous yet peaceful resistance to the government's violent assaults against the parishes, laity and clergy. The heart of the matter was the growing sense of personal communion with their local father, Bishop Kung, and with their Holy Father, Pope Pius XII, which was much more than mere collective enthusiasm or fear. It was a spiritual bond between those fed on the same revealed Word and who received the Word Incarnate in the Eucharist that forged this unity among themselves, with their bishop who was the visible heart of the community of believers, and with the Successor of Saint Peter. In his reflections about the life of the Church in Shanghai at this very moment, which he experienced as a Jesuit seminarian at the time, Father Jean Lefeuvre, S.J. paraphrased the words of Saint Ignatius of Antioch in his Letter to the Church in Smyrna, written as he was a prisoner being dragged to Rome for martyrdom by the Roman government in the first years of the second century: [125]

> The good shepherd knows his sheep and the sheep know him. The Bishop truly is within the Church of Shanghai as the [local] bishop was with those who received the words from Saint Ignatius of Antioch, "Follow the bishop, as Jesus Christ followed the Father. . . Where the bishop appears, there let the people be, just as where Jesus Christ is, there is the Catholic Church. . . It is well to revere God and the bishop. He who honors the bishop is honored by God. He who does anything without the knowledge of the bishop worships the devil." [126]

Father Lefeuvre continued, referring to Bishop Kung,

> In the eyes of the faithful, he became an angel of the Lord; ceaselessly bearing witness to the entire Church. The Church became the realized Chinese ideal of the family: expecting the courage and goodness of a father. [127]

The personal appeal of Bishop Kung was that he not only understood the Chinese notion of the family, he lived it. Having grown up in a Catholic Chinese

---

[124] *Mission Bulletin*, Vol. VII, May, 1955, No. 5, p. 445.
[125] Lefeuvre, *Shanghai,* p. 211.
[126] Ignatius of Antioch, *Letter to the Smyrneans*, VIII, 1-2; IX, 1.
[127] Lefeuvre, *Shanghai*, p. 211.

family, he felt the importance of his mother and father, as well as the intimate relationship with his siblings and with earlier and future generations of the family, reaching backward and forward for decades, linking all members both past, present and future.

As the Communist government strove to destroy the family in Chinese society, replacing it with loyalty to the State, Bishop Kung and Pope Pius XII were forging a spiritual family—the Catholic Church. The mother of the Church-family was the Blessed Virgin Mary, who was the very heart of mercy. The father of the local Church-family was Bishop Kung; the father for the universal Church-family, the Holy Father. All this made perfect sense to Chinese Catholics, and Bishop Kung understood this clearly, believed it fervently, and defended it strenuously. [128]

The relationship Bishop Kung had with the Catholics of Shanghai, and their respect for and dedication to him, is clearly shown in a letter by a Chinese religious sister who was there, witnessed everything, and was later imprisoned:

> Bishop Kung had notified us [the Legion of Mary and the Catholic students] not to join meetings conducted by Communists even meetings of ordinary nature; that was to show his firm resistance of [sic] the Communist's government. The government invited Bishop [Kung] to have a meeting, which Bishop flatly refused to attend. He also ordered that children wearing the 'red scarf' [Communist youth insignia] were not to be given Holy Communion, if they would approach the Communion Rail wearing the scarf which was the signal of joining the children's youth corp. The Bishop conducted a solemn Way of the Cross in Siccawei Cathedral for those who died of faith during the Communists [sic] regime; all these incensed the fury and hatred of the Communists against the Church and himself. Still they would ponder their time, they just let things going on, apparently they seemed to be 'dumb and blind'. Meantime, in all the churches, all the Masses, devotions, etc. . .were packed with people.
>
> The Faithful were reserving all the spiritual strength they would need at the time when they would be called upon to give testimony of their Faith. With bishop's wise guidance the priests did not spare themselves in giving themselves to the faithful the necessary spiritual weapons. The way that most of the Faithful stood for their faith, at least at the time when I was home, is something one cannot forget easily! Whether they were imprisoned, or remained out of it, they were all suffering for their Faith in such a way, I would say, they were martyrs! (bloodless martyrdom). We were taken by force

---

[128] Lefeuvre, Ibid., p. 212-213.

(as some of us were literally called as criminals, so we had no freedom) to see the Exhibition of the Catholic Crimes.

As I was taken from one department to another (also saw my own picture with my crimes there) till to the end of the long line, I found myself stood in front of a picture of His Excellency Bishop I. Kung of Shanghai, taken with the policeman holding his collar, arresting him as a criminal. . . . I have no words to describe to you my thoughts then. [129]

Arrests: Strike the Shepherd and the Sheep will Scatter

As revealed by a Shanghai government document, plans were completed by the late summer of 1955 to launch a "full-scale attack against the reactionary power of the Shanghai Catholic Church." [130] Working committees were established to destroy the "Kung Pin-Mei clique". It was all methodically and logically pursued, as outlined in detail in government documents. The government would divide and conquer the Church in Shanghai, first by attacking the Catholic youth, as narrated in a report following the violent mass arrests of September 1955:

> In conducting the preparatory stage, another important aspect is that beginning in early August we united our work with the Elimination of Counterrevolutionary Movement in the schools and the Suppression of Counterrevolutionaries Movement in society. Concerning the Kung Pin-mei counterrevolutionary clique, we conducted our war by attacking his defensive perimeter. First, we decimated the core leadership of the Catholic Youth—whom the enemy had previously used in the battles as the main force of their mass counter-attacks. They were the college and university students in the "Catholic Youth" organization and part of the main pillar of the reactionaries in society. With the same goal in mind, the different colleges began their intensive thought struggle against 250 of the "Catholic Youth". We controlled their activities. We divided and broke down 240 of them, and we won over 40 of the core leaders, who, after rebelling within [the Catholic Youth movement], came to our side so that we could use them. [From them] we accumulated and enhanced our materials to destroy the Kung Pin-mei clique.

---

[129] October 20, 1958, Sister Candida to Joseph Kung, Cardinal Kung Foundation Archives.
[130] Quoted in Mariani, *Church Militant*, p. 142.

Grade 5, Saint John's Catholic School, Stamford, Connecticut
1955, praying for Persecuted Christians in China.

Basilica of Saint John Archives

At the same time, because of the Suppression of Counter-revolutionaries Movement, the government arrested a group of counterrevolutionaries hidden in the Catholic Church and other counterrevolutionaries guilty of other social crimes, in order to clear barriers to launch the whole movement. [131]

Among the documents and information collected by the government were lists of priests who had attended the two annual retreats led by Bishop Kung for the diocesan clergy. During the summer weeks, individual leaders of the Catholic Youth groups were interrogated and arrested, as were priests and religious. By September, all was ready for the nationwide movement against the Catholic Church, and it would begin in Shanghai.

Realizing the full scale public attack against Bishop Kung, as seen in the press, radio announcements, public loud speaker announcements and posters plastered on walls around the city, everyone sensed the arrest of Bishop Kung was imminent. His mother came to see him. She warned him to protect himself, and, weeping, warned that she feared never seeing him again. Bishop Kung comforted his mother, telling her, "Do not hope to see me again. You should be happy and proud that your son is a prisoner for Christ."[132] His mother died at the Kung Family home in Shanghai, while the Bishop was imprisoned. The government never permitted his family to inform him of his mother's death. He learned about it only after his release, when his youngest brother was able to speak with him after his decades of imprisonment.

Late on the night of September 8th and into the early hours of the 9th, 1955, the Communist forces struck. Hundreds of police raided all Catholic parishes, convents, the seminary and all Catholic institutions in Shanghai simultaneously, as well as a number of homes of leading Catholic laypersons. They arrested Bishop Kung, a number of priests and hundreds of lay Catholics. The Shanghai Communist "Catholic" paper *The Courier Dove* made the announcement of the arrest of Bishop Kung Pin-Mei in its morning edition of September 9th:

> This group, with Kung Pin-mei as their leader, directed by imperialist spies, cloaked in religion and employed the Catholic Church of Shanghai as their cover, pursued their activities across China and sought important information about military, political and economic activities in China in order to pass them to imperialist espionage organizations. [133]

The paper also reported the three charges against Bishop Kung:

---

[131] 1956 *Introduction concerning the Shanghai Catholic Work*, quoted in Mariani, *Church Militant*, pp. 145-146.
[132] Stamford, August 25, 2012, Joseph Kung to Msgr. Stephen DiGiovanni, Basilica Archives.
[133] Quoted in *Mission Bulletin*, Vol. VII, November, 1955, No. 9, p. 821.

1. Resisting orders of the Committee of Military Affairs regarding the Legion of Mary; preventing the members of the Legion from registering with the police. Also, he organized a Party of Patriotic Revolutionaries and a Committee of Young Chinese Revolutionaries and Anti-Communists, as well as sending agents throughout China for destructive activities against the government;

2. Spreading anti-revolutionary rumors with evil intent; sheltering anti-revolutionary elements in the cathedral and in other places; praying to God for Catholics who had been condemned by the Communists;

3. Raising anti-revolutionary elements to assemble in order to create public disorders, and to combat "patriotic" Catholics, who joined the government church; giving Catholics orders like "Stand firm" or "Never betray" or "Fight to the bitter end against the Communists."

But, depending upon the newspaper consulted, as subsequent issues of the *Mission Bulletin* point out, the accusations changed, along with fabricated details, dates and names supporting the fraudulent charges.

The Shanghai daily secular newspaper, *Sin Weh Jih Pao* of September 9th, carried the same story as *The Courier Dove*, and concluded that the police actions and arrests were carried out by the government "In order to destroy this anti-government group of Kung Pin-Mei at its very roots, and to exterminate all anti-revolutionary elements that are hidden by the Catholic Church." [134]

Scanty news reports came through to Hong Kong a few days after the arrests, but no confirmation was had until the arrival of Father Luis Bolumburu relating the extent of the arrests: 23 priests, and between 200-300 leading Catholic laypersons along with Bishop Kung. [135] Reports of the arrests appeared in Western newspapers slowly. *Time Magazine* made mention of Father Bolumburu in a brief article on October 3rd, quoting him as having said that Catholics in Shanghai continued to attend church faithfully, "not because there is religious freedom in Communist China, but because the Catholics are courageous." [136] The *Osservatore Romano* reported the arrests on October 8th, and this report formed the basis of the brief announcement, buried deep inside the paper, by the *New York Times* the next day. [137] The *New York Times* published another brief article on December 11th, again buried on page 32, acknowledging its source as the radio broadcasts from Moscow reporting that "Kung Pin-Mei, Roman Catholic Bishop of Shanghai, and his principal accomplices, had been charged with being spies and subversive

---

[134] Ibid., p. 821
[135] *Mission Bulletin*, Vol. VII, November, 1955, No. 9, p. 805.
[136] *Time Magazine*, October 3, 1955. http://www.time.com/timeprintout/0,8816,807698,00.html
[137] *New York Times*, October 9, 1955, p. 24.

plotters." [138]   The *Times* quoted the Moscow report that "secret police who arrested the Bishop and his aides had captured radio equipment and papers proving they were working for free China [Taiwan] and certain foreign powers. It charged also that they were plotting a counter-revolutionary uprising."

The *Mission Bulletin* commented on an article in its *Lettre De Famille* section, published in the September number of the *China Reconstructs*, an English language periodical for foreigners. Its author was allegedly a Roman Catholic doctor still in Shanghai after the September 8th arrests. He stated there was no persecution, that the churches were open and filled for Masses. The *Bulletin* editors believed this was propaganda, informing the readers that "a propaganda campaign was released and launched in all the media of China against Kung and his clergy." [139]   Then they commented specifically on the *Lettre* itself, and generally on the lack of the world's response to the persecution of the Catholic Church in China:

> Was it a gamble that this article was published in a periodical for foreigners, precisely in September? Was it a gamble that these massive arrests, not only in Shanghai, but especially there, because Shanghai was the last center which had not yet been destroyed or paralyzed, but throughout all of China;--was it by chance that these arrests took place while Chinese-American negotiations were taking place? The foreign press announced with great flourish the liberation of fliers, civil prisoners and others unjustly held elsewhere; there is even talk of a 'change of heart', of an expansion of vision, of a sweetening and of goodness. . . while the mass arrests in Shanghai pass unnoticed. [140]

During the subsequent weeks, the arrested priests, Catholic leaders and members of the Catholic youth were subjected to interrogations, group indoctrination classes, imprisonment or house arrest. [141] All were shown newspapers proclaiming Bishop Kung's betrayal of Catholics and of the country, whose policies for the Diocese of Shanghai were anti-revolutionary lies, part of a massive espionage plot. The Bishop of Shanghai had used the priests and Catholics, hiding under the "cloak of religion", cynically taking advantage of their natural goodness and faith to undermine the People's revolution. Soon, his title as Bishop of Shanghai was no longer used by the media; rather he was repeatedly

---

[138] *New York Times*, December 11, 1955, p. 32.
[139] *Mission Bulletin*, Vol. VII, November, 1955, No. 9, p. 819.
[140] Ibid., p. 820.
[141] Ibid., p. 806.

titled "the criminal Kung Pin-Mei", or his name linked with "criminal activities." [142]

On September 9th, the Communist officials summoned all 54 Chinese priests left in Shanghai to a meeting at which the charges against Bishop Kung were clarified:

> 1) Bishop Kung would not allow Catholic children to join Communist groups; 2) the Bishop had close relations with the foreign imperialists (foreign priests, such as the Jesuits); 3) the Bishop opposed the campaign against the Legion of Mary; 4) the Bishop would not participate personally nor allow others to participate in various *patriotic* movements; 5) the Bishop denied the Sacraments to *patriotic Catholics* (members of the government church). [143]

The *Bulletin* editor opined that two other possible reasons for the arrests had been the Bishop's refusal to pay for repairs to church properties that the Communists planned to confiscate, and his refusal to permit his Chinese priests "to take the indoctrination course, i.e. take the first steps toward joining the puppet, so-called *progressive church*, also called, *independent church*. This, Bishop Kung refused to do, hence the unleashing of the storm."

The most damaging "evidence" against the Bishop and the Church in Shanghai was provided by the former Jesuit Superior, Father Fernand Lacretrelle, S.J. He was imprisoned for a little more than 13 months, and released in July 1954, during which time he was interrogated 550 times. By the time he was expelled to Hong Kong, he was a broken man. During his imprisonment, he was forced to write a 769- page statement, and later a taped "confession", implicating Bishop Kung and the Church in Shanghai, providing names and dates and activities of the leading priests and laypeople. The taped confession was later played to priests and Catholic laypersons during their interrogations, group indoctrination courses and throughout prisons. All knew Father Lacretelle as a saintly priest. Once his taped voice was heard saying that Bishop Kung had nearly destroyed the Church and that the government was saving "the Church in Shanghai from the road of death on which Kung Pin-Mei was leading it", the government's accusations against the Bishop appeared to be confirmed, and resulted in breaking the spirit and resolve of many. [144]

Twenty-eight mass meetings were held during the first two weeks of September, during which Catholics who had "seen the light" and joined forces

---

[142] Lefeuvre, *Shanghai*, p. 220.

[143] *Mission Bulletin*, Vol. VII, December, 1955, No. 10, p. 885.

[144] Quoted in Mariani, *Church Militant*, p. 163.

with the Communists spoke to 20,000 Catholics encouraging them to abandon the Kung Pin-Mei clique and join the patriotic Catholic movement. [145]

It was during one such meeting on September 12th of thousands of Catholics, guarded by armed police, when mass accusations were made against Bishop Kung, his priests and loyal Catholic laypersons. An eyewitness described the scene:

> After all sorts of accusations were thrown at the Bishop, he was asked to speak. But the bishop remained silent. Then they thrust him in front of the mike and kept urging him to say something. The bishop seeing that there would be no end to this, raised his head and shouted, "Long live Christ" several times. The crowd, mostly students followed up by shouting: "Long live the bishop", but could only shout twice because the soldiers raised their rifles and Tommy guns and pointed them ordering them to keep quiet or they would open [fire]. Then they pulled the bishop away from the mike and pushed him roughly into the waiting lorry and drove off. The bishop was dressed in a Chinese short jacket and trousers and had his hands tied behind his back. [146]

By the end of September, the government felt sufficiently confident in its success to convene a massive victory rally at the Candrome, the Shanghai dog racing track on Sunday, September 25, 1955. There 15,000 Catholics and 40 priests were assembled. Bishop Kung was not present. This "Shanghai Catholic Big Meeting" featured a former Jesuit priest, Father Kang who denounced Bishop Kung, vowing to promote an independent Catholic Church in Shanghai. [147] The slogan of the meeting, endlessly repeated over the sound system was "Strongly, Radically, Completely, Totally, let us liquidate the counter-revolutionaries hidden in the church and Kung Pin-Mei their leader." [148]

On October 2nd, the government staged a Mass at Christ the King Church "for the success of the coup against Monsignor Kung and his reactionary group." The priests organizing the Mass were those who had co-operated with the establishment of the government's Patriotic Church, and hundreds of local Catholics were forced to attend. [149]

During the subsequent weeks, the priests were subjected to further government pressure, resulting in their forced written denunciation of Bishop

---

[145] Ibid., p. 155.
[146] *Bamboo Wireless*, April 1956, pp. 3-4, quoted in Mariani, *Church Militant*, p. 160.
[147] *Mission Bulletin*, Vol. VII, December, 1955, No. 10, p. 886
[148] *Mission Bulletin*, Vol. IX, January, 1957, No. 1, p. 51.
[149] *Mission Bulletin*, Vol. VIII, January, 1956, No. 1, p. 83-84.

Kung, which was published by the *People's Daily* on December 10th. [150] While some of the priests' signatures were falsified, and the documents the priests signed were weaker than those actually published, the damage was complete, especially when the signatures were made public by the *People's Daily* on December 11th, [151] below a government text thanking God "for His wise guidance in that the People's Government had taken proper measures to save our Church in Shanghai from the road of death on which Kung Pin-Mei was leading it." [152]

Another mass meeting was arranged by the government to further destroy Bishop Kung's credibility before Shanghai's Catholics. [153] As Bishop Kung stood on the stage, he was denounced for three hours by a number of seminarians and nuns recently released from prison. As a Carmelite nun who witnessed the spectacle later recalled, Bishop Kung "had to listen to a storm of accusations hammered by the screams of the mob. . . . The Bishop remained calm and silent and at a certain time held his hand over his heart." [154] There were other eyewitness reports claiming numerous "great public trials" at which Bishop Kung was forced to appear, but the Chinese government denied these. [155]

Pressure continued to be applied by the People's Republic to convince the Chinese people about the absolute necessity that the government continue to prosecute Bishop Kung and his clique. On November 10, 1955, a lengthy letter allegedly written by the Catholic Clergy of Shanghai to explain their case was printed throughout China. Opening, "Respected Fathers, Beloved Fellow Catholics!" it narrates the events of September 8, 1955, and supports the government actions. It is pure Communist propaganda, designed to confuse the weakened Catholic community and the non-Catholic majority in Shanghai, that they might support the government's actions.

> Jesus said 'Render to Caesar the things that are Caesar's and to God what is God's' (*Mt*, xxii, 21). In being patriotic, we are abiding by the sacred teaching of Jesus, a concrete manifestation of our love of our religion.
>
> The People's Government has correctly implemented the policy of freedom of religious belief, and does not interfere with our purely religious affairs, as well as our religious link with His Holiness. Nor

---

[150] *Mission Bulletin*, Vol. VIII, March, 1956, No. 3, pp. 223-227.

[151] Ibid., pp. 220-223.

[152] Ibid., p. 222.

[153] *America*, November 23, 1963, p. 652: "Bishop Kung was arrested, Sept. 8, 1955, along with many of his faithful clergy and laity. The first attempt at a show trial boomeranged against his captors."

[154] *Bamboo Wireless*, March 1956, pp.1-2, quoted in Mariani, *Church Militant*, p. 167.

[155] *Sunday Examiner*, September 5, 1958, *Three Years in Gaol, Anniversary of the Arrest of the Bishop of Shanghai*, p. 3.

does it force us to abandon our belief. The Government respects our Catholic Church, and protects proper religious activities.

But Kung Pin-Mei and his ilk resort to all measures to stop us from loving our country, demanding of us 'not to see, not to listen, and not to speak', to be separated from the new society.

Kung Pin-Mei and his colleagues exploit the name of religion to engage in such political activities which sabotage the State, and these acts are certainly not those to be done by a Bishop, a priest. [156]

Having discredited Bishop Kung and advanced the breaking down of Catholics of Shanghai, the government next established its own version of the Catholic Church, the Chinese Catholic Patriotic Association. Programs of "re-educating" both clergy and laity now began. Their purpose was to convince Catholics that the government Patriotic Association was the authentic local Catholic Church, which allowed them to be both loyal to the new order in China while maintaining their spiritual ties with the pope in Rome. On the Ides of March 1956, the Chinese government convened its version of a church council. A group of priests who had "converted" dutifully followed government orders and elected their own Bishop of Shanghai, informing Rome a few days later, requesting papal approval. They telegrammed Rome that, "Bishop Ignatius Kung has been imprisoned according to the law of anti-patriotism; hence Francis Xavier Tsang was canonically elected Vicar Capitular of the Diocese of Shanghai." The telegram was signed by Ignatius Zi, "President of the Council". Both Tsang and Zi were diocesan priests of Shanghai, and, as the *Mission Bulletin* opined, "It is feared they have been constrained by the Reds to condemn their Bishop whom they had served faithfully when they were free." [157]

Rome's response was immediate, and took the form of telegram from Cardinal Fumasoni-Biondi, Prefect of the Congregation of the Propagation of the Faith: "After the unjust imprisonment of the most worthy Bishop of Shanghai, Ignatius Kung, the diocese shall continue to be ruled according to the norms of Canon 429 of Canon Law." That canon reads: "Should the Episcopal see be impeded by the imprisonment, arrest, exile, or incapacity of the bishop, so that he cannot communicate with his diocesans by letter, the government of the diocese, so long as the Holy See does not dispose otherwise, shall rest in the hands of the vicar general or some other ecclesiastic designated by the bishop." The Vicar General of Shanghai was still Monsignor Sylvester Tsu who "was still in the city when Bishop Kung was arrested last September." And, referring to the secret *terna* drawn up by Bishop Kung months before, in anticipation of his arrest, the *Mission*

---

[156] *Mission Bulletin*, Vol. VIII, March, 1956, No. 3: the full and lengthy text, along with other Communist propaganda against Bishop Kung, is found on pp. 220-229.
[157] *Mission Bulletin*, Vol. VIII, May, 1956, p. 332.

Bulletin reported that there were also other priests "designated to govern the diocese should it become necessary." [158]

Since the legitimate and "most worthy" Bishop of Shanghai was imprisoned unjustly by the government, the "election" by the "council" of local priests had no validity, because Canon 429, when read in its entirety, provided a solution, and that manufactured by the Chinese government did not suffice. [159] Ignatius Kung Pin-Mei was still the legitimate Catholic Bishop of the Diocese of Shanghai, regardless of the government's judgment or ferocity of protest.

Whatever of the decision by Rome, the Church's buildings, properties, educational, charitable and medical institutions and all resources were confiscated and in the control of the Chinese government and its Chinese Catholic Patriotic Association. "Bishop" Tsang presided over the Diocese of Shanghai, appearing in the various churches of the city in full pontifical vestments. The hope of the government was that if it all looked Catholic, and operated as if nothing had happened, the Catholics of Shanghai would calm down and support the government's Church. But there were still priests in Shanghai still loyal to Rome and to Bishop Kung. One report stated that

> The Chinese pastors of Saint Teresa and Our Lady of Peace Churches refuse to offer Mass publicly. When the Communists sought to make them do so they replied that only Bishop Kung had the power to do that, and that when the Bishop came out of jail and ordered them to again offer Mass in public, they would do so. [160]

The Congregation of Propaganda Fide issued a directive on March 1, 1957. It stated that the legitimate Ordinary of the Diocese of Shanghai, who was also the legitimate Apostolic Administrator of the Diocese of Soochow and of the Archdiocese of Nanking was imprisoned unjustly by the Chinese government. Because of this, special faculties were granted to a specific group:

> The Sacred Congregation of Propaganda Fide grants special faculties to all and to only those priests who remaining in peace and communion with the Holy See, live in the Dioceses of Shanghai, Soochow, and the Archdiocese of Nanking in China.

> Since the legitimate Ordinaries in the above-mentioned Dioceses are no longer present, either impeded or absent, and can in no way be approached, and because those who actually take their place did not obtain this office according to special instructions issued to this end, or because they allowed themselves to be illegitimately assigned;

---

[158] Ibid.
[159] *Mission Bulletin*, Vol. VIII, May, 1956, No. 5, p. 332.
[160] *Mission Bulletin*, Vol. IX, June, 1956, No. 6, p. 464.

This Sacred Congregation

Wishing to provide for the welfare of the souls and the administration of the above-mentioned Churches, grants the following faculties, for the duration of these circumstances, to all priests of both clergy of the Diocese of Shanghai and of Soochow and the Archdiocese of Nanking, on condition that these priests have kept and will keep peace with the Holy See. [161]

Then were listed four grants: Any priest in communion with Rome "could exercise the office of pastor", even if a government priest claimed to hold that office in any parish. These priests, in communion with Bishop Kung and, therefore with Rome, were given jurisdiction to hear confessions, grant any necessary dispensations for the celebration of the sacraments or from absolution from canonical censure, for the good of souls that the needs of the faithful might be supplied even in these extraordinary times of crisis.

The Propaganda Fide even notified the Chinese Catholic Patriotic Association of its decision, in writing. The government response was not a happy one. The Ministry for Religious Affairs issued a statement that Rome's decision "is a scheme concocted by the Vatican in the form of religion that interferes with our country's internal affairs, violates its sovereignty, and damages our patriotic movement against imperialism." [162]

Rome's decision was prompted by concern for the salvation of souls of the Catholics in those dioceses who were being subjected to government persecution. The life of grace was more important than relations with the government of China. The decree was also designed to instruct Catholics about the reality of the government Patriotic Association as a schismatic entity, whose bishops were invalidly and illicitly appointed and consecrated. In reality, the decree served also to confirm the anger raised among Shanghai Catholics by the government's installation of their own bishop. They never accepted him, and referred to "Bishop" Tsang as "the usurper." [163]

As the first anniversary of the September 8th arrests drew near, the government toned down its relentless attacks against the Church. Only a handful of missionaries remained in jail, so that many people began to believe the government persecution had ended. A new organization had formed with no mention of "church" in its title, the "Preparatory Committee of the Patriotic Conference of Chinese Catholics." While the government insisted that it had nothing to do with religion, only Catholics were "permitted" to join. Imprisoned Chinese bishops and priests were pressured to join and to accept posts of

---

[161] *Mission Bulletin*, Vol. IX, October, 1957, No. 8, p. 533.
[162] Ibid., pp. 553-554.
[163] Ibid., p. 554.

responsibility in the organization, but Catholic laypersons were assured "that the movement is not in any way opposed to the Catholic Faith, that it is merely a civic society, hence all true Catholics should regard it as a patriotic duty to join." [164] But the faithful were not so gullible, and understood the government's poorly designed deceit. Their Bishop was still in jail, and neither they nor the Communist Party could ignore or forget that.

> Bishop Kung has been in prison for one year, and rumors have it he will soon be released. Will he still be Ignatius Kung, the valiant defender of the Christian city, or simply the shadow of his former self, broken by a long, clever persecution and subtle torture? On the occasion of the anniversary, the entire Catholic world should join hands with this prisoner of Christ, undoubtedly one of the greatest figures of the Eastern Church. That Peking has not simply ignored the small Catholic minority in China is proof that they have realized that the Catholic Church, though small in numbers, posed a real menace to their regime. To allow citizens, no matter how few, to continue to live in the belief that a person has a higher destiny than to serve the State, Communism could not permit that, hence the crackdown. [165]

In pursuit of its new tack to control the Catholic Church instead of destroying it outright, the government hosted a meeting of their newly created Chinese Catholic hierarchy, clergy, and laity in Peking in late 1957. The Bureau of Religious Affairs then issued a statement:

> In order not to obstruct the interests of the country, its independence and its honor, it is necessary to maintain purely religious relations with the Holy See, and to obey the Pope only in matters of doctrine, belief and to observe ecclesiastical laws but it is necessary to cut off radically all economic and political relations with the Holy See. [166]

There were no economic or political ties between China and the small Vatican City State. And, in light of Pope Pius' insistence that the Church was not limited to directives about liturgical or pious practices, but judgments concerning daily life, including the responsibility of governments, this obviously was part of the Chinese government's preparation for a complete termination of all ties of Chinese Catholics with the pope in Rome. Since the cornerstone of the Chinese government's program was its complete intrusion into and subjugation of individual conscience, the Church's links with her Head had to be broken completely.

---

[164] *Mission Bulletin*, Vol. IX, January, 1957, No. 1, p. 53.
[165] Ibid., p. 51-52.
[166] *Mission Bulletin*, Vol. IX, November, 1957, No. 9, 5, p. 75.

On June 29, 1958, the Solemnity of Saints Peter and Paul, Pope Pius XII issued another encyclical "On Communism and the Church in China" (*Ad Apostolorum Principis*).[167] It was made public two months later, only after the encyclical had been disseminated throughout China.

The Pope began by recalling the words of Pope Pius XI more than two decades earlier when he welcomed to the Tomb of Saint Peter those Chinese priests he would consecrate to be the first native-born bishops of the Church in China, as a sign of communion between China and the Successors of Saint Peter:

> You have come, Venerable Brethren, to visit Peter, and you have received from him the shepherd's staff, with which to undertake your apostolic journeys and to gather together your sheep. It is Peter who with great love has embraced you who are in great part Our Hope for the spread of the truth of the Gospel among your people.

Pius reminded his readers of his earlier letter and encyclical, then asserting the non-political agenda of the Church, written when the Chinese government began its persecution of the Church. Now he writes "to draw attention to the fact that the Church in your lands in recent years has been brought to still worse straights." But, the faith of the Church in China has been "unflinching" before their persecutors. The most recent development is the creation of a religious association "to which has been attached the title of *patriotic*, and Catholics are forced to be part in it." He continued,

> For under the appearance of patriotism, which in reality is just a fraud, this association aims primarily at making Catholics gradually embrace the tenets of atheistic materialism, by which God Himself is denied and religious principles are rejected.

Continuing, the Pope mentioned "a very serious matter that fills Our heart—the heart of a Father and universal Pastor of the faithful—with a grief that defies description." That is, "the dissemination among the people . . . that Catholics have the power of directly electing their bishops." This is not true. Here he quoted from his earlier encyclical, *Ad Sinarum gentem*, that bishops are chosen by God through the successor of Saint Peter, which is a sign and safeguard for the communion of the faithful with the Successor of Saint Peter. Then he quoted Our Lord in the Gospel of John, "He who enters not by the door into the sheepfold, but climbs up another way, is a thief and a robber" [*John* 10:1].

The Chinese government claimed that the episcopal sees of China were vacant, and bishops were needed, hence their election. But the Holy Father replied clearly:

---

[167] The Encyclical can be found in Appendix 10.

It is obvious that no thought is being taken of the spiritual good of the faithful if the Church's laws are being violated, and further, there is no question of vacant sees, as they wish to argue in defense, but of episcopal sees whose legitimate rulers have been driven out or now languish in prison or are being obstructed in various ways from the free exercise of their power of jurisdiction.

It is surely a matter for grief that while holy bishops noted for their zeal for souls are enduring so many trials, advantage is taken of their difficulties to establish false shepherds in their place so that the hierarchical order of the Church is overthrown and the authority of the Roman Pontiff is treacherously resisted. [168]

Pope Pius XII's last encyclical, issued just two weeks later on July 14th, *Meminisse Iuvat*, was a call for universal prayer for the persecuted Church throughout the world. Lamenting the continued absence of peace throughout the world, he called upon all to pray:

There must, then, be a return to Christian principles if we are to establish a society that is strong, just, and equitable. It is a harmful and reckless policy to do battle with Christianity, for God guarantees, and history testifies, that she shall exist forever. Everyone should realize that a nation cannot be well organized or well ordered without religion. [169]

Despite the words and warnings of the Holy Father, the Chinese government continued to name its own bishops, while stepping up the indoctrination and re-education programs, as well as the arrests of Catholic priests and laypersons. [170] Part of the re-education and indoctrination efforts included a stringent program of propaganda to besmirch the work of the Holy Father, of Bishop Kung and of all priests remaining loyal to them. The final resistance would be smashed. [171]

Bishop Kung's own niece, Margaret Chu, offers an example of the government's tactics. She belonged to an underground catechism group. She was given a name of a young woman interested in joining the group, and she and the other members welcomed her. She was a government spy, who asked Margaret to mail the sermons of a Jesuit priest to one of her friends. Margaret did, but,

---

[168] Mariani, *Church Militant*, p. 184: Bishop Kung was rumored to have personally handed the letter of excommunication to the Vicar General of Nanjing, Father Li Weiguang, in 1954 for having supported the government's initiatives to establish an independent Chinese Church, which he championed in his Nanjing Manifesto of 1953.
[169] Claudia Carlen, *The Papal Encyclicals 1939-1958*, p. 374.
[170] *Mission Bulletin*, Vol. XI, December 1959, No. 10, p. 1066: By 1959 there were 26 "bishops" who had been "consecrated" by the Chinese government and positioned in dioceses throughout China.
[171] *Mission Bulletin*, Vol. XI, April 1959, No. 4, p. 396.

unknown to her, she was mailing the sermons to a government official. She was arrested and began indoctrination meetings. During the first, on May 28, 1958, her captors demanded she sign a denunciation of her uncle, Bishop Kung. She refused, and was arrested in September, ultimately spending 20 years in Chinese labor camps. [172]

1959 marked the tenth anniversary of the Communist takeover of China. To underscore the great revolutionary strides made by the government, the Chinese press repeated the accusations against Bishop Kung imprisoned as "a traitor. . . for the good of 600 million Chinese, inclusive of Catholics". [173]

In Shanghai, various moves were made by the government in preparation for events of the coming year: the seminary at Zikawei, which had trained missionary priests for China for more than 100 years, was given a new function. In 1957 it became a center for the indoctrination of Catholic youth; in 1958, the museum of Anti-Catholic Purposes was moved from the International Hotel to the seminary, with exhibitions moving from city to city to alert the citizens of the truth about the Catholic Church with particular reference to the crimes of Bishop Kung and the Jesuits of Shanghai. In late 1959, in observance of the Communist anniversary, the seminary became the center of the Communist People's Committee.

In a large public ceremony in the cathedral of Nanking on November 15, 1959, the Chinese government created four new schismatic bishops. This was the public culmination of the second Congress of the Patriotic Association of Chinese Catholics, bringing the total of schismatic bishops in China to 31, consecrated in violation of the express prohibition of the Holy See. The significance of this action was that all four would be bishops in the Kiangsu Province, on the northern coast of China, as a direct attack against the authority of Bishop Kung, the legitimate Apostolic Administrator of the Archdiocese of Nanking. [174]

Subsequently, armed soldiers were stationed at the doors of all the city's Catholic churches, turning people away, declaring "There is no longer any religion in China." Catholic churches were closed, used for political meetings, movies or Communist propaganda theatrical performances. The churches were opened only for staged Masses for the foreign press, with non-Catholics brought in to play their part as parishioners, all for the cameras, to prove to outsiders that the freedom of religion did exist in China. Despite the threat of labor camps and imprisonment, only twenty priests in all Shanghai had gone over to the Patriotic Association, and only they were permitted to offer public Masses or provide the sacraments. "We

---

[172] Margaret Chu, *A Catholic Voice out of China*, p. 252, http://www.cardinalkungfoundation.org/ar/ACatholicVoiceOutofChina.php

[173] *Asia*, Vol. XII, January, 1960, No. 1, p. 83.

[174] *Asia*, XII, March, 1960, No. 3, p. 312.

offer Mass spiritually", one Catholic was reported to say. Faithful Catholics stayed away, practicing their faith in their family homes, quietly. A great paradox developed whereby non-attendance at Mass in China became a mark of fidelity to the Church. The government told the Catholics throughout the country that they must "adapt their religious life to the needs of production", which meant that they would work continuously, with no time for religion, not even on Sundays. [175]

Forced indoctrination classes continued, in which scores of nuns, priests and laypersons were incarcerated, sometimes for weeks at a time. These were divided into three areas of study: patriotism in general; Bishop Kung and his crimes; the pope as an instrument of imperialists. At the end of the classes, all were forced to sign a document or face public trials.

In early 1960, Bishop Kung was offered one last chance to co-operate with the Chinese government by denouncing the pope, and recognizing the Chinese Catholic Patriotic Association. He refused, once again, telling the chief prosecutor who visited him in prison,

> If I were to consider, it would have meant in my mind that perhaps it might be possible to leave the Holy Father and still remain as a Catholic. My better judgment told me that this was an impossibility.[176] I am a Roman Catholic Bishop. If I denounce the Holy Father, not only would I not be a Bishop, I would not even be a Catholic. You can cut off my head, but you can never take away my duties.[177]

Public Trial and Condemnation of a Faithful Witness

Bishop Kung was tried in Shanghai's Municipal Intermediate People's Court on March 16-17, 1960, along with thirteen other defendants accused of being his co-conspirators, forming what the government charged as the "Kung Pin-mei traitorous counterrevolutionary clique." [178] The court verdict referred to evidence of the alleged subversive activities of Bishop Kung and his associates: "After a search had been made, every type of gun, bullets, radio receivers, gold currency, and American dollars, used for pursuing their criminal activities, all are hereby totally confiscated."

---

[175] *Asia*, Vol. XII, February, 1960, No. 2, pp. 203-205

[176] *Soul Magazine*, July-August 1993, *An Interview with Cardinal Kung*, p. 19.

[177] Cardinal Kung Foundation.

[178] September 8th Editorial Board, *Blessings of the Divine Bounty of "September 8th": In commemoration of the 40th Anniversary of the "Sept. 8th" persecution of the Catholic Church in Mainland China 1955-1995*, Taipei 1999, pp. 57-60 provide excerpts of the official verdict.

Bishop Kung was accused of being named Bishop of Shanghai as part of a plan masterminded by Bishop James Walsh, the Maryknoll missionary who was charged with heading the "reactionary" Catholic Central Bureau in Shanghai, in league with Archbishop Anthony Riberi, the exiled Apostolic Internuncio to China, and Father George Germain, S.J., and Father Jin Luxian, S.J., all joined to Catholic relief efforts headed by Francis Cardinal Spellman of New York as part of a greater American plot. The verdict read:

> On the basis of the evidence for criminal activities on the part of Ignatius Kung's counter-revolutionary and anti-government organization, our court is perfectly cognizant of the fact that the accused, Ignatius Kung, is the leader of this counter-revolutionary and anti-government organization, hiding under the cloak of religion, he is collaborating with the imperialists in the betrayal of his mother land, and has served as an important tool for the imperialists to overthrow the people's democratic political rights of our country, to such an extent that he has accomplished serious violations of the country's interests.

> In this case each defendant, has infringed the People's Republic's law against counter-revolutionary activities, Article No. 3, Item No. 1, Article No. 5, Item No. 1, No. 2, No. 6 of Article No. 7, Article No. 10, Article No. 13, Article No. 14 and Article No. 17, all of which criminal activities are punishable by law.

> Our court in accordance with the concrete circumstances of the defendant's criminal activities, and with respect to any expression of repentance on the part of the accused subsequent to their arrest, has decided to pass the following judgment [sic]: The accused, Ignatius Kung, is the head and leader of the counter-revolutionary and anti-government organization; he is in league with the imperialists, betrayed his motherland, and his crimes are of a very serious nature. But after his case had been brought forward, when confronted with actual circumstantial evidence, he did not deny his role, and furthermore he had something to reveal on the subject of how the imperialists under the cover of religion plotted subversive actions.

> Under the magnanimity of the law we hereby sentence him to lifetime imprisonment, and hereby strip him for life of all his political rights. [179]

---

[179] Ibid., p. 60.

The March 17th verdict of the trial was immediately trumpeted to the Western press by the Communist government, quite a contrast to the near total silence by the government when Bishop Kung was arrested nearly five years earlier. The *New York Times* reported the verdict as a life sentence for treason as "a leader of a counter-revolutionary group." [180] Unlike their reports of the arrest of Bishop Kung five years earlier, this story was not buried far back in the paper, and, even the *Times* got it right, understanding that the Bishop's crime had nothing to do with revolution against the Chinese state. The free world understood well that the condemnation of Bishops Kung and Walsh was an attempt by the Chinese government "to equate loyalty to the Holy See with treason in the minds of the people."[181]

Years later, Cardinal Kung recalled,

> I was sentenced to life imprisonment under the pretext of 'treason'. This 'treason' consisted of my refusal to renounce the Holy Father, my refusal to sever ties between my dioceses [as Ordinary of Shanghai and Apostolic Administrator of Soochow and Nanjing] and the Holy Father, and my refusal to give leadership to the establishment of a "Chinese Catholic Patriotic Association" in China, which would be completely under the control of the Communist government. [182]

The Venerable Archbishop Fulton J. Sheen clearly stated the reality of Bishop Kung's witness:

> God never leaves the Church without witnesses—and a witness is one who suffers persecution or martyrdom for the Faith. The Chinese Mindszenty is Bishop Ignatius Kung, the Bishop of Shanghai. The Reds arrested and tortured him, brought him out clothed in black underwear before a howling mob shouting for his death. The Communists organized Red protests in the Shanghai Stadium where banners were carried reading: "Kill the counter revolutionist Kung, who hides under the cloak of religion."
>
> The West has its Mindszenty, but the East has its Kung. God is glorified in His saints.[183]

---

[180] *New York Times*, March 18, 1960, p. 3.

[181] *Asia*, Vol. XII, May, 1960, No. 5, p. 532.

[182] *Soul Magazine*, July-August 1993, *An Interview with Cardinal Kung*, p. 18.

[183] *Mission Magazine,* January-February 1957, *China Has its Mindszenty*, p. 7. Joseph Cardinal Mindszenty (1892-1975) had been arrested in Hungary by the Communist government, which subjected him to a show trial for treason, and sentenced him to life imprisonment.

The Vatican was swift in its condemnation of the sentences given down to the two bishops. *L'Osservatore Romano* editorialized,

> There is no need to stress that this serious condemnation constitutes a persecuting regime's premeditated vendetta against pastors whose only guilt is their steadfast loyalty to their vocations as Catholic priests and to their missions as bishops.
>
> We are faced once again with terroristic juridical actions which violate divine and human justice in the most blatant way and dishonor the very people who are responsible for them or who are their accomplices.
>
> The names of these two bishops. . . are added to the names of all the other victims of the Communist martyrology in China and elsewhere, because the persecution in China is only one aspect of the ruthless oppression carried out against Catholicism in the name of Marxism-Leninism in so many parts of the world. [184]

An article appeared in the Hong Kong daily newspaper, *Chan Po*, soon after the trial. The author, who claimed to have no religious faith, offered his observations about Bishop Kung and the government's condemnation. He wrote,

> How long will this indomitable old man spend his life in prison!? He will see the light of day again only when all the people of China see the light of day again.
>
> Red China has sentenced Kung Pin-Mei for life. Logically speaking it should be a victory for the Chinese Communists. But I say definitely that the victory belongs to Bishop Kung Pin-Mei. [185]

The anonymous author then narrated a visit he made to Shanghai in the autumn of 1952. As he was walking through the city on a Sunday, he noticed crowds entering the cathedral, and greater crowds standing outside. He asked what was happening and was told that Bishop Kung was preaching. He continued,

> At the time I did not understand what it meant, but after the Bishop's arrest it occurred to me that it must have been the bishop's reputation that drew so many people there that day. This fact showed what a great influence Bishop Kung Pin-Mei had over the people in Shanghai. And this was what the Chinese Communists were most afraid of. But why did they have to wait until 1955 to arrest him? They had their reasons.

---

[184] Quoted in *Asia*, Vol. XII, June, 1960, No. 6, p. 645.
[185] Ibid., p. 649: the article is entitled, *Victory Belongs to Bishop Kung*.

March 16-17, 1960: Chinese government show trial of Bishop Kung
and other Catholic priests.

Bishop Kung is the central defendant in the photograph at left.

When the Chinese Communists started the Separation of Religion from Imperialistic Influence Movement, they thought of Kung Pin-Mei because the Bishop was appointed by the Vatican. Leading Chinese Communists had visited him several times, trying to persuade him to be the spokesman against the Vatican and to accuse the Vatican of being the handmaid of American imperialists. With his strong influence over the Catholics, it would have been a great help to the Communists in their anti-religion movement if Bishop Kung had acceded to their request. But Bishop Kung was firm in his refusal.

The Chinese Communists did not know that he could be so firm. They hoped that harsh treatment might bend him to their design. But as time passed and there was no sign of softening, the Chinese Reds lost hope. Thus this life sentence after six years of "persuasion".

The Chinese Communists thought that a life sentence would be a severe punishment. But this is of no consequence to a man of faith.

Victory does not go to those who hold power and force; but to those who have faith. [186]

Soon after the sentencing, during the 10-day national Congress of the Patriotic Association, a new Bishop of Shanghai was to be elected by delegates from Shanghai. It was reported that 850 lay Catholics, religious sisters and priests, all of whom had endured re-education classes, were forcibly gathered from every district of the Diocese of Shanghai to elect a new bishop. The Shanghai delegates made a joint report, directly attacking Bishops Kung and Walsh.

The Catholics of Shanghai have risen up. The secret plan of American imperialism, which under cover of religion, uses the See of Rome, have again been violently attacked. We Catholics of Shanghai stand resolutely with all the Catholics of China and approve the direction of the Communist Party and follow the road of socialism. We shall advance courageously, holding aloft the banners of the general line, of the great forward leaps of the Popular Communes. We shall rid ourselves of the control of the Holy See, we shall completely sweep out the rest of the Kung Pin-mei clique. In order to realize a free, independent and autonomous Church of Shanghai we shall elect and consecrate our bishops as have other Catholics of China. We shall choose our patriotic chief, and then, the bishop of the Diocese of Shanghai will put an end, forever to the evil control of the See of Rome, the tool of American imperialism.

---

[186] Ibid., p. 650.

We are persuaded that we shall, if united under the direction of the Communist Party and of all the people of China, smash to pieces the intrigues of American imperialism and of the See of Rome. Let us fight against American imperialism and the See of Rome. The victory belongs to the People of China. [187]

They elected Father Chang Chia-Shu, S.J., agreeing "that Shanghai's Catholics, like all Chinese Catholics, must be free from all Vatican control and run the Church independently." [188]

Decades of Imprisonment

Following his trial in 1960, Bishop Kung was hurried off to prison, where he was not seen or heard from by the outside world until his transfer to house arrest in the care of the Chinese Catholic Patriotic Association in 1985. Rumors, however, continued, as did reports of him from fellow prisoners who later spoke or wrote about the Bishop. In 1962, news reports from Hong Kong claimed the Bishop to be either seriously ill or dead. The Western media picked up the story, as well. One publication quoted a fellow prisoner's letter smuggled from jail describing their shared sufferings:

> I have been fasting for six years. . . and with that I am yoked for work worthy of the Pharaohs. We must wear ourselves out for the 'Great Paradise' [promised by the Communists]. It is truly luciferous. Yet, I have the conviction that a new day will shine again soon. [189]

Another article noted:

> To visit Christians imprisoned for the faith was a treasured work of charity in the days of the Roman persecutions. But the communists rarely allow such small mercies as were granted by the pagans of old. The only service that can be paid today's witnesses is to keep alive their memory, particularly when little or nothing is known of their whereabouts or their condition.
>
> Bishop Kung's real offense was that he refused to lead a schismatic move against the Pope.

---

[187] *Asia*, Vol. XII, October, 1960, No. 8, pp. 888-889.
[188] *Asia*, Vol. XII, September, 1960, No. 7, p. 765.
[189] *University Bulletin*, October 14, 1962, *Bishop, Captive of China Reds, Feared Ill or Dead*.

> There is little new to report except that, clearly, the Bishop of Shanghai remains adamant in his refusal to bow or to bend. The world's Christian community is indebted to him for his example of steadfastness. [190]

At first, Bishop Kung was never alone in prison because he shared the cell with others: "Six pairs of feet in my face during the nights", he told a reporter for *La Croix* in 1988. For a time he was moved from prison to prison, finally ending in the Ward Street Jail in Shanghai, where he endured nearly 29 years of isolation, forbidden to celebrate Mass, read the Bible or any book, or to receive visitors. [191] No human contact was permitted him. After his release, he later reported that, unknown to him, representatives of various international humanitarian agencies petitioned the government to visit him, but were all denied. Even the prison guards had been ordered to turn their heads away from his cell door when passing by; "even that degree of contact with other human beings was denied to him." After interviewing Bishop Kung years later, one reporter wrote that the Bishop understood that "incarceration was to be a part of his vocation." [192]

As trials of Catholics increased, more and more priests, religious sisters and bishops were jailed. One sister in a North China prison described life in these prisons, which gives some idea of Bishop Kung's situation. She wrote,

> All the sisters as well as the bishops and priests are taking part in work in the fields. This lasts from six in the morning until nine at night. At midday we take our meals in turns so that work is not interrupted.

> Those who dig the ground change teams every 20 minutes and those who are breaking stones every 10 minutes. When wells are being dug, supper is passed over and work continues on an empty stomach until 9:30 every evening. [193]

A report about Bishop Kung came from a fellow prisoner at the forced labor camp at White Grass Mountain in southern Anhui, central China. Dr. Yih Leefah, a Chinese-American research professor and a Methodist, was arrested in 1963 when he returned to Shanghai to be with his dying father. The camp housed 30,000 political prisoners from the major cities of China, including Bishop Kung. Yih was assigned to shoveling pig excrement to be used as fertilizer. Seeing his case as hopeless, he confided to Bishop Kung that he was considering suicide. Yih recalled, "Bishop Kung kept on praying, morning and evening, while he was out working with the water buffaloes." Some prisoners reported to the guards that the

---

[190] *America*, November 11, 1963, *Absent From Vatican II*, p. 652.
[191] *La Croix*, August 1988, Dorian Malovic, *L'Eveque de Shanghai Decouvre Vatican II*. August 26, 1988.
[192] *America*, July 29, 1995, George Anderson, S.J., *Witnessing for the Faith in China's Prisons*, p. 17.
[193] *Asia*, Vol. XII, June, 1960, No. 6, p. 654.

Bishop was praying, which was a forbidden activity, so the Bishop was made to take part in a "struggle session."

> He [Bishop Kung] stood calmly, his head down, showing no emotion while I had to insult him. I said, 'You old fool, why should you pray, if there is a god in heaven you would not be here.' Then he [Kung] looked at me with very disappointed but loving eyes, like Jesus must have looked at Peter when Peter denied him three times after he had been arrested. I felt terrible.

A few days later, Yih encountered the Bishop in the fields. The Bishop told the man he forgave him for his actions during the "struggle session". Bishop Kung also encouraged Yih "not to give up his struggle for life." [194]

Another account comes from Philip Watt, imprisoned with Bishop Kung until 1975. He once worked in the Shanghai Cable Company, but was arrested like so many others as a counter-revolutionary. He was sentenced to a labor camp and found Bishop Kung to be one of his cellmates. He claimed he knew nothing of the Bishop's identity, since the Bishop was arrested twenty years earlier, and the Chinese press never mentioned him. Watt wrote that "the Chinese prison officials particularly despised [Kung]." Watt recounted that he had been an Episcopalian, "but that the heroic loyalty to the Holy Father that the imprisoned priests had shown and their love of the Catholic faith impressed him so much that he decided to convert to the Catholic Church." [195] He continued, "In the prison, every three or four days, he [Kung] was allowed to take a walk."

According to Watt, in spite of the hatred that the Chinese prison officials had for Cardinal Kung, "he was treated a little different because of international pressure." Watt said that when President Nixon visited China, high ranking Chinese officials told him [Kung], "Nixon is asking about you. We'll let you go, if you cut off your relationship with the pope." Cardinal Kung, though, refused their offer, said Watt.

Another report came from a man imprisoned in the Ward Street Jail in Shanghai along with Bishop Kung from 1975-1979. [196] The man was not a Catholic, yet came to admire his fellow prisoner, even though their meetings were infrequent and brief.

> Due to his special situation, Bishop Kung was housed in a small cell, measuring about 30 square feet. The prison guard would unlock his door in the morning and let him out for a few minutes in the prison yard. Because I was young and strong, I was assigned to the prison's

---

[194] Fox Butterfield, *China: Alive in the Bitter Sea*, New York 1982, p. 368.
[195] Maggie Garcia, *Renounce the Pope! In Prison with Cardinal Kung*, September 2001.
[196] *World Daily News*, March 31, 1996, courtesy of the Cardinal Kung Foundation.

general work team to deliver the big wooden barrel of water and rice to the prisoners for every meal. I met Kung each day in my rounds.

I once asked Kung, "Each prisoner is given 3 ounces of rice for each meal (twice daily) and is always mad with hunger. Why do you only ask for 2 ounces of rice on your own?" Kung smiled and replied, "3 ounces is not enough and everyone is always starving and angry, and one would not be given more rice. Since I, on my own, asked for only 2 ounces of rice, I had the control of my own situation. Therefore, I do not feel anger with my hunger." I thought that was a strange theory, and I later tried to imitate him. Strange enough, after I had my 2 ounces of rice, I felt hungry all the same, but I was not angry. I know that if I wanted to, I could have another ounce.

After Mao's death, a lot of political prisoner's cases were reviewed and many prisoners released. One afternoon, Kung was also called to the prison office, but returned after a few minutes. I was very curious and asked him what had happened that he should return so quickly. He calmly told me, "They wanted me to admit my crimes and in doing so, I would be granted leniency. How could this be possible? This is not something we can talk and negotiate. If that was possible, I would have talked and negotiated years ago and would never end up here."

I was full of admiration for his integrity. However, knowing that he has already been in prison for over 20 years, I felt very bad that he will continue to be here.

When I was released from prison, he did not say goodbye to me. He nodded at me from a distant, and pointed to the sky. I knew that he was saying, "We will meet again in heaven."

I am wondering now how Cardinal Kung would feel in heaven watching the Vatican negotiating with the Communist government, the party that he refused to negotiate with.

After his release in 1988, Cardinal Kung spoke briefly and infrequently of his imprisonment. "When we were in jail, we had no Holy Mass, no sacraments and no religious books. However, we had our fingers to recite the Rosary which gave us strength and grace during the ten, twenty or thirty years of imprisonment." [197]   When he was in solitary confinement, the Bishop later

---

[197] *Soul Magazine*, July-August 1993, *An Interview with Cardinal Kung*, p. 21.

recalled, he made the traditional 30-day Jesuit retreat every month, and prayed the entire 15 decades of the Rosary daily. [198]

During his thirty years of imprisonment, Bishop Kung wrote out prayers, the Canon of the Mass and meditations written in Chinese characters from memory on small scraps of rice paper. Most were confiscated and destroyed, but his meditations on the Stations of the Cross survived, smuggled out of China during the years. His Meditation on the Crucifixion of Jesus was first made public at his funeral in 2000. [199]

Bishop Kung's Appeal for Justice

In 1979 Bishop Kung made his first written appeal of the March 17, 1960 verdict against him. At the time of its composition, the Bishop had been in jail 24 years and two months. In his appeal document, the Bishop gave as reasons why he had not submitted an appeal, that "it is too difficult for me to recall what had happened", and that before the law was promulgated mandating an annual written appeal "whoever did not accept the court sentence and refused to reform became a target to be criticized. Therefore, I could not appeal, even though I had been victimized by false accusations, nor was it prudent for me to expose the court's error." [200] Now that the law had changed, and annual appeals made mandatory, Bishop Kung complied. The form he decided upon was to "present to the government the false charges as stated in the verdict so that the government might clarify and distinguish right from wrong with the full force of the law to re-establish the rightful place of the Catholic Church." [201]

He continued,

> Personal merit or punishment does not matter much to me. My ultimate goal is that the Chinese people should be able to practice the human right of religious freedom as claimed in the [Chinese] constitution. My argument is that the Church has the right to protect the integrity of its fundamental religious belief, and that the nation has no right to forcibly alter the basic religious belief of the Church.
>
> During my five-year term of appointment, the major contradiction between the government and religion was that the government

---

[198] *Catholic New York*, July 9, 1998, Claudia McDonnell: *Cardinal Ignatius Kung marks 97th birthday, 10 Years of Freedom in the United States.*
[199] An English translation of Bishop Kung's *Stations of the Cross* can be found in Appendix 13.
[200] *Bishop Kung's Appeal Document, Submitted to the Beijing People's Supreme Court*, pp. 1-2, Cardinal Kung Foundation Archives.
[201] An English translation of Bishop Kung's complete Appeal Letter is found in Appendix 12.

promotes the Three-Self Reforms Movement, which forces Roman Catholics to denounce the Holy Father, whereas the Church insists on protecting unwavering loyalty to the Church and the pope.

The Bishop next answered questions about his approach to the government's Three-Self Reform Movement and its insistence that the Catholic Church cut ties with the pope and become a truly Chinese institution by having only Chinese bishops govern the Church, Chinese priests to preach, and Chinese citizens to raise funds without foreign subsidies. His answer:

> These methods have been the wishes of all Catholics and have been the three basic principles of the popes of the past generations. More than forty parishes managed by Chinese bishops have already practiced these, especially in our Shanghai diocese which has had sufficient manpower and financial resources to fulfill these three principles. Why did we have to promote other reforms? Are there other purposes? Could it have been to ask Chinese Catholics to separate from the pope? [202]

In light of the *Oppose Monarchy, Be Patriotic* campaign which expelled all foreign priests, and the 1957 government creation of the government's own version of the Catholic Church, the Chinese Catholic Patriotic Association, Bishop Kung reflected that there was a possible ulterior motive on the part of the Chinese government. He then moved to substantive examples:

> The first chairman of the [Chinese Catholic Patriotic Association] Pi-Shu-Shi of the Shen Yang Archdiocese and others sent a telegram directly to the Pope to announce the severance of the relationship between the government and himself. Self-ordaining bishops, self-managed church, and the first self-founded Chinese schismatic church proved to be the actual disguise of the Three-Self Reforms.

To underscore his point, Bishop Kung reiterated that the author of this appeal was not a foreigner, but a native-born Chinese bishop, well-educated in the intellectual traditions of China. Bishop Kung then quoted from an ancient Chinese literary classic to underscore his point about the Chinese government's true intentions and actions. He quoted the *Book of Odes*—which he studied when a child: "Only God knows the unknown chance. Before it rains, clouds gather first". Emphasizing that he was Chinese born, and hinting that he was more familiar with authentic Chinese culture than his captors, Bishop Kung referred to Confucius and his teaching on loyalty. Besides his deep Faith, another reason for his unwavering fidelity to the Holy See was his classical Chinese education, which had inculcated

---

[202] *Bishop Kung's Appeal Letter*, p. 2

in him a deep sense "of the virtue of loyalty", and that he preferred death rather than betray the Successor of Saint Peter.

He then gave a specific example of the Communist government's attempts to destroy the Catholic Church. In January, 1951, the government confiscated Aurora University, turned out the Jesuits, and named two former Catholics, Yang Shih-Da the new dean, and Hu Guang Yiao as administrator. This was soon followed by the Suppression of Counter-Revolutionaries Movement, and the implementation of the Regulations for the Suppression of Counter-Revolutionaries as the law of the country. Bishop Kung continued that the Catholic student body did not agree with these changes, so Bishop Kung asked Hu Guang Yiao to swear before the Catholic students that he would be faithful to the Church to restore the students' faith in him. The man refused. "This was the life and death of the contradiction between government and religion. I was arrested because of this."

Another specific example the Bishop gave was the government's repeated invitations to Kung to "reform" the Church in Shanghai by cutting his relationship with the pope. Bishop Kung then wrote that the night before his trial, the Shanghai court prosecutor, Lu Ming asked him again to sever all ties with the Holy See

> . . . so that I could have happiness and well-being in my old age. I replied that I absolutely would not consider exchanging my religion for a life of ease.

> Who would not want to live and hate to die? But there is more value in a man's justice and morality and in a disciple's completeness of faith. There is a hatred worse than death itself if people of loyalty and virtue rebel against the Lord, if disciples desert Jesus Christ. To separate from the Holy See, the only representative of Jesus Christ in the world, is to throw away the root of the Catholic faith and become pagan. Being without the Pope would be like a corpse without a head, a tree without roots, a stream without source, and a religious vampire without transcendent life. This is a most serious dilemma for which billions sacrificed their lives in battle throughout Catholic history. Therefore, in the spring of 1950 the most respected Prime Minister Zhou said "Catholics who would sever their political and economic relationship with the Roman Catholic Pope are allowed to keep a pure religious relationship with the Pope, which is a reasonable promise." Unfortunately, this has not been carried on. I had replied frankly to the court prosecutor that I absolutely would not sever the religious relationship with the Pope now, or ever in the

future. Therefore, this was the reason that I was sentenced to life in prison on March 19 [sic], 1960. [203]

Bishop Kung then challenged the government to study the practice of religious liberty in other countries, "in order to verify whether or not the [government] reins of power have the right to change a disciple's basic religious doctrines in order to turn him from his religion to become a schismatic". He then moved to a consideration of the laws of China:

> The Great Chairman Mao taught us that religion would not be destroyed by the government, and that people should not be forced to abandon their religious practices. Therefore, based on the law of the country and Chairman Mao's teaching, there is no legal foundation for the country to reform religion. If there is no such right, is it not unconstitutional to force a religion to change its doctrines and rules?
>
> I hope the government, based on the principle of governing by law, will investigate and correct its practices in order that the international fame of our nation as tolerant of various religions will be renewed, so that the millions of followers of the world's religions and the billions of people around the whole world will support China.

The Bishop then returned to the question of the charges made against him and the verdict condemning him to life imprisonment:

> The government realized that it had no legal right to reform the Church and to found a schismatic church; therefore, the verdict did not mention that I led Church members to resist the Three Forms Movement. Instead, the major accusations were that I was 1. a leader of a counter-revolutionary group; 2. a co-conspirator with imperialists; and 3. a traitor to my motherland. This was done to publicize and exaggerate my legitimate work to the proportion of a heinous crime and so that the verdict would appear legal and verified.

Bishop Kung then demanded specifics and details to prove the government's accusations against him. If he was a leader organizing a counter-revolutionary group, then the government should be able to provide the specific name of the group, its regulations and its membership. Other than the fifteen bishops and priests charged as members of the so-called counter-revolutionary group, there were no other details. The Church cannot be held responsible for groups outside its control. Those sponsored by the Church are religious

---

[203] *Bishop Kung's Appeal Letter*, p. 3

organizations and nothing more. The Bishop firmly asserted "I have never belonged to any group or organization not permitted by law." The Bishop continued that, except for five priests of the Diocese of Shanghai, he had no knowledge about nor jurisdiction over the others named in the indictment, and could not be held responsible for anything they may have done. If he contacted imperialist groups or agents, which groups and which agents? As for being a traitor, the Bishop categorically denied that it would be impossible for him ever to "betray the motherland in which I was born and on whose soil I was raised." Accused of hiding arms and munitions, he denied the charge and asked why the evidence had never been actually produced in court, other than a fabricated list of items.

Further in the document, the Bishop stated that the Diocese of Shanghai had meetings of the clergy to discuss the government's land reform program in light of Catholic teaching. While some priests voiced criticism of the government policy during the meetings, the accusations were false that stated Rome and the Diocese of Shanghai worked to undermine the government's program. The Bishop gave as evidence the fact that he had given over to the local government the land holdings of the Diocese of Shanghai one year earlier, as a demonstration of co-operation with the government.

The Bishop flatly denied the accusation of treason against his homeland. Admitting that he had preached and written about the Kingdom of God, but that was standard Catholic doctrine and had no political implications whatsoever, nor did he join in any counter-revolutionary plots to overthrown the communist government.

The final charge against him concerned funding for revolutionary activities. Kung answered by pointing to the fact that, years earlier, during one of the periods when government hostilities against the Church were slightly eased, he actually believed the government's claims to implement religious freedom. He repented then of his earlier hard line, and, as a sign of co-operation, turned over to the government the entire mission fund of the Diocese, totaling 1,830 taels of gold. [204] However, immediately after this, the government accused him of amassing wealth to fund counter-revolutionary plots, and the government claimed that the money Bishop Kung gave them had actually been discovered by the government and confiscated. They demanded that the Bishop admit to this. He refused to make this false statement.

---

[204] One tael of gold equals 37.80 grams, which in today's gold market is valued at $54.42. http://www.traditionaloven.com/metal/precious-metals/gold/convert-tael-of-gold-to-ounce-oz-of-gold.html

In this appeal document, Bishop Kung concluded by stating he had been disappointed and mistreated by the government's unjust actions, and requested that his case be reviewed. [205]

He made this appeal in 1979, while still in the Ward Street Jail in Shanghai, where he would remain until his release into house arrest in 1985. In that year, the government once again tried to cut a deal with the aging and weakened Bishop: his freedom in exchange for his heading the Chinese Catholic Patriotic Association. He refused. As his jailer later recalled, Bishop Kung told him that "so long as there is still one priest, nun or Christian in jail for the faith, he will stay in jail; he will be the last one to leave jail." [206]

Bishop Kung later recalled what was termed "the most difficult moment during your 30 years in jail" during an interview following his release. Joseph Kung, Bishop Kung's nephew and translator, recalled the Bishop's reply,

> The most painful time for him was when Bishop Jin, S.J. the then patriotic Auxiliary Bishop of Shanghai, who was the previous seminary rector serving under Bishop Kung, was sent by the government to visit him in jail, in an attempt to persuade Bishop Kung to change his position and to leave the Holy Father. [207]

Rome Remembers

On October 7, 1974, Pope Paul VI wrote a letter to Bishop Kung on the 25th anniversary of the Bishop's episcopal consecration. The Pope wrote that, even though Bishop Kung was hidden from the world in the isolation of his prison cell, "It is in no way hidden from Us how much you have achieved from the very outset of your episcopacy, nor are We unaware that your outstanding merits of life and rectitude of conscience presently endure intense sorrow."[208] Unbeknown to Bishop Kung, as he was composing and submitting his Letter of Appeal, the Church had not forgotten him. Blessed Pope John Paul II announced a consistory for June 30, 1979 to add new members to the Sacred College of Cardinals. The usual protocol was followed concerning the publication of the nominees and the ceremonial imposition of the cardinal's *birettum*. However, at the conclusion of June 29, 1979 consistory, the Holy Father made a solemn announcement in Latin

---

[205] Beatrice Leung, *Sino-Vatican Relations: Problems in Conflicting Authority, 1976-1986*, New York, 1992, p. 167.

[206] Michael Chu, *Report about the Church in China*, March 2, 1979, quoted in Mariani, *Church Militant*, p. 208.

[207] Stamford, August 25, 2012, Joseph Kung to Msgr. Stephen DiGiovanni, Basilica Archives.

[208] Bishop Kung never knew of this letter, and saw the letter only after he arrived in Stamford, Connecticut following his release by the Chinese government. The text can be found in Appendix 11.

that *"praeter hos, qui nominati sunt, adlegere in Collegium vestrum decrevimus alium, quem tamen in pectore reservamus et quandocumque aribitrio nostro renuntiabimus* (Besides these who have been named, we have decided to include another, whom we have reserved in our heart, and which we shall make public when it is opportune)". [209]

In October, 1981, a Chinese government Protestant bishop, K.H.Ting, heading the Chinese delegation to a church conference in Montreal, asked a Vatican representative if the rumors that the pope would name Bishop Kung a cardinal were true. He then observed that the conferral of the cardinal's red hat on this religious prisoner would embarrass China. The comment was made because Kung had been relentlessly manifesting his attitude of non-conformity, protesting in letters of appeal to the government that he was innocently condemned, and that the Chinese government delayed his release, because of the suspicion that he would receive the red hat. [210]

A former colleague of Bishop Kung in Shanghai, Father Camille Graff, S.J., wrote and published an open letter to the Bishop in September 1984, recalling the approaching thirtieth anniversary of Bishop Kung's arrest. [211]

> In August, this year, you have entered your 84th year of age. You have been a Priest for 55 years, and of them 35 years as a Bishop of the Church of Jesus Christ. Almost half of your life in prison, in a long 'offertory' of yourself. A long "Holy Sacrifice" in union with Christ on His Cross. By love of Him. By love of His Church. By love of the Church in Shanghai, which has been entrusted to you by the Vicar of Christ on earth: the Bishop of Rome. And nothing has been able to shatter your faith in the true Church of Christ. God knows and History will know for ever that it is the only one true reason for your incarceration.

> So, you refused the "Schism" and went to prison. Many other Bishops and Priests went too. Your 30 years in prison already is [sic] and shall be for the future, the true seed of the Catholic Church in China. Others have already died. But thanks to you all, the true Catholic [Church] goes on and develops on Mainland China. Unseen by many. But really living and growing.

On July 3, 1985, Bishop Kung was moved from the Ward Street Jail. The next day, the news was published in major papers throughout the West. Unlike his arrest and imprisonment, this news was trumpeted by the Chinese government,

---

[209] Quoted in Leung, *Sino-Vatican Relations,* p. 208.
[210] Ibid., p. 209.
[211] Taiwan, September 4, 1984, *Open Letter* by Fr. Camille Graff, S.J. See:
http://www.cardinalkungfoundation.org/ar/TwoOpenLetterstoBishopKung.php

claiming that the aged Bishop was "remorseful" and "repentant" of his crimes against the State, and had signed a document expressing his change of heart. Despite his years rejecting government offers "that tied his release to a public repudiation of the Vatican", the government claimed that Bishop Kung "had finally made the deal that could have secured his release many years ago." Now, the Chinese government, through its Patriotic Catholic Association, "an organization that runs the Catholic churches under close official scrutiny, depicted the prelate as having abandoned the posture that made him the concern of Catholics' prayers worldwide." [212] The Chinese government even told the press that Bishop Kung "had kissed the ring of the Patriotic Bishop of Shanghai, and promised to act under his guidance." [213] The government falsely reported also that Bishop Kung promised to have no contact with the Vatican after his release from prison.

Despite these false statements by the Chinese government, Bishop Kung was not free. He was to be under house arrest in Shanghai at the residence of a former colleague, Father Aloysius Jin, with whom he endured years of imprisonment for refusing to break communion with the Holy Father. Jin finally accepted the terms of the government in 1982, renounced his loyalty to the pope, was released and created the Bishop of Shanghai by the government. The People's "bishop" of Shanghai was now the jailer of the legitimate Bishop of Shanghai, Bishop Ignatius Kung.

However, the Western media, and Catholics around the world, had their doubts about the government story. "But the ambiguous wording and the absence from the agency's account of any direct statement to that effect by the Bishop suggested that the [Chinese] authorities, not the Bishop, might have relented." [214]

In August 1985, Father Camille Graff, S.J., wrote another open letter to Bishop Kung.

> Of course we are told by your jailer that you have "admitted your crimes;" And as a matter of fact, you have been given to the "Patriotic Association of the Catholic Church" to be watched over, under the responsibility of the Bishop—and his two Auxiliary Bishops—who have usurped your Episcopal See of Shanghai. Although we were asked to believe that it is a "liberation", no one is allowed to see you, except your new jailer. [215]

---

[212] *New York Times*, July 5, 1985: *China Depicts Freed Cleric as Repentant.*

[213] *Time Magazine*, July 15, 1985, *China: Freedom for a Catholic Bishop.* http://www.time.com/time/magazine/article/0,9171,959671,00.html

[214] *New York Times*, July 4, 1995, John Burns, *China Releases a Catholic Bishop Who was Jailed Nearly 30 Years*, p. 28.

[215] http://www.cardinalkungfoundation.org/ar/TwoOpenLetterstoBishopKung.php

Father Graff continued that one of the two government auxiliary bishops of Shanghai, during a visit to Hong Kong a few weeks after Bishop Kung's release into the custody of the Patriotic Association, admitted to reporters that Bishop Kung "actually had not" denounced the Holy Father nor acknowledged the Patriotic Association.

The reality was that the government released Bishop Kung fearing he might die in prison and be acknowledged a martyr. The media had some inkling that this was the case, especially since the Bishop was forbidden to speak to anyone, especially to the press. [216] He, himself later told the press, "I was placed in the custody of the 'Patriotic Association' which I had steadfastly opposed. I had no freedom of movement during my 'parole.' I was not allowed to go out alone." [217]

His days under house arrest were quiet ones. The Bishop had his own room. He rose each morning at 5:00 a.m. and offered private Mass at 5:30 a.m. He spent his days in prayer and reading Scripture, practicing *taijichaun* three times daily for exercise. [218] Even during his time under house arrest, he remained faithful to the Holy Father. He related that during this time, a candidate for the priesthood asked him if he should enroll in the seminary, recently re-opened by the government. Bishop Kung responded, "I told him only he can make that decision but asked him if he wanted to spread the gospel according to Jin [the government Bishop of Shanghai, and Bishop Kung's jailer] or the gospel according to the Holy Father. He decided not to become a priest of the Patriotic Church." The author of the interview wrote that the Bishop smiled as he said this. [219]

The Bishop was permitted visitors, but only his family and some friends, and only if approved by the Patriotic Association. After repeated refusals by the government, Jaime Cardinal Sin, Archbishop of Manila was finally permitted to visit Bishop Kung. This was the first time since his arrest in 1955 that Bishop Kung was allowed to be visited by a Catholic bishop, despite the repeated requests during the decades of his imprisonment.

The Patriotic Association used the visit in an attempt to publicize the good treatment Bishop Kung was receiving at their hands. A formal banquet was arranged, with Cardinal Sin seated at one end of a long banquet table and Bishop Kung at the other end, separated from each other by more than twenty Patriotic Association officials and their government bishops. During the dinner, Cardinal Sin suggested that each person sing a brief song to celebrate their "friendship visit", as it was being called by the government press. When Bishop Kung's turn

---

[216] *Wall Street Journal*, July 25, 1985, *Mr. Lin in Washington*.

[217] *Soul Magazine*, July-August 1993, *An Interview with: Cardinal Kung*, p. 18.

[218] *The Washington Post*, January 10, 1988, Daniel Southerland, *Freed Chinese Bishop Vows Loyalty to Vatican*.

[219] *San Francisco Chronicle*, May 1, 1989, Don Lattin, Bitter *Rivals Vie for Bishop of Shanghai*.

had come, the Cardinal invited him to follow the example of those before him, and sing a song. In the presence of his captors and informants, Bishop Kung looked directly at Cardinal Sin and sang *Tu es Petrus et super hanc petram edificabo Ecclesiam meam* (You are Peter and upon this rock I will build my Church) [Matt 16:18]. By this, Bishop Kung conveyed to Cardinal Sin, even without further conversation, his continued devotion and loyalty to the Successor of Saint Peter.

Immediately following the banquet, Aloysius Jin LuXian, the Chinese Catholic Patriotic Association's Bishop of Shanghai, rebuked Bishop Kung for this, demanding of him, "What were you doing, showing your position!?" Bishop Kung replied, "It is not necessary to show my position. My position has never changed." Upon his return to the Philippines, Cardinal Sin immediately transmitted Bishop Kung's message to the Holy Father as he understood it during that evening's banquet: "This man of God never faltered in his love for his Church or his people despite unimaginable suffering, isolation, and pain." [220]

Given to His Family: A Witness to the World from Stamford

On January 5, 1988, the Chinese government suddenly announced the termination of Bishop Kung's house arrest. The Bishop's health was worsening, and the government feared he might be proclaimed a martyr if he died while in Chinese custody. Bishop Kung's nephew, Joseph Kung traveled to China to accompany the Bishop to his home in Stamford, Connecticut, while his wife, Agnes, coordinated the logistics of his move, communicating with the State Department and the Apostolic Nunciature in Washington, D.C.

Bishop Kung arrived in Stamford in May, 1988. Bishop Walter W. Curtis, Bishop of Bridgeport, generously agreed to assist Bishop Kung by accepting him into the priests' retirement facility, the Queen of Clergy Residence, attached to Saint Joseph's Hospital in Stamford, under the supervision of Sister Daniel Marie McCabe, C.S.J., President of the hospital.

Once Bishop Kung had arrived in Stamford, many requested to visit with him. One was Father John Houle, S.J., who had been ordained by Bishop Kung in Shanghai, and then was imprisoned by the Communist government for nearly five years, and then expelled from China. Father Houle had suffered greatly in prison, enduring severe back injuries. In 1988, he was stationed in San Francisco, and wanted to see "his bishop". He flew into New York City, and had planned to travel by car to stay with the Jesuit Community at Fairfield University, with another priest ordained in Shanghai by Bishop Kung, Father John Schmotzer, S.J. But,

---

[220] Stamford, August 25, 2012, Joseph Kung to Msgr. Stephen DiGiovanni, Basilica Archives.

after the eight hour flight, Father Houle's injuries prevented his traveling farther than Stamford, and Joseph and Agnes Kung took care of him in their home. Agnes informed Father Schmotzer that the elderly priest would not arrive in Fairfield that night, and she expressed her surprise that Father Houle would endanger his fragile health by taking such a long journey. Father Schmotzer rebuked Agnes, telling her, "If you had met the young Bishop Kung in the 1950's, you would have risked everything to come to see your bishop."

That same evening, Father Schmotzer suffered a heart attack and died. Bishop Kung, although himself weak, having arrived in the United States only two months earlier, and after only one month his release from Saint Joseph Hospital, insisted on traveling to Fairfield University to bless his priest, Father Schmotzer, "much to the surprise of the Jesuit Community in Fairfield." This was the first public appearance of Bishop Kung, to pray for the soul of one of his priests he had ordained in Shanghai. [221]

Monsignor John Horgan, a priest of the Diocese of Bridgeport, became the confessor to Bishop Kung soon after his arrival. Monsignor spoke French, and so served as the Bishop's translator, since the Bishop spoke no English. Monsignor told me that soon after the arrival of Bishop Kung, a visitor came to the hospital asking to visit him. Since he was dressed as a bishop, Bishop Kung readily agreed to see him, and asked Monsignor Horgan to stay and act as his translator. The visitor was "Bishop" Robert McKenna, O.P. He was a priest of the Order of Preachers who broke with the Church after the Second Vatican Council, and who, in 1986 arranged to be ordained a bishop, without Vatican mandate, by Bishop Guerard des Lauriers, who had been excommunicated years before. He then began his own traditionalist schismatic chapel located in the town of Monroe, Connecticut. Now "Bishop" McKenna presented himself to the exiled Bishop of Shanghai, relating his story, asking Bishop Kung to support his apostasy.

Monsignor Horgan told me that, once Bishop Kung understood who his visitor was and what he wanted, and as the man prattled on about the illegitimacy of Second Vatican Council and that there had been no valid pope since Pope Pius XII, Bishop Kung turned to Monsignor Horgan to ask, "Does this man know what I have been through these past decades? Does he really expect that I could or would give my blessing to his schism and disloyalty to the successor of Saint Peter after having suffered imprisonment rather than betray the Pope?" Bishop Kung then thanked Father McKenna for his visit, and instructed Monsignor Horgan to explain who Bishop Kung was, and that he would offer his prayers for the man, but never bless his disloyalty, apostasy and schism. [222]

---

[221] Stamford, August 25, 2012, Joseph Kung to Msgr. Stephen DiGiovanni, Basilica Archives.

[222] Monsignor Horgan and Cardinal Kung became close friends. Upon the Cardinal's death in 2000, to honor his friend, Monsignor Horgan officially changed his surname to Horgan-Kung.

The following September 8 was the thirty-third anniversary of the Communist mass arrest of Catholics in Shanghai. To commemorate this, his first anniversary of the event when he was not imprisoned and could offer Mass, Bishop Kung offered Mass in the chapel of Saint Joseph's Hospital and preached his first public sermon since his 1955 arrest. [223]

In May the following year, Bishop Kung traveled to Rome to meet with Blessed Pope John Paul II. "During that meeting, I was told by the Holy Father that I had been elevated in 1979, *in pectore*, to the College of Cardinals. I kept this a secret until our Holy Father announced it to the world on May 29, 1991." [224] That consistory was the first since the collapse of Communism across Eastern Europe, and included three prelates from the former Warsaw Pact countries of Romania, Czechoslovakia and East Germany. Bishop Kung, Archbishop Alexandru Todea and Bishop Jan Chryzostom Korec had all endured years of imprisonment by Communist regimes. "It was clear in another way that the Vatican wanted to give special acknowledgment to those who had suffered under Communism." [225] The Chinese government responded angrily that the pope was "meddling in its internal affairs by appointing a Chinese priest as a Catholic cardinal." [226]

During the Consistory of June 28th, as Cardinal Kung stepped forward to receive the red *birettum* from the Holy Father, the crowd jumped to their feet and broke into sustained applause for eight minutes in recognition of his fidelity and long-suffering for the Church. The cardinalatial robes he wore had been those of Terence Cardinal Cooke, given to Cardinal Kung by John Cardinal O'Connor, Archbishop of New York. [227]

The next day, Cardinal Kung offered Mass for Catholics in China at the Church of the Queen of Angels and Queen of Martyrs. [228] On the morning of July 1st, the Holy Father received Cardinal Kung and his family in the Sala of Saint Ambrogio in the Apostolic Palace. He addressed the Cardinal:

> Your Eminence:
>
> I give joyful thanks to Almighty God for your presence here today in the company of members of your family and some of your friends and well-wishers. Your participation in Friday's Consistory was the

---

[223] An English translation of the full text can be found in Appendix 13.

[224] *Soul Magazine*, July-August, 1993, *An Interview with Cardinal Kung*, p. 18.

[225] *New York Times*, May 30, 1991, Clyde Haberman, *Pope Names 22 Cardinals; Chinese Prelate Is Identified.*

[226] *New York Post*, June 18, 1991.

[227] *Catholic New York*, August 5, 1999, Stephen Steele, *'Loving Symbol', Cardinal Kung, longtime China prisoner, honored at Mass.*

[228] An English translation of the full text can be found in Appendix 16.

realization of an intention which has been with me since the beginning of my Pontificate, since the Consistory of June 30, 1979.

At that time, I felt that the whole Church could not but honor a man who has given witness by word and deed, through long suffering and trials, to what constitutes the very essence of life in the Church: participation in the divine life through the apostolic faith and evangelical love.

The bonds of faith, hope and love which unite the baptized with the Lord and with each other have an essential and visible manifestation in the communion which links the particular Churches to the Church of Rome and to the successor of Peter.

As the Second Vatican Council stated: "Just as, by the Lord's will, Saint Peter and the other apostles constituted one apostolic college, so in a similar way the Roman Pontiff as the successor of Peter, and the bishops as the successors of the Apostles are joined together. . . by the bonds of unity, charity and peace" (*Lumen Gentium*, 22).

Your Eminence's elevation to the College of Cardinals is a tribute to your humble perseverance in this necessary communion with Peter.

By honoring you the Holy See honors the whole faithful Church in China. With what prayerful longing and love do I follow the life of the loyal Chinese Catholic communities!

My desire to have you as a member of the College of Cardinals was, in 1979, and continues today to be the expression of my heartfelt esteem, openness and good will towards the great Chinese family.

I express the hope that this event which is a source of joy for the whole Church will be seen as a sign of our desire to foster that dialogue which can benefit the cause of harmony and peace among all the peoples of the world. [229]

Following his audience with the Holy Father, Cardinal Kung offered his first Mass in his titular church of San Sisto II, who was a pope and martyr during the third century imperial persecution of the Emperor Valerian. [230]

---

[229] *L'Osservatore Romano*, July 2, 1991.
[230] An English translation of the full text can be found in Appendix 17.

The new Cardinal's coat of arms.
Upon the map of China rests the Shrine and Our Lady of She Shan.
The motto reads,
"There may be one fold and one shepherd."

Blessed Pope John Paul II met with Ignatius Cardinal Kung,
his family and friends in the Sala San Ambrogio in the Apostolic Palace
of the Vatican on July 1, 1991.

The final years of Cardinal Kung's life were lived quietly in Stamford at the home of Joseph and Agnes Kung from December 15, 1997 until his death two years and three months later in March 2000. He continued his life of prayer and offered daily Mass at his nephew's home for the Church in China, and occasionally in local parishes.

He had numerous visitors, including many Chinese lay persons who remembered the Cardinal in Shanghai, some having endured imprisonment, or who had been members of the various Sodalities, especially the Legion of Mary. The priest who had been instrumental in re-establishing the Legion of Mary in Shanghai in the 1940's and 1950's was Father Aedan McGrath, an Irish Columban Missionary priest who had been imprisoned and expelled from the country. During the 1990's, Father McGrath came three times to visit the Cardinal, despite his advanced age and infirmity, and stayed with the Cardinal at the Kung home.

Joseph Kung recalled that Fr. McGrath still spoke the Shanghai dialect fluently. During his three visits, he and the Cardinal spoke privately. He also concelebrated Mass with the Cardinal for former members of the Shanghai Legion of Mary, preaching in the Shanghai dialect. [231]

In March, 1998, while the then-Chairman of China, Jiang Zemin, was visiting the United States, Cardinal Kung appealed to him in writing to allow religious freedom in China and to release Catholics held in Chinese jails and labor camps. His letter was hand-delivered to Zemin by Representative Nancy Pelosi during a breakfast of senior officials of the United States Government welcoming the Chairman. Chairman Zemin responded to this appeal by confiscating the passport of the 97-year-old Cardinal, officially exiling him from his homeland and diocese.

In 1999, the year of his 70th anniversary of priestly ordination, 50th anniversary as a bishop, and 20th as a cardinal, Joseph Cardinal Ratzinger, Prefect for the Congregation for Doctrine of the Faith, along with hundreds of others from around the world sent him greetings:

> In your decades of fidelity to the Church, you have followed the example of Christ the Good Shepherd, and even in the face of great suffering, have not ceased to proclaim the truth of the Gospel by your words and example. For your faithful witness to Christ, the church is deeply grateful. [232]

His last months were filled with pain, as he was dying of stomach cancer. His last words were, "God save me, Holy Mother save me." Ignatius Cardinal

---

[231] Stamford, August 25, 2012, Joseph Kung to Msgr. Stephen DiGiovanni, Basilica of Saint John Archives.
[232] Cardinal Kung Foundation Archives.

Kung died on March 12, 2000 at the age of 98 in the Stamford home of Agnes and Joseph Kung.

The funeral for Cardinal Kung was held in the Church of Saint John the Evangelist in Stamford on March 18, 2000. The night before, the body of the Cardinal lay in state in the church. Bishop (now Cardinal) Edward M. Egan, then Bishop of Bridgeport, celebrated Mass. "Cardinal Kung will forever be in the prayers and hearts of our diocese," he said. "It has been a privilege to host the cardinal here in our diocese since 1988 when he was released from 30 years of imprisonment and solitary confinement under the communist regime in China in testimony to his faith."

The Holy Father, Blessed Pope John Paul II, sent Francis Cardinal Stafford, President of the Pontifical Council for the Laity, as his personal representative for the funeral Mass which attracted some 1,700 mourners. Former President (and Ambassador to China) George H.W. Bush and first lady, Barbara Bush, sent a letter, which was read at the funeral by the president's brother, Prescott Bush of Greenwich, Connecticut, expressing their condolences to the Kung family. "Despite the adversities that life put in his way," Prescott Bush read, "Cardinal Kung stands forever as an example of courage and faith."

Cardinal Paul Shan Kuo-hsi of Taiwan paid tribute to his brother priest. "I think that Cardinal Kung could feel, in his last moment of earthly life, that 'I have fought the good fight, I have finished this race, I have kept the faith'", Cardinal Shan said in his homily. In both English and Mandarin, Cardinal Shan praised Cardinal Kung's devotion to God as a good shepherd of his flock and a faithful soldier of Christ.

Ignatius Cardinal Kung's life spanned the twentieth century. He was a witness to the reality of the Incarnate and Triune God in a world determined to destroy even the memory of God; in a world dedicated to itself in materialism, both in Communist China and in the Capitalist West. His witness was to the reality of God and the Church founded by Christ that bears the mandate to make God present in every forum of human life, even in the family, society, government and labor. He preferred imprisonment and suffering, rather than acquiesce to the Communist program to exclude God from the world. His years of witness to Christ and His Church, his loyalty to the Successor of Saint Peter, his dedication to the Catholics of Shanghai, and his decades of suffering and imprisonment made him one of the great confessors of the Faith.

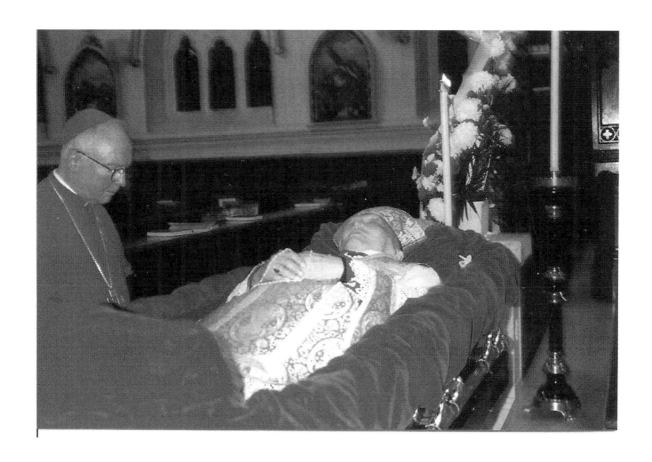

Ignatius Cardinal Kung lay in state in the Basilica of Saint John the Evangelist in Stamford, Connecticut, March 17, 2000.

Francis Cardinal Stafford represented Pope John Paul II, presiding at the funeral on March 18, 2000.

Appendix 1

Bishop Kung's remarks during his Episcopal Consecration, October 7, 1949, as the first Bishop of Soochow.[233]

On this day of my consecration, many sentiments move my heart. But only one word: "thank you," which sums up everything—especially to my students.

Each day, Christians offer beautiful prayers recalling five gracious actions of God in His gifts of creation, incarnation, redemption, mercy and the Church. Priests add another, which is gratitude for their priestly ordination. And today, I ask you to join me in making a 7th act of recognition: give thanks to our Almighty and Merciful God for the fullness of the priesthood which has come to be conferred on me by His Excellency the Internuncio.

Reconnaissance pour le Saint Pere et son representant:

Your Excellency represents our Holy Father Pius XII. Please send him the homage of my filial gratitude. I thank him above all for his confidence in me. Better than anyone else, He knows our situation. Despite this, he has created a new diocese. Is this not a palpable proof of his paternal confidence in the vitality of the Diocese of Shanghai? And it is He who holds the rudder of this new barque, as if repeating Christ's order "Put out into the deep." This confidence, while honoring me, also gives me the courage and the daring itself to assume the weighty responsibility of the episcopate, without worrying about other considerations.

Your Excellency, you yourself represent the presence of our common Father. By receiving from your hands the episcopal consecration, I have the intimate sense of the bonds that unite us to the Chair of Saint Peter. Thank you for this consecration. I promise you, and through you I promise the Vicar of Christ, obedience and fidelity.

Pour l'Eveque et la Mission de Shanghai:

However someone is missing from these festivities. Our well-loved Father is no longer. [Bishop Haouisee, Bishop of Shanghai died in 1948]. He should be here among us: he worked so hard for the arrival of this day. 19years ago he ordained me a priest. His whole life, I know--and this remains a great strength for me—that he loved me greatly. It is with much more than mere sadness that I weep at his absence.

---

[233] *China Missionary Bulletin*, Vol. II, Feb 1950, No. 2, p 136-138.

Nevertheless, I have fooled myself. Not only, are we convinced that he is here, invisible yet present, but I have discovered him visibly in the person of his collaborator, Monsignor Henry. Monsignor, you both worked together—with such a union of heart and soul! Monsignor Internuncio, he has reminded us, in his letter to Father Lacretelle, with that disinterest about our becoming a bishop, while you had prepared the division of the Diocese of Shanghai. I know the love you have for this diocese. I received this beautiful Diocese of Soochow from your hands, and I wish to thank you with all my heart. They all thank you, Monsignor and I thank the entire ancient Mission of Shanghai.—It was 350 years ago when the great Ricci visited our city. He himself dreamt of establishing here the base camp for his many journeys. In 1748—just 200 years ago, --Fathers Herniquez and Attimis and others received the martyr's crown. Then followed generations of missionaries of both branches of the clergy, who fraternally cultivated the field of labor, watering it with their own sweat, and with their own tears, and with their own blood. So many Fathers of the ancient Society of Jesus are buried in the hills of Zangsoh. My dear friend, Father Ignace Zen has joined them. At Tsangking, two of my co-workers rest awaiting the resurrection: Fr. Joachim King, [shot by Japanese in 1937, for protecting consecrated virgins who were threatened by the troops], a martyr of Christian chastity, and Father Thaddee Tsang, carried away prematurely.

Pour la Compagnie de Jesus:

To the Society of Jesus I owe my entire Christian and priestly formation. My Reverend Fathers, it is your Society that raised me from Baptism to the Episcopate. I owe my entrance into the Church beneath the mantle of your blessed Father: who gave me his name. Since then, not a single day, have I been without the maternal providence of his Society.

So many of your Fathers are no longer here to receive my thanks. They have better: they see the face of God. From their place above, may they protect me.

But I am delighted to be able to greet here today Fathers Chevestrier, Lefebvre, Vincent Zi, Couturier: may they be blessed for their efforts expended to form me in the Christian and clerical life.

Monsignor Henry, was my first prefect at the College of Saint Ignatius in which sprouted my priestly vocation. Immense is my gratitude to you, Monsignor, and to my Alma Mater—may I be worthy to see much greater prosperity under the vigorous efforts of the present rector, my friend, Father Beda Chang.

My dear and venerated Father Bonay, I wish to say only a simple "thank you", but one greatly felt. You were my seminary rector; with maternal care you directed me at 19 years of age toward the priestly life.

Father Maumus, whom I thank infinitely, taught me to savor the marrow of Ignatian spirituality. I see Father Germain, the well-spring where one may find supernatural strength, that knightly sense of duty in the service of God, that I have daily admired in you at the Aurora: wholehearted in your work, magnanimous before adversity, joyful in sacrifice. You have formed, thereby, not only technical engineers, doctors and lawyers, but also a bishop.

The Father Superior has given me precious relics of my holy patron. I will carry them daily in my pectoral cross, next to my heart engraved with all the blessings I have received from the Society. I would like to shower many more with my thanks. I offer my thanks to Fathers Lacretelle and Burckhart, and ask them to send my thanks to the Father General, and that the Father General may consider me as an adopted son of our Holy Founder, who loves your Society, more tenderly, possibly, than a novice, but certainly with a very clear conscience about everything, as I should.

Pro Confratribus e clero saeculari:

To my brothers in the diocesan clergy of Shanghai, there is too much for me to say: for us the work is not understood by the number of words spoken, but much more by how much charity joins us. I invoke the memory of the Fathers who in the Diocese of Soochow worked and died. There is much to do now: to them, I express my undying thanks from my heart.

Much thanks goes to Father Mathiae Tsang, Ecclesiasical Superior of Tong Ka Dou for his most generous assistance. If I have received any experience in mission work, I learned it from this *vicar forane* of the district of Nekaoghiao. I hope that in the future he will grant me his counsel in all things.

Father Joseph Sen, Superior of the College of St. Aloysius and his assistant Father Paul Tseu, and to all the Fathers in that College, I thank you from the depths of my heart for the sweat of your labor, from the time I was named until today.

How can I repay you, O my brothers in Christ? You gave me this pastoral staff as a sign of your unity in fraternal charity. By your sympathy and generosity, you have been for me a staff. You will be for me always a staff in times of joy and a bastion in adversity by your prayers. To each and every one of you I appeal, first to Fathers Tsang and Ignatio Zi, *vicars forane*, now subjects of the Diocese of Soochow. Never can our diocese forget you. And so, you will stand in the sight of your new bishop and you will speak for me, your least brother!

Duc in Altum:

Now I must go to my diocese: but we will not be separated. We will remain joined in the charity of Christ, just as we are joined now.

Christ yesterday, today and tomorrow: so too with us. Brothers we were yesterday, brothers we remain today: brothers we will be tomorrow, in Christ Our Lord.

So, to you the helpers of all: first, Father Luca Tsang, my Vicar General, and then all my clergy, through the intercession of Blessed Mary Our Lady of Lourdes, Queen of the Most Holy Rosary, and the intercession of our holy Father Saint Ignatius, may Our Lord reign: *Duc in altum* [Put out into the deep], and I confidently respond, *In Verbo tuo, laxabo rete* [At your Word, I will lower the net].

Appendix 2

Pope Pius XI, *Divini Redemptoris*, Encyclical on Atheistic Communism, March 19, 1937.[234]

To the Patriarchs, Primates, Archbishops, Bishops, and other Ordinaries in Peace and communion with the Apostolic See.

Venerable Brethren, Health and Apostolic Benediction.

The promise of a Redeemer brightened the first history of mankind, and the confident hope aroused by this promise softened the keen regret for a paradise which had been lost. It was this hope that accompanied the human race on its weary journey, until in the fullness of time the expected Savior came to begin a new universal civilization, the Christian civilization, far superior even to that which up to this time had been laboriously achieved by certain more privileged nations.

Nevertheless, the struggle between good and evil remained in the world as a sad legacy of the original fall. Nor has the ancient tempter ever ceased to deceive mankind with false promises. It is on this account that one convulsion following upon another has marked the passage of the centuries, down to the revolution of our own days. This modern revolution, it may be said, has actually broken out or threatens everywhere, and it exceeds in amplitude and violence anything yet experienced in the preceding persecutions launched against the Church. Entire peoples find themselves in danger of falling back into a barbarism worse than that which oppressed the greater part of the world at the coming of the Redeemer.

This all too imminent danger, Venerable Brethren, as you have already surmised, is Bolshevistic and atheistic Communism, which aims at upsetting the social order and at undermining the very foundations of Christian civilization.

I.   ATTITUDE OF THE CHURCH TOWARDS COMMUNISM
Previous Condemnations

In the face of such a threat, the Catholic Church could not and does not remain silent. This Apostolic See, above all, has not refrained from raising its voice, for it knows that its proper and social mission is to defend truth, justice and all those eternal values which Communism ignores or attacks. Ever since the days

---

[234] Claudia Carlen, *The Papal Encyclicals 1903-1939*, Ypsilanti, MI, 1990. pp. 537-554.

when groups of "intellectuals" were formed in an arrogant attempt to free civilization from the bonds of morality and religion, Our Predecessors overtly and explicitly drew the attention of the world to the consequences of the de-Christianization of human society. With reference to Communism, Our Venerable Predecessor, Pius IX, of holy memory, as early as 1846 pronounced a solemn condemnation, which he confirmed in the words of the *Syllabus* directed against "that infamous doctrine of so-called Communism which is absolutely contrary to the natural law itself, and if once adopted would utterly destroy the rights, property and possessions of all men, and even society itself" [*Qui Pluribus*, Nov. 9, 1864].

Later on, another of Our predecessors, the immortal Leo XIII, in his Encyclical *Quod Apostolici Muneris*, defined Communism as "the fatal plague which insinuates itself into the very marrow of human society only to bring about its ruin" [*Quod Apostolici Muneris*, December 28, 1878]. With clear intuition he pointed out that the atheistic movements existing among the masses of the Machine Age had their origin in that school of philosophy which for centuries had sought to divorce science from the life of the Faith and of the Church.

During Our Pontificate We too have frequently and with urgent insistence denounced the current trend to atheism which is alarmingly on the increase. In 1924 when Our relief-mission returned from the Soviet Union We condemned Communism in a special Allocution which We addressed to the whole world [*Nostis qua praecipue*, December 18, 1924]. In Our Encyclicals *Miserentissimus Redemptor* [May 8, 1928], *Quadrageismo Anno* [May 15, 1931], *Caritate Christi* [May 3, 1932], *Acerba Animi* [September 29, 1932], *Dilectissima Nobis* [June 3, 1933], We raised a solemn protest against the persecutions unleashed in Russia, in Mexico and now in Spain. Our two Allocutions of last year, the first on the occasion of the opening of the International Catholic Press Exposition, and the second during Our audience to the Spanish refugees, along with Our message of last Christmas, have evoked a world-wide echo which is not yet spent. In fact, the most persistent enemies of the Church, who from Moscow are directing the struggle against Christian civilization, themselves bear witness, by their unceasing attacks in word and act, that even to this our Papacy has continued faithfully to protect the sanctuary of the Christian religion, and that it has called public attention to the perils of Communism more frequently and more effectively than any other public authority on earth.

To Our great satisfaction, Venerable Brethren, you have, by means of individual and even joint pastoral letters, accurately transmitted and explained to the faithful these admonitions. Yet despite Our frequent and paternal warning the peril only grows greater from day to day because of the pressure exerted by clever agitators. Therefore We believe it to be Our duty to raise Our voice once more, in a still more solemn missive, in accord with the tradition of this Apostolic See, the Teacher of Truth, and in accord with the desire of the whole Catholic world, which makes the appearance of such a document but natural. We trust that the echo of Our voice will reach every mind free from prejudice and every heart sincerely desirous of the good of mankind. We wish this the more because Our words are now receiving sorry confirmation from the spectacle of the bitter fruits of subversive ideas, which We foresaw and foretold, and which are in fact multiplying fearfully in the countries already stricken, or threatening every other country of the world.

Hence We wish to expose once more in a brief synthesis the principles of atheistic Communism as they are manifested chiefly in Bolshevism. We wish also to indicate its method of action and to contrast with its false principle as the clear doctrine of the Church, in order to inculcate anew and with greater insistence the means by which the Christian civilization, the true *civitas humana*, can be saved from the satanic scourge, and not merely saved, but better developed for the well-being of human society.

II.   COMMUNISM IN THEORY AND PRACTICE

The Communism of today, more emphatically than similar movements in the past, conceals in itself a false messianic idea. A pseudo-ideal of justice, of equality and fraternity in labor impregnates all its doctrine and activity with a deceptive mysticism, which communicates a zealous and contagious enthusiasm to the multitudes entrapped by delusive promises. This is especially true in an age like ours, when unusual misery has resulted from the unequal distribution of the goods of this world. This pseudo-ideal is even boastfully advanced as if it were responsible for a certain economic progress. As a matter of fact, when such progress is at all real, its true causes are quite different, as for instance the intensification of industrialism in centuries which were formerly almost without it, the exploitation of immense natural resources, and the use of the most brutal methods to insure the achievement of gigantic projects with a minimum of expense.

The doctrine of modern Communism, which is often concealed under the most seductive trappings, is in substance based on the principles of dialectical and historical materialism previously advocated by Marx, of which the theoricians of Bolshevism claim to possess the only genuine interpretation. According to this doctrine there is in the world only one reality, matter, the blind forces of which evolve into plant, animal and man. Even human society is nothing but a phenomenon and form of matter, evolving in the same way. By a law of inexorable necessity and through a perpetual conflict of forces, matter moves towards the final synthesis of a classless society. In such a doctrine, as is evident, there is no room for the idea of God; there is no difference between matter and spirit, between soul and body; there is neither survival of the soul after death nor any hope in a future life. Insisting on the dialectical aspect of their materialism, the Communists claim that the conflict which carries the world towards its final synthesis can be accelerated by man. Hence they endeavor to sharpen the antagonisms which arise between the various classes of society. Thus the class struggle with its consequent violent hate and destruction takes on the aspects of a crusade for the progress of humanity. On the other hand, all other forces whatever, as long as they resist such systematic violence, must be annihilated as hostile to the human race.

Communism, moreover, strips man of his liberty, robs human personality of all its dignity, and removes all the moral restraints that check the eruptions of blind impulse. There is no recognition of any right of the individual in his relations to the collectivity; no natural right is accorded to human personality, which is a mere cog-wheel in the Communist system. In man's relations with other individuals, besides, Communists hold the principle of absolute equality, rejecting all hierarchy and divinely-constituted authority, including the authority of parents. What men call authority and subordination is derived from the community as its first and only font. Nor is the individual granted any property rights over material goods or the means of production, for inasmuch as these are the sources of further wealth, their possession would give to one man power over another. Precisely on this score, all forms of private property must be eradicated, for they are at the origin of all economic enslavement.

Refusing to human life any sacred or spiritual character, such a doctrine logically makes of marriage and the family a purely artificial and civil institution, the outcome of a specific economic system. There exists no matrimonial bond of a juridico-moral nature that is not subject to the whim of the individual or of the collectivity. Naturally, therefore, the notion of an indissoluble marriage-bond is ridiculed. Communism is particularly characterized by the rejection of any link that binds woman to the family and the home, and her emancipation is proclaimed as a basic principle. She is withdrawn from the family and the care of her children, to be thrust instead into public life and collective production under the same conditions as man. The care of home and children then devolves upon the collectivity. Finally, the right of education is denied to parents, for it is conceived as the exclusive prerogative of the community, in whose name and by whose mandate alone parents may exercise this right.

What should be the condition of a human society based on such materialistic tenets? It would be a collectivity with no other hierarchy than that of the economic system. It would have only one mission: the production of material things by means of collective labor, so that the goods of this world might be enjoyed in a paradise where each would "give according to his powers" and would "receive according to his needs." Communism recognizes in the collectivity the right, or rather, unlimited discretion, to draft individuals for the labor of the collectivity with no regard for their personal welfare; so that even violence could be legitimately exercised to dragoon the recalcitrant against their wills. In the Communistic commonwealth morality and law would be nothing but a deprivation of the existing economic order, purely earthly in origin and unstable in character. In a word, the Communists claim to inaugurate a new era and a new civilization which is the result of blind evolutionary forces culminating in a humanity without God.

When all men have fully acquired the collectivist mentality in the Utopia of a really classless society, the political State, which is now conceived by Communists merely as the instrument by which the proletariat is oppressed by the capitalists, will have lost all reason for its existence and will "wither away". However, until that happy consummation is realized, the State and the powers of the State furnish Communism with the most efficacious and most extensive means for the achievement of its goal.

Such, Venerable Brethren, is the new gospel which Bolshevistic and atheistic Communism offers the world as the glad tidings of deliverance and salvation! It is a system full of errors and sophisms. It is in opposition both to reason and to Divine Revelation. It subverts the social order, since it means the destruction of its foundations because it ignores the true origin and purpose of the State; because it denies the rights, dignity and liberty of human personality.

How is it possible that such a system, long since rejected scientifically and now proved erroneous by experience, how is it, We ask, that such a system could spread so rapidly in all parts of the world? The explanation lies in the fact that too few have been able to grasp the nature of Communism. The majority instead succumb to its deception, skillfully concealed by the most extravagant promises. By pretending to desire only the betterment of the condition of the working classes, by urging the removal of the very real abuses changeable to the liberalistic economic order, and by demanding a more equitable distribution of this world's goods (objectives entirely and undoubtedly legitimate), the Communist takes advantage of the present world-wide economic crisis to draw into the sphere of his influence even those sections of the populace which on principle reject all forms of materialism and terrorism. And as every error contains its element of truth, the partial truths to which We have referred are astutely presented according to the needs of the time and place, to conceal, when convenient, the repulsive crudity and inhumanity of Communistic principles and tactics. Thus the Communist ideal wins over many of the better-minded members of the community. These in turn become the apostles of the movement among the younger intelligentsia who are still too immature to recognize the intrinsic errors of the system. The preachers of Communism are also proficient in exploiting racial antagonisms and political divisions and oppositions. They take advantage of the lack of orientation characteristic of modern agnostic science in order to burrow into the universities, where they bolster up the principles of their doctrine with pseudo-scientific arguments.

If we would explain the blind acceptance of Communism by so many thousands of workmen, we must remember that the way had been already prepared for it by the religious and moral destitution in which wage-earners had been left by liberal economics. Even on Sundays and holy days, labor-shifts were given no time to attend to their essential religious duties. No one thought of building churches within convenient distance of factories, nor of facilitating the work of the priest. On the contrary, laicism was actively and persistently promoted, with the result that we are now reaping the fruits of the errors so often denounced by Our Predecessors and by Ourselves. It can surprise no one that the Communistic fallacy should be spreading in a world already to a large extent de-Christianized.

There is another explanation for the rapid diffusion of the Communistic ideas now seeping into every nation, great and small, advanced and backward, so that no corner of the earth is free from them. This explanation is to be found in the propaganda so truly diabolical that the world has perhaps never witnessed its like before. It is directed from one common center. It is shrewdly adapted to the varying conditions of diverse peoples. It has at its disposal great financial resources, gigantic organizations, international congresses, and countless trained workers. It makes use of pamphlets and reviews, of cinema, theater and radio, of schools and even universities. Little by little it penetrates into all classes of the people and even reaches the better-minded groups of the community, with the result that few are aware of the poison which increasingly pervades their minds and hearts.

A third powerful factor in the diffusion of Communism is the conspiracy of silence on the part of a large section of the non-Catholic press of the world. We say conspiracy, because it is impossible otherwise to explain how a press usually so eager to exploit even the little daily incidents of life has been able to remain silent for so long about the horrors perpetrated in Russia, Mexico and even in a great part of Spain; and that it should have relatively so little to say concerning a world organization as vast as Russian Communism. This silence is due in part to shortsighted political policy, and is favored by various occult forces which for a long time have been working for the overthrow of the Christian Social Order.

Meanwhile the sorry effects of this propaganda are before our eyes. Where Communism has been able to assert its power—and here We are thinking with special affection of the people of Russia and Mexico—it has striven by every possible means, as its champions openly boast, to destroy Christian civilization and the Christian religion by banishing every remembrance of them from the hearts of men, especially of the young. Bishops and priests were exiled, condemned to forced labor, shot and done to death in inhuman fashion; laymen suspected of defending their religion were vexed, persecuted, dragged off to trial and thrown into prison.

Even where the scourge of Communism has not yet had time enough to exercise to the full its logical effects, as witness Our beloved Spain, it has, alas, found compensation in the fiercer violence of its attack. Not only this or that church or isolated monastery was sacked, but as far as possible every church and every monastery was destroyed. Every vestige of the Christian religion was eradicated, even though intimately linked with the rarest monuments of art and science. The fury of Communism has not confined itself to the indiscriminate slaughter of Bishops, of thousands of priests and religious of both sexes, it searches out above all those who have been devoting their lives to the welfare of the working classes and the poor. But the majority of its victims have been laymen of all conditions and classes. Even up to the present moment, masses of them are slain almost daily for no other offense than the fact that they are good Christians or at least opposed to atheistic Communism. And this fearful destruction has been carried out with a hatred and a savage barbarity one would not have believed possible in our age. No man of good sense, nor any statesman conscious of his responsibility can fail to shudder at the thought that what is happening today in Spain may perhaps be repeated tomorrow in other civilized countries.

Nor can it be said that these atrocities are a transitory phenomenon, the usual accompaniment of all great revolutions, the isolated excesses common to every war. No, they are the natural fruit of a system which lacks all inner restraint. Some restraint is necessary for man considered either as an individual or in society. Even the barbaric peoples had this inner check in the natural law written by God in the heart of every man. And where this natural law was held in higher esteem, ancient nations rose to a grandeur that still fascinates—more than it should—certain superficial students of human history. But tear the very idea of God from the hearts of men, and they are necessarily urged by their passions to the most atrocious barbarity.

Thus, unfortunately, is what we now behold. For the first time in history we are witnessing a struggle, cold-blooded in purpose and mapped out to the least detail, between man and "all that is called God" [*II Thess* II, 4]. Communism is by its nature anti-religious. It considers religion as "the opiate of the people" because the principles of religion which speak of a life beyond the grave dissuade the proletariat from the dream of a Soviet paradise which is of this world.

But the law of nature and its Author cannot be flouted with impunity. Communism has not been able, and will not be able, to achieve its objectives even in the merely economic sphere. It is true that in Russia it has been a contributing factor in rousing men and materials from the inertia of centuries, and in obtaining by all manner of means, often without scruple, some measure of material success. Nevertheless We know from reliable and even very recent testimony that not even there, in spite of slavery imposed on millions of men, has Communism reached its promised goal. After all, even the sphere of economics needs some morality, some moral sense of responsibility, which can find no place in a system so thoroughly materialistic as Communism. Terrorism is the only possible substitute, and it is terrorism that reigns today in Russia, where former comrades in revolution are exterminating each other. Terrorism, having failed despite all to stem the tide of moral corruption, cannot even prevent the dissolution of society itself.

In making these observations it is no part of Our intention to condemn *en masse* the people of the Soviet Union. For them We cherish the warmest paternal affection. We are well aware that not a few of them groan beneath the yoke imposed on them by men who in very large part are strangers to the real interests of the country. We recognize that many others were deceived by fallacious hopes. We blame only the system, with its authors and abettors who considered Russia the best-prepared field for experimenting with a plan elaborated decades ago, and who from there continue to spread it from one end of the world to the other.

III.   DOCTRINE OF THE CHURCH IN CONTRAST

We have exposed the errors and the violent, deceptive tactics of Bolshevistic and atheistic Communism. It is now time, Venerable Brethren, to contrast with it the true notion, already familiar to you, of the *civitas humana* or human society, as taught by reason and Revelation through the mouth of the Church, *Magistra Gentium*.

Above all other reality there exists one supreme Being: God, the omnipotent Creator of all things, the all-wise and just Judge of all men. This supreme reality, God, is the absolute condemnation of the impudent falsehoods of Communism. In truth, it is not because men believe in God that He exists; rather because He exists do all men whose eyes are not deliberately closed to the truth believe in Him and pray to Him.

In the Encyclical on Christian education [*Divini Illius Magistri*, December 31, 1929], We explained the fundamental doctrine concerning man as it may be gathered from reason and Faith. Man has a spiritual and immortal soul. He is a person, marvelously endowed by his Creator with gifts of body and mind. He is a true "microcosm," as the ancients said, a world in miniature, with a value far surpassing that of the vast inanimate cosmos. God alone is his last end, in this life and the next. By sanctifying grace he is raised to the dignity of a son of God, and incorporated into the Kingdom of God in the Mystical Body of Christ. In consequence he has been endowed by God with many and varied prerogatives: the right to life, to bodily integrity, to the necessary means of existence; the right to tend toward his ultimate goal in the path marked out for him by God; the right of association and the right to possess and use property.

Just as matrimony and the right to its natural use are of divine origin, so likewise are the constitution and fundamental prerogatives of the family fixed and determined by the Creator. In the Encyclical on Christian Marriage [*Casti Connubii*, December 31, 1930] and in Our other Encyclical on Education, cited above, we have treated these topics at considerable length.

But God has likewise destined man for civil society according to the dictates of his very nature. In the plan of the Creator, society is a natural means which man can and must use to reach his destined end. Society is for man and not vice versa. This must not be understood in the sense of liberalistic individualism, which subordinates society to the selfish use of the individual; but only in the sense that by means of an organic union with society and by mutual collaboration the attainment of earthly happiness is placed within the reach of all. In a further sense, it is society which affords the opportunities for the development of all the individual and social gifts bestowed on human nature. These natural gifts have a value surpassing the immediate interests of the moment, for in society they reflect the divine perfection, which would not be true were man to live alone. But on final analysis, even in this latter function, society is made for man, that he may recognize this reflection of God's perfection, and refer it in praise and adoration to the Creator. Only man, the human person, and not society in any form is endowed with reason and a morally free will.

Man cannot be exempted from his divinely-imposed obligations toward civil society, and the representatives of authority have the right to coerce him when he refuses without reason to do his duty. Society, on the other hand, cannot defraud man of his God-granted rights, the most important of which We have indicated above. Nor can society systematically void these rights by making their use impossible. It is therefore according to the dictates of reason that ultimately all material things should be ordained to man as a person, that through his mediation they may find their way to the Creator. In this wise we can apply to man, the human person, the words of the Apostle of the Gentiles, who writes to the

Corinthians on the Christian economy of salvation: "All things are yours, and you are Christ's and Christ is God's" [*I Cor* III, 23]. While Communism impoverishes human personality by inverting the terms of the relation of man to society, to what lofty heights is man not elevated by reason and Revelation!

The directive principles concerning the social-economic order have been expounded in the social Encyclical of Leo XIII on the question of labor [*Rerum Novarum*, May 15, 1891]. Our own Encyclical on the Reconstruction of the Social Order [*Quadragesimo Anno*, May 15, 1931] adapted these principles to present needs. Then, insisting anew on the age-old doctrine of the Church concerning the individual and social character of private property, We explained clearly the right and dignity of labor, the relations of mutual aid and collaboration which should exist between those who possess capital and those who work, the salary due in strict justice to the worker for himself and for his family.

In this same Encyclical of Ours We have shown that the means of saving the world of today from the lamentable ruin into which a moral liberalism has plunged us, are neither the class-struggle nor terror, nor yet the autocratic abuse of State power, but rather the infusion of social justice and sentiment with Christian love into the social-economic order. We have indicated how a sound prosperity is to be restored according to the true principles of a sane corporative system which respects the proper hierarchic structure of society; and how all the occupational groups should be fused into a harmonious unity inspired by the principle of the common good. And the genuine and chief function of public and civil authority consists precisely in the efficacious furthering of this harmony and coordination of all social forces.

In view of this organized common effort towards peaceful living, Catholic doctrine vindicates to the State the dignity and authority of a vigilant and provident defender of those divine and human rights on which the Sacred Scriptures and the Fathers of the Church insist so often. It is not true that all have equal rights in civil society. It is not true that there exists no lawful social hierarchy. Let it suffice to refer to the Encyclicals of Leo XIII already cited, especially to that on State powers [*Diuturnum Illud*, June 20, 1881], and to the other on the Christian Constitution of States [*Immortale Dei*, November 1, 1885]. In these documents the Catholic will find the principles of reason and the Faith clearly explained, and these principles will enable him to defend himself against the errors and perils of a Communistic conception of the State. The enslavement of man despoiled of his rights, the denial of the transcendental origin of the State and its authority, the horrible abuse of public power in the service of a collectivistic terrorism, are the very contrary of all that corresponds with natural ethics and the will of the Creator, Who has mutually ordained them one to the other. Hence neither can be exempted from their correlative obligations, nor deny or diminish each other's rights. The Creator himself has regulated this mutual relationship in its fundamental lines, and it is by an unjust usurpation that Communism arrogates to itself the right to enforce, in place of the divine law based on the immutable principles of truth and charity, a partisan political program which derives from the arbitrary human will and is replete with hate.

In teaching this enlightening doctrine the Church has no other intention than to realize the glad tidings sung by the Angels above the cave of Bethlehem at the Redeemer's birth: "Glory to God. . . and. . . peace to men. . ." [*Luke* II, 14], true peace and true happiness, even here below as far as is possible, in preparation for the happiness of heaven—but to men of good will. This doctrine is equally removed from all extremes of error and all exaggerations of parties or systems which stem from error. It maintains a constant equilibrium of truth and justice, which it vindicates in theory and applies and promotes in practice, bringing into harmony the rights and duties of all parties. Thus authority is reconciled with liberty, the dignity of the individual with that of the State, the human personality of the subject with the divine delegation of the superior; and in this way a balance is struck between the due dependence and well-ordered love of a man for himself, his family and country, and his love of other families and other peoples, founded on the love of God, the Father of all, their first principle and last end. The Church does not separate a proper regard for temporal welfare from solicitude for the eternal. If she subordinates the former to the latter according to the words of her divine Founder, "Seek ye first the Kingdom of God and His Justice, and all these things shall be added unto you" [*Matt* V, 3], she is nevertheless so far from being unconcerned with human affairs, so far from hindering civil progress and material advancement, that she actually fosters and promotes them in the most sensible and efficacious manner. Thus even in the sphere of social-economics, although the Church has never proposed a definite technical system, since this is not her field, she has nevertheless clearly outlined the guiding principles which, while susceptible of varied concrete applications according to the diversified conditions of times and places and peoples, indicate the safe way of securing the happy progress of society.

The wisdom and supreme utility of this doctrine are admitted by all who really understand it. With good reason outstanding statesmen have asserted that, after a study of various social systems, they have found nothing sounder than the principles expounded in the Encyclicals *Rerum Novarum* and *Quadagesimo Anno*. In non-Catholic countries, men recognize the great value to society of the social doctrine of the Church. Thus, scarcely a month ago, an eminent political figure of the Far East, a non-Christian, did not hesitate to affirm publicly that the Church, with her doctrine of peace and Christian brotherhood, is rendering a signal contribution to the difficult task of establishing and maintaining peace among the nations. Finally, We know from reliable information that flows into this Center of

Christendom from all parts of the world, that the Communists themselves, where thy are not utterly depraved, recognize the superiority of the social doctrine of the Church, when once explained to them, over the doctrines of their leaders and their teachers. Only those blinded by passion and hatred close their eyes to the light of truth and obstinately struggle against it.

But the enemies of the Church, though forced to acknowledge the wisdom of her doctrine, accuse her of having failed to act in conformity with her principles, and from this conclude to the necessity of seeking other solutions. The utter falseness and injustice of this accusation is shown by the whole history of Christianity. To refer only to a single typical trait, it was Christianity that first affirmed the real and universal brotherhood of all men of whatever race and condition. This doctrine she proclaimed by a method, and with an amplitude and conviction, unknown to preceding centuries; and with it she potently contributed to the abolition of slavery. Not bloody revolution, but the inner force of her teaching made the proud Roman matron see in her slave a sister in Christ. It is Christianity that adores the Son of God, made Man for love of man, and become not only the "Son of the Carpenter" but Himself a "Carpenter" [*Matt* XIII 55]. It was Christianity that raised manual labor to its true dignity, whereas it had hitherto been so despised that even the moderate Cicero did not hesitate to sum up the general opinion of his time in words of which any modern sociologist would be ashamed: "All artisans are engaged in sordid trades, for there can be nothing ennobling about a workshop" [Cicero, *De Officiis*, I, 42].

Faithful to these principles, the Church has given new life to human society. Under her influence arose prodigious charitable organizations, great guilds of artisans and workingmen of every type. These guilds, ridiculed as "medieval" by the liberalism of the last century, are today claiming the admiration of our contemporaries in many countries who are endeavoring to revive them in some modern form. And when other systems hindered her work and raised obstacles to the salutary influence of the Church, she was never done warning them of their error. We need but recall with what constant firmness and energy Our Predecessor, Leo XIII, vindicated for the workingman the rights to organize, which the dominant liberalism of the most powerful States relentlessly denied him. Even today the authority of this Church doctrine is greater than it seems; for the influence of ideas in the realm of facts, though invisible and not easily measured, is surely of predominant importance.

It may be said in all truth that the Church, like Christ, goes through the centuries doing good to all. There would be today neither Socialism nor Communism if the rulers of the nations had not scorned the teachings and maternal warnings of the Church. On the bases of liberalism and laicism they wished to build other social edifices which, powerful and imposing as they seemed at first, all too soon revealed the weakness of their foundations, and today are crumbling one after another before our eyes, as everything must crumble that is not grounded on the one corner stone which is Christ Jesus.

IV. DEFENSIVE AND CONSTRUCTIVE PROGRAM

This, Venerable Brethren, is the doctrine of the Church, which alone in the social as in all other fields can offer real light and assure salvation in the face of Communistic ideology. But this doctrine must be consistently reduced to practice in every-day life, according to the admonition of St. James the Apostle: "Be ye doers of the word and not hearers only, deceiving your own selves" [*James* I, 22]. The most urgent need of the present day is therefore the energetic and timely applications of remedies which will effectively ward off the catastrophe that daily grows more threatening. We cherish the firm hope that the fanaticism with which the sons of darkness work day and night at their materialistic and atheistic propaganda will at least serve the holy purpose of stimulating the sons of light to a like and even greater zeal for the honor of the Divine Majesty.

What then must be done, what remedies must be employed to defend Christ and Christian civilization from this pernicious enemy? As a father in the midst of his family, We should like to speak quite intimately of those duties which the great struggle of our day imposes on all the children of the Church; and We would address Our paternal admonition even to those sons who have strayed far from her.

As in all the stormy periods of the history of the Church, the fundamental remedy today lies in a sincere renewal of private and public life according to the principles of the Gospel by all those who belong to the Fold of Christ, that they may be in truth the salt of the earth to preserve human society from total corruption.

With hearts deeply grateful to the Father of Light, from Whom descends "every best gift and every perfect gift" [*James* I, 17], We see on all sides consoling signs of this spiritual renewal. We see it not only in so many singularly chosen souls who in these last years have been elevated to the sublime heights of sanctity, and in so many others who with generous hearts are making their way towards the same luminous goal, but also in the new flowering of a deep and practical piety in all classes of society even the most cultured, as We pointed out in Our recent Motu Proprio *In multis solaciis* of October 28 last, on the occasion of the reorganization of the Pontifical Academy of Sciences.

Nevertheless, We cannot deny that there is still much to be done in the way of spiritual renovation. Even in Catholic countries there are still too many who are Catholics hardly more than in name. There are too many who fulfill more or less faithfully the more essential obligations of the religion they boast of professing, but have no desire of knowing it better, of deepening their inward conviction, and still less of bringing into conformity with the external gloss the inner splendor of a right and unsullied conscience, that recognizes and performs all its duties under the eye of God. We know how much Our Divine Savior detested this empty pharisaic show, He Who wished that all should adore the Father "in spirit and in truth" [*John* IV, 23]. The Catholic who does not live really and sincerely according to the Faith he professes will not long be master of himself in these days when the winds of strife and persecution blow so fiercely, but will be swept away defenseless in this new deluge which threatens the world. And thus, while he is preparing his own ruin, he is exposing to ridicule the very name of Christian.

And here We wish, Venerable Brethren, to insist more particularly on two teachings of Our Lord which have a special bearing on the present condition of the human race: detachment from earthly goods and the precept of charity. "Blessed are the poor in spirit" were the first words that fell from the lips of the Divine Master in His sermon on the mount [*Matt* V, 3]. This lesson is more than ever necessary in these days of materialism athirst for the goods and pleasures of this earth. All Christians, rich or poor, must keep their eye fixed on heaven, remembering that "we have not here a lasting city, but we seek one that is to come" [*Hebrews*, XIII, 14]. The rich should not place their happiness in things of earth nor spend their best efforts in the acquisition of them. Rather, considering themselves only as stewards of their earthly goods, let them be mindful of the account they must render of them to their Lord and Master, and value them as precious means that God has put into their hands for doing good; let them not fail, besides, to distribute of their abundance to the poor, according to the evangelical precept [*Luke* XI, 41].

Otherwise there shall be verified of them and their riches the harsh condemnation of St. James the Apostle: "Go now, ye rich men; weep and howl in your miseries which shall come upon you. Your riches are corrupted, and your garments are moth-eaten; your gold and silver is cankered; and the rust of them shall be for a testimony against you and shall eat your flesh like fire. You have stored up to yourselves wrath against the last days. . ." [*James* V, 1-3].

But the poor too, in their turn, while engaged, according to the laws of charity and justice, in acquiring the necessities of life and also in bettering their condition, should always remain "poor in spirit" [*Matt* V, 3], and hold spiritual goods in higher esteem than earthly property and pleasures. Let them remember that the world will never be able to rid itself of misery, sorrow and tribulation, which are the portion even of those who seem most prosperous. Patience, therefore, is the need of all, that Christian patience which comforts the heart with the divine assurance of eternal happiness. "Be patient, therefore, brethren", we repeat St. James, "until the coming of the Lord. Behold the husbandman waits for the precious fruit of the earth, patiently bearing until he receive the early and the later rain. Be you therefore also patient and strengthen your hearts, for the coming of the Lord is at hand" [*James* V, 7-8]. Only thus will be fulfilled the consoling promise of the Lord: "Blessed are the poor!" These words are no vain consolation, a promise as empty as those of the Communists. They are the words of life, pregnant with a sovereign reality. They are fully verified here on earth, as well as in eternity. Indeed, how many of the poor, in anticipation of the Kingdom of Heaven already proclaimed their own: "for yours is the Kingdom of Heaven" [*Luke* VI, 20], find in these words a happiness which so many of the wealthy, uneasy with their riches and ever thirsting for more, look for in vain!

Still more important as a remedy for the evil we are considering, or certainly more directly calculated to cure it, is the precept of charity. We have in mind that Christian charity, "patient and kind" [*I Cor* XIII, 4], which avoids all semblance of demeaning paternalism, and all ostentation; that charity which from the very beginning of Christianity won to Christ the poorest of the poor, the slaves. And We are grateful to all those members of charitable associations, from the conferences of St. Vincent de Paul to the recent great relief organizations, which are perseveringly practicing the spiritual and corporal works of mercy. The more the working men and the poor realize what the spirit of love animated by the virtue of Christ is doing for them, the more readily will they abandon the false persuasion that Christianity has lost its efficacy and that the Church stands on the side of the exploiters of their labor.

But when on the one hand We see thousands of the needy, victims of real misery for various reasons beyond their control, and on the other so many round about them who spend huge sums of money on useless things and frivolous amusement, We cannot fail to remark with sorrow not only that justice is poorly observed, but that the precept of charity also is not sufficiently appreciated, is not a vital thing in daily life. We desire therefore, Venerable Brethren, that this divine precept, this precious mark of identification left by Christ to His true disciples, be ever more fully explained by pen and word of mouth; this precept which teaches us to see in those who suffer Christ Himself, and would have us love our brothers as Our Divine Savior has loved us, that is, even at the sacrifice of our selves, and, if need be, of our very life. Let all then frequently meditate on those words of the final sentence, so consoling yet so terrifying, which the Supreme Judge will pronounce on the day of the Last Judgment: "Come, ye blessed of my Father . . . for I was hungry and you gave me to eat; I was thirsty and you gave me to drink. . . Amen, I say to you, as long as you did it to one of these my least brethren you did it to me" [*Matt* XXV, 34-40]. And the reverse: "Depart from me, you cursed, into everlasting fire. . . for I was hungry and you gave me not to eat; I was thirsty and you gave me not to drink. . . Amen, I say to you, as long as you did not to one of these least, neither did you do it to me" [*Matt* XXV, 41-45].

To be sure of eternal life, therefore, and to be able to help the poor effectively, it is imperative to return to a more moderate way of life, to renounce the joys, often sinful, which the world today holds out in such abundance; to forget self for love of the neighbor. There is a divine regenerating force in this "new precept" (as Christ called it) of Christian charity [*John* XIII, 34]. Its faithful observance will pour into the heart an inner peace which the world know not, and will finally cure the ills which oppress humanity.

But charity will never be true charity unless it takes that "he who loves his neighbor has fulfilled the law" and he gives the reason: "For, You shall not commit adultery, You shall not kill, You shall not steal. . . and if there be any other commandment, it is comprised in this word: You shall love your neighbor as yourself" [*Romans* XIII, 8, 9]. According to the Apostle, then, all the commandments, including those which are of strict justice, as those which forbid us to kill or to steal, may be reduced to the single precept of true charity. From this it follows that a "charity" which deprives the workingman of the salary to which he has a strict title in justice, is not charity at all, but only its empty name and hollow semblance. The wage-earner is not to receive as alms what is his due in justice. And let no one attempt with trifling charitable donations to exempt himself from the great duties imposed by justice. Both justice and charity often dictate obligations touching on the same subject-matter, but under different aspects; and the very dignity of the workingman makes him justly and acutely sensitive to the duties of others in his regard.

Therefore We turn again in a special way to you, Christian employers and industrialists, whose problem is often so difficult for the reason that you are saddled with the heavy heritage of an unjust economic regime whose ruinous influence has been felt through many generations. We bid you be mindful of your responsibility. It is unfortunately true that the manner of acting in certain Catholic circles has done much to shake the faith of the working-classes in the religion of Jesus Christ. These groups have refused to understand that Christian charity demands the recognition of certain rights due to the workingman, which the Church has explicitly acknowledged. What is to be thought of the action of those Catholic employers who in one place succeeded in preventing the reading of Our Encyclical *Quadragesimo Anno* in their local churches? Or of those Catholic industrialists who even to this day have shown themselves hostile to a labor movement that We Ourselves recommended? Is it not deplorable that the right of private property defended by the Church should so often have been used as a weapon to defraud the workingman of his just salary and his social rights?

In reality, besides commutative justice, there is also social justice with its own set obligations, from which neither employers nor workingmen can escape. Now it is of the very essence of social justice to demand for each individual all that is necessary for the common good. But just as in the living organism it is impossible to provide for the good of the whole unless each single part and each individual member is given what it needs for the exercise of its proper functions, so it is impossible to care for the social organism and the good of society as a unit unless each single part of each individual member—that is to say, each individual man in the dignity of his human personality—is supplied with all that is necessary for the exercise of his social functions. If social justice be satisfied, the result will be an intense activity in economic life as a whole, pursued in tranquility and order. This activity will be proof of the health of the social body, just as the health of the human body is recognized in the undisturbed regularity and perfect efficiency of the whole organism.

But social justice cannot be said to have been satisfied as long as workingmen are denied a salary that will enable them to secure proper sustenance for themselves and for their families; as long as they are denied the opportunity of acquiring a modest fortune and forestalling the plague of universal pauperism; as long as they cannot make suitable provision through public or private insurance for old age, for periods of illness and unemployment. In a word, to repeat what has been said in Our Encyclical *Quadragesimo Anno*: "Then only will the economic and social order be soundly established and attain its ends, when it offers, to all and to each, all those goods which the wealth and resources of nature, technical science and the corporate organization of social affairs can give. These goods should be sufficient to supply all necessities and reasonable comforts, and to uplift men to that higher standard of life which, provided it be used with prudence, is not only not a hindrance but is of singular help to virtue"

It happens all too frequently, however, under the salary system, that individual employers are helpless to ensure justice unless, with a view to its practice, they organize institutions the object of which is to prevent competition incompatible with fair treatment of the workers. Where this is true, it is the duty of contractors and employers to support and promote such necessary organizations as normal instruments enabling them to fulfill their obligations of justice. But the laborers too must be mindful of their duty to love and deal fairly with their employers, and persuade themselves that there is no better means of safeguarding their own interests.

If, therefore, We consider the whole structure of economic life, as We have already pointed out in Our encyclical *Quadragesimo Anno*, the reign of mutual collaboration between justice and charity in social-economic relations can only be achieved by a body of professional and inter-professional organizations, built on solidly Christian foundations, working together to effect, under forms adapted to different places and circumstances, what has been called the Corporation.

To give to this social activity a greater efficacy, it is necessary to promote a wider study of social problems in the light of the doctrine of the Church and under the aegis of her constituted authority. If the manner of acting of some Catholics in the social-economic field has left much to be desired, this has often come about because they have not known and pondered sufficiently the teachings of the Sovereign Pontiffs on these questions. Therefore, it is of the utmost importance to foster in all classes of society an intensive program of social education adapted to the varying degrees of intellectual culture. It is necessary with all care and diligence to procure the widest possible diffusion of the teachings of the Church, even among the working-classes. The minds of men must be illuminated with the sure light of Catholic teaching, and their wills must be drawn to follow and apply it as the norm of right living in the conscientious fulfillment of their manifold social duties. Thus they will oppose that incoherence and discontinuity in Christian life which We have many times lamented. For there are some who, while exteriorly faithful to the practice of their religion, yet in the field of labor and industry, in the professions, trade and business, permit a deplorable cleavage in their conscience, and live a life too little in conformity with the clear principles of justice and Christian charity. Such lives are a scandal to the weak, and to the malicious a pretext to discredit the Church.

In this renewal the Catholic Press can play a prominent part. Its foremost duty is to foster in various attractive ways an ever better understanding of social doctrine. It should, too, supply accurate and complete information on the activity of the enemy and the means of resistance which have been found most effective in various quarters. It should offer useful suggestions and warn against the insidious deceits with which Communists endeavor, all too successfully, to attract even men of good faith.

On this point We have already insisted in Our Allocution of May 12th of last year, but We believe it to be a duty of special urgency, Venerable Brethren, to call your attention to it once again. In the beginning Communism showed itself for what it was in all its perversity; but very soon it realized that it was thus alienating the people. It has therefore changed its tactics, and strives to entice the multitudes by trickery of various forms, hiding its real designs behind ideas that in themselves are good and attractive. Thus, aware of the universal desire for peace, the leaders of Communism pretend to be the most zealous promoters and propagandists in the movement for world amity. Yet at the same time they stir up a class-warfare which causes rivers of blood to flow, and, realizing that their system offers no internal guarantee of peace, they have recourse to unlimited armaments. Under various names which do not suggest Communism, they establish organizations and periodicals with the sole purpose of carrying their ideas into quarters otherwise inaccessible. They try perfidiously to worm their way even into professedly Catholic and religious organizations. Again, without receding an inch from their subversive principles, they invite Catholics to collaborate with them in the realm of so-called humanitarianism and charity; and at times even make proposals that are in perfect harmony with the Christian spirit and the doctrine of the Church. Elsewhere they carry their hypocrisy so far as to encourage the belief that Communism, in countries where faith and culture are most strongly entrenched, will assume another and much milder form. It will not interfere with the practice of religion. It will respect liberty of conscience. There are some even who refer to certain changes recently introduced into Soviet legislation as a proof that Communism is about to abandon its program of war against God.

See to it, Venerable Brethren, that the Faithful do not allow themselves to be deceived! Communism is intrinsically wrong, and no one who would save Christian civilization may collaborate with it in any undertaking whatsoever. Those who permit themselves to be deceived into lending their aid towards the triumph of Communism in their own country, will be the first to fall victims of their error. And the greater the antiquity and grandeur of the Christian civilization in the regions where Communism successfully penetrates, so much more devastating will be the hatred displayed by the godless.

But, "unless the Lord keep the city, he watches in vain that keeps it" [*Ps CXXVI*, 1].

And so, as a final and most efficacious remedy, We recommend, Venerable Brethren, that in your dioceses you use the most practical means to foster and intensify the spirit of prayer joined with Christian penance. When the Apostles asked the Savior why they had been unable to drive the evil spirit from a demoniac, Our Lord answered: "This kind is not cast out but by prayer and fasting" [*Matt* XVII, 20]. So, too, the evil which today torments humanity can be conquered only by a world-wide crusade of prayer and penance. We ask especially the Contemplative Orders, men and women, to redouble their prayers and sacrifices to obtain from Heaven efficacious aid for the Church in the present struggle. Let them implore also the powerful intercession of the Immaculate Virgin who, having crushed the head of the serpent of old, remains the sure protectress and invincible "Help of Christians."

V.   MINISTERS AND CO-WORKERS IN CATHOLIC SOCIAL ACTION

To apply the remedies thus briefly indicated to the task of saving the world as We have traced it above, Jesus Christ, our Divine King, has chosen priests as the first-line ministers and messengers of His Gospel. Theirs is the duty, assigned to them by a special vocation, under the direction of their Bishops and in filial obedience to the Vicar of Christ on earth, of keeping alight in the world the torch of Faith, and of filling the hearts of the Faithful with that supernatural trust which has aided the Church to fight and win so many other battles in the name of Christ: "This is the victory which overcomes the world, our Faith" [*I John* V: 4].

To priests in a special way We recommend anew the oft-repeated counsel of Our Predecessor, Leo XIII, to go to the workingman. We make this advice Our own, and faithful to the teachings of Jesus Christ and His Church, We thus complete it: "Go to the workingman, especially where he is poor; and in general, go to the poor." The poor are obviously more exposed than others to the wiles of agitators who, taking advantage of their extreme need, kindle their hearts to envy the rich and urge them to seize by force what fortune seems to have denied them justly. If the priest will not go to the working man and to the poor, to warn them or to disabuse them of prejudice and false theory, they will become an easy prey for the apostles of Communism.

Indisputably much has been done in this direction, especially after the publication of the Encyclicals *Rerum Novarum* and *Quadragesimo Anno*. We are happy to voice Our paternal approval of the zealous pastoral activity manifested by so many Bishops and priests who have with due prudence and caution been planning and applying new methods of apostolate more adapted to modern needs. But for the solution of our present problem, all this effort is still inadequate. When our country is in danger, everything not strictly necessary, everything not bearing directly on the urgent matter of unified defense, takes second place. So must we act in today's crisis. Every other enterprise, however attractive and helpful, must yield before the vital need of protecting the very foundation of the Faith and of Christian civilization. Let our parish priest, therefore, while providing of course for the normal needs of the Faithful, dedicate the better part of their endeavors and their zeal to winning back the laboring masses to Christ and to His Church. Let them work to infuse the Christian spirit into quarters where it is least at home. The willing response of the masses, and results far exceeding their expectations, will not fail to reward them for their strenuous pioneer labor. This has been and continues to be our experience in Rome and in other capitals, where zealous parish communities are being formed as new churches are built in the suburban districts, and real miracles are being worked in the conversion of people whose hostility to religion has been due solely to the fact that they did not know it.

But the most efficacious means of apostolate among the poor and lowly is the priest's example, the practice of all those sacerdotal virtues which We have described in Our Encyclical *Ad Catholici Sacerdotii* [December 20, 1935]. Especially needful, however, for the present situation is the shining example of a life which is humble, poor and disinterested, in imitation of the Divine Master Who could say to the world with divine simplicity: "The foxes have holes and the birds of the air nests, but the Son of Man has nowhere to lay His head" [*Matt* VIII, 20]. A priest who is really poor and disinterested in the Gospel sense may work among his flock marvels recalling a Saint Vincent de Paul, a Cure of Ars, a Cottolengo, a Don Bosco and so many others; while an avaricious and selfish priest, as We have noted in the above-mentioned Encyclical, even though he should not plunge with Judas to the abyss of treason, will never be more than empty "sounding brass" and useless "tinkling cymbal" [*I Cor* XIII, 1]. Too often, indeed, he will be a hindrance rather than an instrument of grace in the midst of his people. Furthermore, where a secular or religious is obliged by his office to administer temporal property, let him remember that he is not only to observe scrupulously all that charity and justice prescribe, but that he has a special obligation to conduct himself in very truth as a father of the poor.

After this appeal to the clergy, We extend Our paternal invitation to Our beloved sons among the laity who are doing battle in the ranks of Catholic Action. On another occasion [May 12, 1936] We have called this movement so dear to Our heart "a particularly providential assistance" in the work of the Church during these troublous times. Catholic Action is in effect a *social* apostolate also, inasmuch as its object is to spread the Kingdom of Jesus Christ not only among individuals, but also in families and in society. It must, therefore, make it a chief aim to train its members with special care and to prepare them to fight the battles of the Lord. This task of formation, now more urgent and indispensable than ever, which must always precede direct action in the field, will assuredly be served by study-circles, conferences, lecture-courses and the various other activities undertaken with a view to making known the Christian solution of the social problem.

The militant leaders of Catholic Action, thus properly prepared and armed, will be the first and immediate apostles of their fellow workmen. They will be an invaluable aid to the priest in carrying the torch of truth, and in relieving grave spiritual and material suffering, in many sectors where inveterate anti-clerical prejudice or deplorable religious indifference has proved a constant obstacle to the pastoral activity of God's ministers. In this way they will collaborate, under the direction of especially qualified priests, in that work of spiritual aid to the laboring classes on which We set so much store, because it is the means best calculated to save these, Our beloved children, from the snares of Communism.

In addition to this individual apostolate which, however useful and efficacious, often goes unheralded, Catholic Action must organize propaganda on a large scale to disseminate knowledge of the fundamental principles on which, according to the Pontifical documents, a Christian Social Order must build.

Ranged with Catholic Action are the groups which We have been happy to call its auxiliary forces. With paternal affection We exhort these valuable organizations also to dedicate themselves to the great mission of which We have been treating, a cause which today transcends all others in vital importance.

We are thinking likewise of those associations of workmen, farmers, technicians, doctors, employers, students and others of like character, groups of men and women who live in the same cultural atmosphere and share the same way of life. Precisely those groups and organizations are destined to introduce into society that order which We have envisaged in Our Encyclical *Quadragesimo Anno*, and thus to spread in the vast and various fields of culture and labor the recognition of the Kingdom of Christ.

Even where the State, because of changed social and economic conditions, has felt obliged to intervene directly in order to aid and regulate such organizations by special legislative enactments, supposing always the necessary respect for liberty and private initiative, Catholic Action may not use the circumstance as an excuse for abandoning the field. Its members should contribute prudently and intelligently to the study of the problems of the hour in the light of Catholic doctrine. They should loyally and generously participate in the formation of the new institutions, bringing to them the Christian spirit which is the basic principle of order wherever men work together in fraternal harmony.

Here We should like to address a particularly affectionate word to Our Catholic workingmen, young and old. They have been given, perhaps as a reward for their often heroic fidelity in these trying days, a noble and an arduous mission. Under the guidance of their Bishops and priests, they are to bring back to the Church and to God those immense multitudes of their brother-workmen who, because they were not understood or treated with the respect to which they were entitled, in bitterness have strayed far from God. Let Catholic workingmen show these their wandering brothers by word and example that the Church is a tender Mother to all those who labor and suffer, and that she has never failed, and never will fail, in her sacred maternal duty of protecting her children. If this mission, which must be fulfilled in mines, in factories, in shops, wherever they may be laboring, should at times require great sacrifices, Our workmen will remember that the Savior of the world has given them an example not only of toil but of self-immolation.

To all Our children, finally, of every social rank and every nation, to every religious and lay organization in the Church, We make another and more urgent appeal for union. Many times Our paternal heart has been saddened by the divergencies—often idle in their causes, always tragic in their consequences—which array in opposing camps the sons of the same Mother Church. Thus it is that the radicals, who are not so very numerous, profiting by this discord are able to make it more acute, and end by pitting Catholics one against the other. In view of the events of the past few months, Our warning must seem superfluous. We repeat it nevertheless once more, for those who have not understood, or perhaps do not desire to understand. Those who make a practice of spreading dissension among Catholics assume a terrible responsibility before God and the Church.

But in this battle joined by the powers of darkness against the very idea of Divinity, it is Our fond hope that, besides the host which glories in the name of Christ, all those—and they comprise the overwhelming majority of mankind—who still believe in God and pay Him homage may take a decisive part. We therefore renew the invitation extended to them five years ago in Our Encyclical *Caritate Christi*, invoking their loyal and hearty collaboration "in order to ward off from mankind the great danger that threatens all alike." Since, as We then said, "belief in God is the unshakable foundation of all social order and of all responsibility on earth, it follows that all those who do not want anarchy and terrorism ought to take energetic steps to prevent the enemies of religion from attaining the goal they have so brazenly proclaimed to the world" [*Caritate Christi,* May 3, 1932].

Such is the positive task, embracing at once theory and practice, which the Church undertakes in virtue of the mission, confided to her by Christ, of constructing a Christian society, and, in our own times, of resisting unto victory the attacks of Communism. It is the duty of the Christian State to concur actively in this spiritual enterprise of the Church, aiding her with the means at its command, which although they be external devices, have nonetheless for their prime object the good of souls.

This means that all diligence should be exercised by States to prevent within their territories the ravages of an anti-God campaign which shakes society to its very foundations. For there can be no authority on earth unless the authority of the Divine Majesty be recognized; no oath will bind which is not sworn in the Name of the Living God. We repeat what We have said with frequent insistence in the past, especially in Our Encyclical *Caritate Christi*: "How can any contract be maintained, and what value can any treaty have, in which every guarantee of conscience is lacking? And how can there be talk of guarantees of conscience when all faith in God and all fear of God have banished? Take away this basis, and with it all moral law falls, and there is no remedy left to stop the gradual but inevitable destruction of people, families, the State, civilization itself."

It must likewise be the special care of the State to create those material conditions of life without which an orderly society cannot exist. The State must take every measure necessary to supply employment, particularly for the heads of families and for the young. To achieve this end demanded by the pressing needs of the common welfare, the wealthy classes must be induced to assume those burdens without which human society cannot be saved nor they themselves remain secure. However, measures taken by the State with this end in view ought to be of such a nature that they will really affect those who actually possess more than their share of capital resources, and who continue to accumulate them to the grievous detriment of others.

The State itself, mindful of its responsibility before God and society, should be a model of prudence and sobriety in the administration of the commonwealth. Today more than ever the acute world crisis demands that those who dispose of immense funds, built upon the sweat and toil of millions, keep constantly and singly in mind the common good. State functionaries and all employees are obliged in conscience to perform their duties faithfully and unselfishly, imitating the brilliant example of distinguished men of the past and of our own day, who with unremitting labor sacrificed their all for the good of their country. In international trade-relations let all means be sedulously employed for the removal of those artificial barriers to economic life which are the effects of distrust and hatred. All must remember that the peoples of the earth form but one family of God.

At the same time the State must allow the Church full liberty to fulfill her divine and spiritual mission, and this in itself will be an effectual contribution to the rescue of nations from the dread torment of the present hour. Everywhere today there is an anxious appeal to moral and spiritual forces; and rightly so, for the evil we must combat is at its origin primarily an evil of the spiritual order. From this polluted source the monstrous emanations of the Communistic system flow with satanic logic. Now, the Catholic Church is undoubtedly pre-eminent among the moral and religious forces of today. Therefore the very good of humanity demands that her work be allowed to proceed unhindered.

Those who act otherwise, and at the same time fondly pretend to attain their objective with purely political or economic means, are in the grip of a dangerous error. When religion is banished from the school, from education and from public life, when the representatives of Christianity and its sacred rites are held up to ridicule, are we not really fostering the materialism which is the fertile soil of Communism? Neither force, however well organized it be, nor earthly ideals however lofty or noble, can control a movement whose roots lie in the excessive esteem for the goods of this world.

We trust that those rulers of nations, who are at all aware of the extreme danger threatening every people today, may be more and more convinced of their supreme duty not to hinder the Church in the fulfillment of her mission. This is the more imperative since, while this mission has in view man's happiness in Heaven, it cannot but promote his true felicity in time.

We cannot conclude this Encyclical Letter without addressing some words to those of Our children who are more or less tainted with the Communist plague. We earnestly exhort them to hear the voice of their loving Father. We pray the Lord to enlighten them that they may abandon the slippery path which will precipitate one and all to ruin and catastrophe, and that they recognize that Jesus Christ, our Lord, is their only Savior: "For there is no other name under heaven given to man, whereby we must be saved" [*Acts* IV, 12].

CONCLUSION

To hasten the advent of that "peace of Christ in the Kingdom of Christ" [*Ubi Arcano*, December 23, 1922] so ardently desired by all, We place the vast campaign of the Church against world Communism under the standard of St. Joseph, her mighty Protector. He belongs to the working-class, and he bore the burdens of poverty for himself and the Holy Family, whose tender and vigilant head he was. To him was entrusted the Divine Child when Herod loosed his assassins against Him. In a life of faithful performance of everyday duties, he left an example for all those who must gain their bread by the toil of their hands. He won for himself the title of "The Just", serving thus as a living model of that Christian justice which should reign in social life.

With eyes lifted on high, our Faith sees the new Heavens and the new earth described by Our first Predecessor, St. Peter [*2 Peter*, III, 13; *Isaiah* LXV, 17; LXVI, 22; *Apoc* XXI, 1]. While the promises of the false prophets of this earth melt away in blood and tears, the great apocalyptic prophecy of the Redeemer shines forth in heavenly splendor: "Behold, I make all things new" [*Apoc* XXI, 5].

Venerable Brethren, nothing remains but to raise Our paternal hands to call down upon you, upon your clergy and people, upon the whole Catholic family, the Apostolic Benediction.

Given at Rome, at St. Peter's, on the Feast of St. Joseph, Patron of the Universal Church, on the 19th of March, 1937, the 16th year of our Pontificate.

PIO PP. XI

Appendix 3

Bishop Ignatius Kung's First Pastoral Letter as Bishop of Shanghai, October 7, 1950. [235]

Nos tres chers Frères:

Hardly one year since our departure for Soochow, we are back in your midst, a father and pastor with his friends. There are good reasons why we dreaded taking up this burden, so heavy for our shoulders. Since the friendship that binds us to you priests, our well-beloved companions, and the sympathy that you have given us lightens our fears, emboldening us to dedicate ourselves to your service: our life henceforth belongs to the Diocese of Shanghai.

On August 9th, we first took possession of the Episcopal seat of Shanghai according to the canonical prescriptions. The solemn enthronement took place on the 13th in our cathedral church of Tongkadou. On the 15th, the Feast of the Assumption of Our Holy Mother, the Episcopal curia was formed: you have without doubt received with joy the nomination of Father Sylvestre Tsu as Vicar General.

Nouvelle page d'histoire:

Today we are pleased to be able, as the first Chinese bishop of Shanghai, to address in writing our clergy and all our faithful.

Our venerable predecessor, Monsignor Haouisee, S.J., spent his entire life building this diocese. He died working. To us remaining, he left not only his work, but also the example of a holy life. His memory will guide us and his prayers will assist us.

After these past two years, and with a calm and supernatural optimism, Father Henry, S.J., will assure the normal working of the diocese. During the turmoil, he has held firm. In the name of the diocese, we respectfully express our most profound gratitude.

The diocesan administration is now effectively placed in the hands of the diocesan clergy. A decisive stage in the life of our diocese is already accomplished. A new page of history begun.

---

[235] *China Missionary Bulletin*, Vol. III (IV), February 1951, No. 2, pp. 97-100.

We invite you, my dear Brothers, let us turn our attention for a moment to the glorious past in order to see our present responsibilities and to prepare for the future.

You are proud of your diocese. You have reason, for it is one of the most beautiful in China. 110,900 Christians. Hundreds of churches and chapels. Notre-Dame de Zose which you love. An efflorescence of works: Schools for all levels; minor and major seminaries; dispensaries and hospitals; asyla for abandoned children and for the aged; pious associations: Marian congregations, the Confraternity of the Rosary, Eucharistic Crusade, Catholic Action; facilities for scientific research, and a Catholic press. Over all, a solidly formed clergy, eminent for your accomplishments, which has proven itself during these troubled times.

Such is the fruit of three and a half centuries of work: Father Cattaneo arrived in our city in 1608.—This is the heritage that has come down to our fathers by the Faith: Franciscans, Dominicans, Discalced Carmelites, Lazarists, mission priests of Propaganda Fide, priests of the Holy Family of Naples, Salesians, and Missionaries of Saint Colomban.

But it is only just to say that the credit for having developed the work to its present state belongs to the Society of Jesus. The return of the Sons of Saint Ignatius had been called for by our ancestors with petitions to the Holy See. And so harkening back to Kiangnan, they tirelessly and with a spirit of carrying on earlier works which characterized them, they worked after 100 years at the construction of the Church in Shanghai. The work continues, and they return with joy into the hands of the clergy that which they formed.

Collaboration des fideles et du clerge:

We take in hand today the work that cost so much labor. Crushing is our responsibility. Our duty, which is also yours, my very dear Brothers, is never to let perish that which actually constitutes the form of the Church in our diocese, of the works and methods for which she pursues the goal of evangelization. We would consider this to be a grave failure. We would consider as a failure no less grave to leave all these works without progress, simply maintaining them as they are. Without a doubt, the task is arduous, especially under the present circumstances. Still, unity provides the strength: with the grace of God, we can accomplish this by the intimate collaboration of the faithful laity and the clergy.

This collaboration is from another source of tradition in our diocese. Was it not Paul Siu Koangk'i who brought Father Cattaneo to our City and who assisted him in the apostolate? It is the good organization of the first saints of the lay apostolate that gave strength to the past. It is that which ought to give us the strength for the future.

And so, our intention, our most dear Brothers, with this letter that inaugurates our episcopate, is to insist on the urgency of the lay apostolate, and we want to speak about the place the work of the faithful has in the apostolate of the hierarchy.

Urgence de l'apostolat laic:

The Apostolate, in effect, is an activity of a strictly religious nature, --and so in no way political. It has as its goal to extend the Kingdom of the Divine Redeemer and to procure, through this, the glory of God and the salvation of souls. This duty is incumbent upon each member of Christ, who, on the Cross, created the thirst for the glory of his Father and to save souls. By birthright, the Christian is an apostle. In a world doubly pagan such as ours, not only in the darkness and shadows of death, without Christ, but even in the influence of those who repudiate Christ, and whose duty is a mere dream, as His Excellency the Internuncio has declared, a character of extreme necessity.

Look around you: the faith is troubled and, for many, shaken. Should we stand before such a spectacle with crossed arms? On the other hand, numerous are those who are moved by the desire for truth about human destiny. Shall we not extend a fraternal hand to them?

In other respects, the apostolate is never a work that one enters upon in a moment of enthusiasm. It is life and the communication of life. It is the Charity of God who communicates Himself to the world through Christ and the Church. To be an apostle, is to open oneself to the gift of God, as a modest instrument of His work, to be able to communicate this gift to the world. To communicate the divine life presupposes that one possesses it abundantly in oneself.

The extension of the Kingdom of Christ is not realized except under the impulse and direction of the Spirit of Christ: charity, humility, renunciation of one's own interests and of one's personal ideas, and obedience to the Hierarchy. One need consecrate everything: time, energy and life itself. Under this condition alone, one is an apostle.

The apostolate is, therefore, the duty of the entire Church; and the lay apostolate, is the participation of the faithful in the apostolate of the Church joining with the Hierarchy and under its direction: pastors and faithful intimately collaborating.

The lay apostolate, therefore, requires being hierarchically organized. In other words, it must be the foundation of Catholic Action, the totality of its organizations of programs and of works that Pius XI, the Pope of the Missions and

Catholic Action, declared very dear to his heart,--by which he defined its meaning and structure.

Modalides de l'Action Catholique:

Our Holy Father Pope Pius XII gloriously reigning, and His Excellency Monsignor Riberi have insisted upon the necessity of organizing the lay apostolate in each diocese. You will remember, my very dear Brothers: how constant the support of our venerable predecessor had been to promote and organize Catholic Action among us. Our diocese is endowed by a Catholic Action organized by the considerable contribution to hierarchic apostolate. We count on the collaboration of the faithful and of the priests, to have and further promote in every home this goal to extend the Kingdom of Christ.

The Church possesses an admirable ability to adapt. So, while the principles of Catholic Action are immutable, the methods of action must be based upon the changing realities of actual circumstances. Catholic Action must be more than a revival of the matchless tradition of the budding Church.

May the pastors in concert with their faithful take the initiative to adapt the organization of Catholic Action so as to respond to today's needs.

Congregations mariales:

The formation of the faithful in the hierarchic apostolate first requires a work of spiritual deepening. Catholic Action is never activism. This is why we ask you to give new life to the work of the Marian sodalities before all else. The revival of this work will place us within the historical direction of our diocese. In 350 years, our diocese has come through a very difficult period. The most dangerous trial was, without doubt, the absence of sufficient numbers of missionaries. Now, thanks to the work of the Marian sodalities, all these difficulties were overcome, one after the other. It was our faithful, formed by these sodalities that had a personal piety and a sense of Christian responsibility.

Do not believe otherwise than that the Marian sodalities did their work while yoked with Catholic Action. This is, according to the words of our Holy Father Pope Pius XII himself, that Catholic Action was undertaken by the inspiration and assistance of the Blessed Virgin. Its work was the deepening of Christian life, and it accomplished this methodically. The means that it placed at the disposal of its members were traditional and formed the tools to be used by those who wished to follow Christ perfectly and completely: spiritual exercises, frequent reception of the sacraments, frequent meetings with a specific spiritual director, and a filial docility to him, a total gift of self to the Blessed Virgin, and a formal promise to work toward that perfection and the perfection of others. The [Marian] sodalists had the right to be considered among the pioneers of Catholic Action.

In the majority of our parishes, this work has existed for some time. You have made this work more alive.—A "Marian Service" operates at the Scholasticate at Zikawei. The directors are attentive to make it conform to this organization. It will be of great assistance to anyone interested in the Marian sodality: its formation of members of the sodalities, organization of work, and its apostolic activities.

As the Sovereign Pontiff said, the Church favors a unity of diversity in the manner in which it conducts the apostolic works it carries on each day, all directed to the same goal, joined in one common fraternal effort, under the direction of the bishops: the diocesan authority of Shanghai will favor all apostolic initiatives undertaken in this spirit.

Les vocations:

Seeing the number of vocations—priests, teaching brothers, religious women novices, gradually diminishing each year: (this year were inscribed only 14 major seminarians, 9 teaching brothers, and 15 religious women novices), our heart shrinks, and the future appears to us distressing.

Given the low number of seminarians in China, His Excellency Monsignor Riberi sounded an alarm last year. You recall the appeal by Monsignor Haouisee calling for priestly vocations. In our churches, prayers should be offered to obtain from God a number of holy priests. Redouble your supplications. Ask also for greater numbers of holy teaching brothers and holy Presentation religious sisters.

In addition to prayers, search out means to develop more vocations. A vocation is a delicate flower. Planted in the hearts of children, it grows and blossoms only after much care. Normally school and family are called upon to collaborate in this education. In theory, the duty of parents is essential, and *a fortiori*, the Christian influence of a school can do little alone.

The giving of children to God constitutes a sorrowful sacrifice for the love of parents. But Christians, cognizant of the honor that God gives them, even when resisting this sacrifice, should consider how this signal grace, this exquisite flower of a vocation, could be developing in the heart of their home. From them they might have the heart to surround the child with a healthy home atmosphere of an ardent love for Christ, of devotion to His Church, of purity and a spirit of sacrifice.

They will find a precious help from the work of the Eucharistic Crusade, the nursery of vocations, that forms children to prayer, to frequent communion, to sacrifice, to the apostolate. Parish priests and parents should encourage children to take part in this. By the concerted efforts of priests and parents, this work will recover its original vigor.

Christianiser les foyers:

Christian parents, my Brethren, Christianize your homes. This is the primary objective of your participation in the apostolate of the Hierarchy. We ask you this in the name of our diocese. The future depends on the Christianization of families. Create an atmosphere of faith; pray in common. Your life should be an example. Family life or social relations should be inspired by the theological virtues: faith, hope, charity.

In this condition, your children will be immunized against all evil influences; their faith will confirm this, and their life will be fundamentally Christian.

Devotion a la Sainte Vierge:

You will find in our coat of arms the Immaculate Virgin and the first church of our diocese, that of Laodaong, a converted pagoda. Our entire infancy has passed under the protective shadow of Our Holy Mother; protection, moreover, that never ceases. We received Episcopal consecration from the hands of His Excellency the Internuncio on the Feast of the Holy Rosary, which is exactly one year ago today.

We have received everything from the Holy Mother. And, during these three hundred years of existence, our diocese owes her a debt of innumerable benefits. To such a sweet Mother, we consecrate our entire diocese: its present and its future, each of its works, each Christian family that makes up this diocese.

Our gaze sees buildings, many of the style as our most venerable church [in Laodaong], but alas, God is absent. By your apostolate, may these be converted to temples of the true God; and may the Reign of Christ be established in our City of Shanghai, which is a crossroads of the world because of our river.

My very dear Brethren, let us all work together, bishop, priests and laity, united in charity. To those who have the honor to understand the Kingdom of

Christ, *Instaurare omnia in Christo*, [Restore all things in Christ] Our Lord asks his Father for the grace of unity in charity: *Ut sint unum* [That all may be one].

We make this prayer ourselves,

Given at Shanghai, October 7, 1950
On the Feast of the Most Holy Rosary
Anniversary of our Episcopal consecration.

IGNATIUS

Bishop of Shanghai

Appendix 4

Bishop Ignatius Kung's Second Pastoral Letter, April 22, 1951.[236]

Lettre Pastorale

Consecration of the Diocese of Shanghai to the Immaculate Heart of Mary

Frères bien-aimes dans le Christ:

In this pastoral letter, we would like to speak with you of the project to consecrate our Diocese of Shanghai to the Immaculate Heart of the Blessed Virgin Mary, and of the means that seem the most effective by which this consecration may truly serve for the Glory of God Almighty, to the praise of the Kingdom of Heaven, and for our health and for our greater sanctification.

The Blessed Virgin Mary, Mother of Our Savior, was chosen by her Divine Son to serve as the mother of all his good disciples. A mother's duty is to clothe and feed her children. Her love for her children inspires her to teach them virtuous habits, to protect them from all harm, to fill them with a fraternal affection, that with them she might share bravely and loyally the pains and joys of the whole family. What's more, it is usually the mother who teaches her children to speak the family's language.

Mary, the mother of Christians, from the first moment when she was asked to cooperate actively in the Redemption, responded perfectly to the holy will of God. "Behold the handmaid of the Lord", she said to the Angel Gabriel. Surely she obeyed with the same eagerness of will to her Son who desired that she be the mother of his disciples. Mary had a place at the side of the Cross of Jesus on Calvary. She confessed without blushing or trembling her great love for Him in that hour of His Passion. She united her heart and her will to the Heart and Will of Jesus, and they offered the same sacrifice to the Father, with the same intentions: that humanity be ransomed from sin and provided with the graces necessary to live a holy life on earth and a happy one for all ages in Heaven.

This union with Jesus has merited for Mary the title of co-redemptrix. She merited for us the graces that are the clothing of our souls: the robe of baptismal innocence that clothes the soul with beauty for the eyes of God. Since her love for Him was so immense and faithful, it is through her hands that Jesus allows these favors to pass to Christians of all times.

---

[236] *China Missionary Bulletin*, Vol. III (IV), October 1951, No. 8, pp. 657-660.

Likewise, Mary, as a good mother, feeds her children. It is from His mother's most pure body that Jesus took his own flesh and blood, which give life and strength to Christians in the Holy Eucharist. At Nazareth, the tireless love of Mary worked to raise a strong Jesus to preach and suffer for us. Christians, devoted to Mary, feel drawn by her to approach the sacraments frequently and to pray often. In this way, she aids us to grow in the likeness of Jesus, and to acquire strength to make known Christ by word and example in our lives.

How does Mary teach us virtuous habits? Above all, by her own example. Christians who meditate on the Mysteries of the Rosary learn from them the spirit of humility of the Virgin of the Annunciation, of her selfless charity in the Visitation, of her serene patience in the Nativity and so forth. . . Anxious for the well-being of her children, she continues teaching them the virtues that are most necessary in certain periods of history, by her apparitions to her chosen beloved children. At Lourdes, she recommended purity; at Fatima, mortification in reparation for sins.

Mary protects her children from evil: this is the one truth of experience for all Christian families after a certain time. The history of our Diocese of Shanghai tells of more than one case when the prayers of Mary actually saved someone from danger or comforted others in time of trial. The basilica and sanctuary in Zose are monuments witnessing to the powerful protection of Mary. One of our most familiar prayers that we pray says: "Remember O Sweet and Blessed Virgin Mary, that never was it known that anyone who sought your protection or sought your intercession [was left unaided]." Every day, throughout the whole world, the Church sees confirmation of the truth of these words.

A strong affection naturally unites children with their mother. Her greatest gift given to us her children is Jesus, the Son of God, as our elder brother. That the human family could be glorified by a brother infinitely good and noble, conferring upon us a new dignity and a pledge of divine life and grace as 'the adopted sons and daughters of God', is that they possess them through the merits of Jesus. Mary, mother of all Christians, watches to prevent all discord among her children. She both inspires and defends them, to be charitable in thought and in word for those members of the family who might be unjustly accused. For if a member is tempted by folly or weakness to leave the family, Mary, as a good Mother, tries to save and call him back.

If a mother ought to teach her children the language of the family, Mary rises eminently as the mother of Christians. The Holy Rosary is Mary's prayer; all Christians learn to say it from a young age; they find it full of the most beautiful praises of God.

By beginning with the *Sign of the Cross*, the Christian is reminded that he is ransomed by the Cross of Jesus. He recalls that the Cross is for us the source of all grace and all glory, a moving witness of the love of Christ, the standard of Christ the King; the Christian realizes that the worst sufferings can be the prelude of a glorious resurrection.

The *Creed* is a profession of Faith, by which the Christian proclaims his belief in the truths that the apostles understood from the lips of Jesus from which they were instructed directly by the Holy Spirit. During twenty centuries, the martyrs carried their witness in favor of this same doctrine: they shed their blood for us in order to hand that Faith down to us in its purity and integrity.

The *Our Father* is the response of Jesus himself to his disciples' request: "Lord, teach us how to pray." No one on earth has a better way to glorify God in reverent prayer than the *Our Father*. He taught us the *Our Father* by which we can approach God to give full homage and to implore His mercy and to request his assistance in all our spiritual and temporal needs. Pope Pius XI said: "How could the Eternal Father refuse to come to our aid, when we pray using the words of His own Son?"

The *Hail Mary* reminds the Christian of the goodness, the purity and the holiness of his Celestial Mother: She is full of grace, blessed among women, the Lord is with Her, Mary is the Mother of God. In this prayer the great love of God for us is so clearly shown, in which He sent His Only Son to earth, to give us the true life. Through the *Hail Mary* we commend ourselves to our Mother, and through Her to God, with all our needs "now and at the hour of our death."

Finally, the *Glory Be* lifts our hearts up to the heart of the Blessed Trinity, and we know that whoever lifts his heart to God lifts also the world around him. All Christians, young or old, educated or illiterate, can and should learn to recite the [Rosary] chaplet fruitfully. Mary desires that the Rosary be a chain connecting all the members of the Mystical Body.

One might occasionally object that the indistinct repetition of the same words runs the easy risk of making this prayer a monotonous and routine formula. But to speak like this, one would have no understanding of the language of love, and to be insensible of the language of children. For in this repetition is love, piety, humility of spirit, and the sweet fragrance of a true simplicity. The Son of God said: "Unless you become like a little child, you will not enter the Kingdom of Heaven."

Our Heavenly Mother has shown her desire to have our daily recitation of the Rosary associated with the Consecration to Her Immaculate Heart. More than that, we meditate and live the Mysteries of the Rosary; we are to feel thrilled to dedicate all our strength to the patronage of Mary our Mother and our Queen.

On June 13, 1917, the Blessed Virgin told the young shepherds of Fatima: "For the salvation of souls, Jesus desires the spreading of devotion to my Immaculate Heart throughout the world. If they do as I say, many souls will be saved and there will be Peace. To escape disasters, I ask that the world be consecrated to my Immaculate Heart."

During the other apparitions at Fatima, She said: "I am the Lady of the Holy Rosary. I come to warn the faithful to amend their lives. You must pray the Rosary every day and pray it well." "Pray! Pray much and make sacrifices for sins. Many are the souls buried in Hell because no one prays or offers sacrifices for them."

His Holiness Pius XII answered the wish of Our Lady, when on December 8, 1942, "In the name of the human family ransomed by God", he entrusted and solemnly consecrated the whole human race to the Immaculate Heart of Mary. By this act of consecration, the Holy Father expressed the hope that Mary would actually guide and direct the lives of all men. But the pontiff saw clearly that that general consecration made by him for everyone, as our Spiritual Father, was not sufficient. He desires that the dioceses, parishes and even the families of the Catholic world unite with him to make in their own name, after fervent preparation and with a personal devotion, the same act of consecration to the Immaculate Heart. In his May 1, 1948 Encyclical he wrote:

"It is our wish, consequently, that wherever the opportunity suggests itself, this consecration be made in the various dioceses as well as in each of the parishes and families. And We are confident that abundant blessings and favors from Heaven will surge forth from this private and public consecration" [*Auspicia Quaedam*, 22].

But, what is the deeper meaning of this consecration to the Immaculate Heart?

First, it signifies that the members of this family have an Interior Spirit of veneration for the immense charity of Mary, and to her perfect purity symbolized by her most pure heart. In the heart of Mary, there are two great flames of love: for God and for mankind. Naturally, of these two flames, the more brilliant is that which burns for God. Mary loved God, not solely as her Creator, her Lord and her Father, as did all the saints, but also with the tenderness of a very holy Mother for her infinitely perfect Son. This love for God was the source of her innocence. There was a total enmity between her and Satan, of which God predicted: "She will strike at your head, and you will strike at her heel" [*Genesis* 3:15]. By a privilege, she was conceived without [Adam's] Original Sin, She had never done even the smallest actual fault, but found her joy in obeying even the slightest manifestation of the divine will with an entire loyalty.

Her love for humankind was also a maternal love. For her, the words of Christ on the Cross, "Woman, behold your son" [*John* 20:26] were like the Annunciation, the beginning of a second maternity. The history of the Church is that of each individual Christian, which is full of favors granted through the intercession of Mary: the graces of purity and of victory over temptations are those that she likes most to obtain for us. Desiring then to honor her charity and her purity, families, by this act of consecration, choose her as their Queen and their Mother. When they address her, they echo the words of Pope Leo XIII in the formula of consecration to the Sacred Heart of Jesus: "We exist for You, and we want to be with You; but to be more surely united with You, see that each of us is freely consecrated today to Your most pure Heart."

Second: By this consecration the family declares its intention to live that type of life that Mary our Mother desires. This personal act of consecration should produce a permanent effect: the state of consecration sets the family apart because it is now specially owned by Mary. Consequently, within a family consecrated to the Immaculate Heart of Mary, the holy laws of marriage are observed; families are again as newly baptized; families will teach their children their prayers, the truths of the Catholic faith and the practice of Christian virtues. If there be prodigal children, they will return to the loving arms of Jesus their Savior. The pagan neighbors will be attracted to the truth and goodness of the Christian life by good example and words of encouragement. The dying will be prepared to depart with a purified and peaceful conscience for their eternal rest, where they hope to see the family reunited again one day in the company of Jesus and Mary. If there are any obstacles to this "consecrated state", these will be swept away before the person making the act of consecration.

Third: Other than the general obligations, the consecration to the Immaculate Heart of Mary implies three other more particular ones: 1) the daily recitation of the five decade Rosary by the family; 2) a daily act of renunciation or of patience offered in reparation for sins against the love of God; 3) attendance at Mass and reception of Holy Communion in honor of Mary on the first Saturday of each month, whenever possible. That Mary desires to see these devotions practiced by families consecrated to her is clear from her words pronounced at Fatima, and from the commentaries of Pope Pius XII about devotion to the Immaculate Heart of Mary.

The daily recitation of the Rosary responds to the urgent needs of Catholics in China today. It will assist Catholic families in knowing their religion better, loving it more intensely, and as a strong safeguard. The urgent invitation of the Immaculate Heart of Mary that the Rosary be prayed daily is a providential sign of her maternal vigilance and of her love for Catholics in China, which tradition shows, after centuries, is enlivened by this special devotion.

It is strongly recommended that the recitation of Family Rosary be joined with a daily reading from Christian doctrine. We have already pointed out how the prayers of the Rosary call to mind the principal truths of our religion. We hope that among each of the families of our diocese, the father, mother or one of the older children would explain to the other family members the *Sign of the Cross*, a part of the *Hail Mary* or *Our Father*, or one of the twelve articles of the *Apostles' Creed*. When these small chats have been given, one might turn to the fifteen Mysteries of the Rosary for material for the daily lesson. These mysteries tell us all about the lives of Jesus and Mary. If we know Jesus and Mary, we will be ignorant of very little that is important in life. "You have the words of eternal life", Saint Peter told Jesus. In the Joyous Mysteries we rejoice with Jesus and Mary; in the Sorrowful Mysteries, we sympathize and enter into his lesson of courage; in the Glorious Mysteries we see before us the hope of a certain and lasting triumph. Once a first series of discussions about Catholic doctrine is completed, another might begin; the treasures of Wisdom and of the knowledge of God are inexhaustible.

The Family Rosary should be recited not only for the spiritual and temporal needs of the family itself, but also for the dear intentions of the entire Church. In the name of these intentions, the graces and strength for suffering souls are provided: for the light of truth against error and ignorance; courage and fidelity for souls exposed to grave temptations; repentance and forgiveness for souls who have fallen into sin. We should pray for our nation that we might enjoy prosperity, that justice and charity relieve the miseries of those who are exposed to poverty, and provide all with a decent standard of living. Above all, when reciting the Rosary, the family makes the words of Pope Saint Pius X their own: "Grant, Lord, peace in our days—peace for our souls, peace for our families, peace for our country, peace among nations. May the rainbow of peace and reconciliation extend its serene light over the earth, sanctified by the life and Passion of Your Divine Son."

Through this daily exercise of faith, grace and the diligent practice of prayer, Catholic families will become a strong interior unity. All families of our parishes and our diocese can but become one in spirit through the truths they learn, and one in heart through the intentions they recommend to God, strengthening their union more and more among themselves and with their pastors. Rising to Heaven, the voices of the Dioceses will form one voice, clearly praising God and Mary, powerful in its request for favors and graces to us whose needs are so urgent and our desire so intense.

It is our intention to solemnly proceed on the fourth Sunday of June to a Consecration of the entire Diocese to the Immaculate Heart of Mary. Since this solemn ceremony expresses a gift of action and not merely of words, we ask all priests of the Diocese to collaborate with us and that you propose and recommend beforehand to the families of your parishes the Consecration to the Immaculate Heart of Mary.

It is our hope and desire that the weeks before the Consecration an intense and fervent preparation be made throughout the Diocese, 1) to obtain a profound interior spirit of love and respect for the perfect charity and purity of Mary; 2) to do whatever is necessary so that our family might become worthy of this Consecration of which we have spoken, that they conform to the desire of Mary that we be faithful to the Commandments of God; 3) that we put into action regularly from this time the three particular obligations that the consecrated families will freely assume: a) daily recitation of the Rosary; b) the daily act of renunciation and reparation for sins committed; c) the reception of Holy Communion during Holy Mass in honor of Mary on the first Saturday of each month, if possible.

May this renewal of religious life and Marian devotion in our Diocese and in each family release an abundance of spiritual and temporal graces for you, through the hands of our mother and mediator, Mary. Strong in our confidence, we extend to you, beloved Brethren in Christ, as a sign of paternal affection, our apostolic blessing.

Given in the Sanctuary of Zose

IGNATIUS KUNG

Bishop of Shanghai

22 April 1951

Feast of Our Lady Queen of the Society of Jesus

Appendix 5

New Year Address by Shanghai Catholic Students to Bishop Kung, January 1, 1952.[237]

The beginning of 1952 symbolizes development and growth in life that is a beautiful image emerging before us. Life in 1952 is one of struggle.

The memory of last year is still very much alive and full of meaning. It was a period of blood and tears, within which sorrow we found sweetness and hope, and in sacrifice, love and joy. We desire the arrival of the Cross. We rejoice because of the unity and the victory of Holy Church. The Diocese of Shanghai under your leadership, Monsignor, begins a very beautiful life. Monsignor, you are the light that enlightens our way in the darkness; You are the guide directing our progress before adversity, before sorrowful events; You have preserved the integrity of the faith and the traditional spirit of the Church; You are the rock of our Church; You have made real the will and the desire of the Pope, Head of the Church. We greet you, our Bishop.

The battle demands sacrifices, the victory claims its prize. The defense of the faith demands blood and tears. Even if the battle and the sacrifice were painful, the depth of the heart is filled with joy. That our sufferings might compare with those of the three hundred years of persecution of the primitive Church in Rome! In light of the intensity of the sufferings of innumerable holy men and women, how small seems our little cross!

We know that these various difficulties are nothing but the beginning: We are just at the first step of our way of the Cross. But, we have no fear, we march forward. The bloody trails of past heroes point out our path, and the love of God urges us to commit ourselves to follow it. We know our weakness, but, confident in God, from weakness we will become strong: we will not lack the grace of God during severe trials.

The Cross is crushing; but it is by the Cross alone that one can safeguard the faith, and strengthen the rhythm of our steps; it is only by the Cross that the flowers of victory can bloom. Dreaming of the unity of the Roman Church, of the future of the Church in China, dreaming of the innumerable future conversions, of the spreading of true religion in China, to the coming of the era of Mary, we smile. Dreaming, we carry our cross, we make our way of the Cross. We are happy, because we have the opportunity to live in this wonderful time. If God wishes to

---

[237] *China Missionary Bulletin*, Vol. IV (V), March, 1952, No. 3, pp. 442-443.

use us as His instruments, then we are content; if we can do something for the Church, then we will be proud!

The beginning of the year symbolized a development and a growth in life. That which develops before us is very beautiful. Life in 1952 is one of struggle. The possibility of 1952 is magnificent.

Happy New Year, Monsignor. Guide our progress.

The Catholic students greet you.

Appendix 6

Pope Pius XII, Apostolic Letter *Cupimus imprimis,* The Catholic Church in China, January 18, 1952. [238]

First of all we want to express to you our ardent affection for the entire population of China, which since time immemorial has distinguished itself among the other peoples of Asia for its business, its literature and the splendor of its civilization, and, after being enlightened by the light of the Gospel, which greatly excels the wisdom of this world, it drew more wealth for its spirit, namely the Christian virtues, which perfect and strengthen the natural virtues themselves. In fact, as you well know, the Catholic religion does not contradict any doctrine that is true, to any public or private institution that has a basis of justice, freedom and love, but, rather, promotes, enhances and improves them. Indeed, in no way is it opposed to the natural character of each people, their particular customs or their culture, but graciously accepts them, gladly beautifying them with new honors.

For this reason, we were extremely saddened to know that among you, the Catholic Church is considered, presented, and fought as an enemy of your people; that its bishops, the other sacred ministers and religious people, unfortunately, so often far from their own homes [as missionaries] are hindered in the free exercise of their duties, as if it was not in the service of heavenly things, nor to cultivate and strengthen souls in virtue, nor to enlighten minds in schools, or to relieve human suffering of infants, children or the elderly in their hospitals and asyla, but, rather, to obey and serve human interests or lust for worldly power.

Therefore, although already in the recent encyclical *Evangelii praecones* [on foreign missions around the world] we addressed all the faithful of the far East who have suffered and are suffering precisely because they were and are deeply attached to their religion, we now turn our hearts to you in this letter, to comfort and exhort you paternally, knowing well your troubles, your anxieties and your hardships. And since the great fortitude of your faith and ardent love for Christ and His Church are equally known to us, we thank God the Father through His Son our Redeemer, who has bestowed upon you from above the strength to support these holy trials for His glory and the salvation of souls.

From all corners of the globe, Catholics turn with admiration of hearts and minds: "Your faith is celebrated throughout the world" [*Rom* 1, 8], and to you can

---

[238] http://www.vatican.va/holy_father/pius_xii/apost_letters/documents/hf_p-xii_apl_19520118_cupimus-imprimis_it.html

be applied the words of the Apostle to the Gentiles: "They were tempted. . . impoverished, distressed, afflicted. . . of which the world was not worthy" [*Heb* 11, 37-38]. Not to your dishonor, but to your glory can be attributed that "for Christ's sake you have been given the gift not only to believe in Him, but to suffer for Him" [*Phil* 1, 29].

Since this is the work of God and of His Holy Church, "do not be frightened by anything of your opponents" [*Phil* 1, 28]; but be steadfast in the strength of spirit that comes not by the work of man but, by the grace of God, obtained by prayer. Offer to God, as a sweet oblation, your sufferings and your sorrows, so that He might will, by His benevolence, finally to grant tranquility and peace to the Church in China, and make known to everyone, which is brighter than the light of the sun, that the Church seeks not the things of this world, but of Heaven, and that by the strength of Her Divine mandate, she directs all her members toward the Heavenly homeland, by practicing of virtue and good works.

As everyone knows, and can easily see, there are certainly those who seek to seize worldly power and who work daily to expand it and to extend its grasp; but the Church neither aspires to this nor seeks it. In fact, it seeks only to preach the truth of the Gospel, by which she adorns the hearts of men, improves them and makes them worthy of Heaven, seeks to promote fraternal concord among its citizens, consoles and comforts as best she can those who suffer, and bolsters and strengthens those foundations of human cooperation with Christian virtues that are more powerful than any weapons. Those who hold to these things are inferior to no one in their love of country; they obey the public authorities and are bound in conscience and according to Divine precepts to render what is due to each, first to God.

The Church does not call to herself only one people or one nation, but loves all people of every race with the supernatural love of Christ, calling her members to unite as brothers. So no one can say that it is at the service of any particular world power. Likewise, neither can she be required to break that unity which her Divine Founder willed to bestow upon her, constituting particular churches to each nation, that they might separate themselves unhappily from the Apostolic See, where Peter, the Vicar of Jesus Christ, continues to live in his successors until the end of time. If any Christian community would wish to do this, it would lose its lifeblood, as a branch cut from the vine [cf *John* 15, 6], unable to produce healthy fruit.

You, venerable brothers and beloved sons, know all this, and so, by your own will strongly oppose all types of dangers, even those now cunningly presented, falsely veiled in truth. We know that foreign missionaries are sent among you that they might provide for the immense needs of your people concerning the Christian religion, or who offer their help to native clergy, which is numerically still insufficient to the present needs. Consequently, as soon as this Apostolic See was able to provide your dioceses with bishops who were your citizens, we readily did so. Already twenty-five years have passed since Our predecessor Pius XI, himself, of happy memory, by his ardent love of the Church in China, consecrated the first six bishops, chosen from among your people here in the Basilica of Saint Peter. And we, ourselves, no less desirous to add to that number and to render longer lasting the progress of your Church, established the sacred Hierarchy in China a few years ago, raising to the dignity of the Roman purple one of your own fellow citizens, for the first time in the annals of history.

If, therefore, all foreign missionaries who have left their homes far behind them to spend themselves laboring in the fields of the Lord are kept far from their missions, as if they were dangerous people, then this will turn most damagingly against the growth of your Church. For if the foreign missionaries come from many nations in which the Catholic Church is flourishing and has developed a passion for the apostolate, then the resulting character of the Catholic Church is universal, and these heralds of the Gospel call for and desire nothing more than to choose your country as their second home, to enlighten it with the light of evangelical doctrine, to introduce Christian customs, to bring it, little by little with the supernatural assistance of charity, finally to bear fruit among you, providing a number of native clergy to bring the Church to that final maturity by which assistance and collaboration from foreign missionaries would no longer be necessary.

By no less evidence can honest people arrive at an understanding that the religious women, even those from among yourselves, as consoling angels, pursue their work in schools, orphanages, hospitals are urged on by Divine love to work in such a way that, renouncing all hope of worldly happiness in order to be wed to the Heavenly Spouse, they treat your children as if their own, especially the poor and abandoned, with a spirit of sweet, supernatural motherhood, and, as much as is in their power, comfort, instruct and educate them.

As you well know, the Catholic Church does all this by the command and mandate of her Divine Founder. She does this, as we say, asking nothing more than the liberty to be able to exercise her duties for the betterment and salvation of all peoples. And if attacked by false accusations, her pastors and followers should not loose heart, but with faith lean upon the promises of Christ expressed in these solemn words: "The gates of Hell will not prevail against her" [Mt 16, 18]; "And behold, I am with you all days even to the end of time" [Mt 28, 20].

You should raise the most ardent prayers to God for the persecutors themselves, so that, by your own goodness, by your light and grace their minds might be illumined, and might move and be directed towards Heavenly truth.

Continue to work in this way, venerable brothers and beloved sons, with fear of the dangers and difficulties, by recalling the sublime words of the Divine Redeemer "Blessed are those who weep, for they will be consoled. Blessed are those who hunger and thirst for justice, for they will be satisfied. Blessed are those who, when people revile and persecute you and say all manner of false things about you on my account. Rejoice and be glad, for your reward in Heaven is great" [*Mt* 5, 5-12]. As the Apostles "went out full of joy. . . for having been judged worthy of abuse for the name of Jesus" [*Acts* 5, 41] in the early days of the Church, so you should not be frightened, but with eyes, mind and hearts turned toward Heaven, be filled with joy and with that Heavenly consolation, that comes from a good conscience, sustained by the firm hope of eternal reward.

Just as during the long course of the centuries your Church has sustained fierce persecutions, so now your soil has been empurpled by the sacred blood of martyrs; now, especially, can you apply to yourselves those famous words, "We become more numerous each time we are mown down. . . and the blood of Christians is seed" [Tertullian, *Apology*, 50].

As anyone can see, everything human, whether sad or happy, weak or strong, will disappear sooner or later. But the society founded by Christ the Lord, under the guidance of the Eternal Father, facing difficulties and opposition, defeats and triumphs, battles and victories, will continue to fulfill its mission of peace and salvation to the end of time: she will, undoubtedly, be opposed, but she will never be vanquished.

Steadfastly confidant in the Divine promises, in no way become fearful; as the sun returns in its splendor after the storms, so too after may trials, much discord and suffering, by the help of God, peace, tranquility and freedom will shine once again upon the Church. In the meantime, joined together by your prayers, and a most intense way, with our supplications and those of all the faithful, let us sweetly beseech the Father of mercies, that he may permit all to happen as quickly and as happily as possible.

Let us pray that we might obtain by our prayers that Heavenly glory now enjoyed by those holy martyrs who already gave example of their heroism to our ancestors, along with the Blessed Virgin Mary, Mother of God, Queen of China, whom you love and venerate with such love and piety. Bring this hope especially to those in grave danger, in anguish, in prison, in exile; and may it be especially present in the help you give to those among you who, having formed peaceful associations, are consecrated to your service, that they might glory in His name, and be granted strength, consolation and assistance.

While we raise our hands to Heaven in supplication, beseeching divine grace for you, bearer of Christian strength, as a pledge of our good will to each of you, venerable brothers, and to all the faithful who have been entrusted do your pastoral care, we cordially impart our Apostolic Blessing in the Lord.

Given in Rome at Saint Peter's, January 18th, the Feast of the Roman Chair of Saint Peter, 1952, the thirteenth of Our Pontificate.

PIO PP. XII

Appendix 7

Banner composed by Bishop Kung for the Catholic Students of Shanghai:

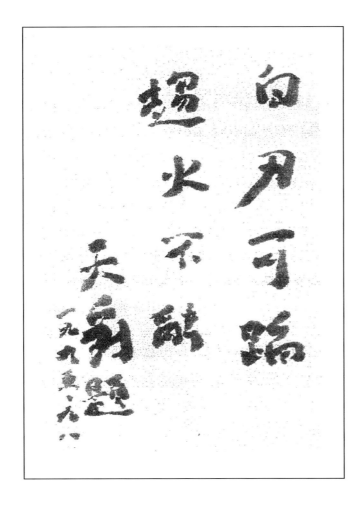

Neither Fire nor Sword Can Take Away My Faith in God

Bishop Kung created this in late 1952 to bolster the faith and courage of the Catholic youth of the city. Cardinal Kung re-created the above copy in 1995, to recall the 40th anniversary of his arrest by the Chinese Communist government. [239]

---

[239] Stamford, August 25, 2012, Joseph Kung to Msgr. Stephen DiGiovanni, Basilica Archives. "September 8th Editorial Board", *Blessings of the Divine Bounty of September 8th: In Commemoration of the 40th anniversary of the "Sept. 8th" Persecution of the Church in Mainland China, 1955-1995*, Taipei 1999, p. 140.

Appendix 8

New Year Address by Shanghai Catholic Students to Bishop Kung, January 1, 1953.[240]

This year, one student was elected to represent the delegation of 1,300 students representing all Catholic youths of the City. The gathering took place in front of Christ the King Church.

Your Excellency: permit me to say a few words.

The splendor of the glorious tears of 1952 still shines on this New Year. We look to 1953 to make us holy; we look to 1953 to be grounded on the tears of holiness. This year will give to the Church a splendid variety of flowers, and it is the love of God that will make them bloom; thanks to your care as a good gardener, they will be overflowing with sweet fragrance and life.

We carry the hope of the Church with pride. And you, Monsignor, you are the solid ground in which is rooted this immovable tree of our hope, the solid ground where this immortal tree sends forth its sap. In the Diocese of Shanghai, Monsignor, you are also the sun that gives light and warmth; where, other than in Rome, the Holy City of our Holy Father the well-loved Pope, from which comes light and warmth, it is you who transmit these to us.

Before the darkness that surrounds us, you shine like a star. You guide China towards the Truth, towards Happiness. The Catholic youth of the schools and universities of Shanghai live, work, suffer, and carry the Cross of Christ, without weakening, to spread the divine Truth.

Through the struggles of last year, God has purified us as one would purify silver, seven times in a crucible. Now our life has left the kingdom of Herod to settle in Nazareth. This life of Nazareth has already a great value, and its grandeur depends upon our willingness to follow along the direction of Your Excellency, which is the will of the Most High.

God doesn't exactly desire our bloody sufferings. He takes no pleasure in the profound sadness of agony. God simply desires the one whom He loves and who accepts His Will.

---

[240] *China Missionary Bulletin*, Vol. V (VI), May 1953, No. 5, pp. 443-444.

If His Holy Will be that we glorify Him by our blood, surely we will not refuse, we will give to the last drop. If His Holy Will is that we render Him glory in an ordinary way, we will live in complete fidelity. Faith and Charity, whether in silence or in action and battle, are the two sides of a life in Christ, pleasing to the Father.

We ask that Your Excellency consider for a moment the life of the Catholic youth whom You govern: We are inseparably united as brothers; we even enjoy a higher level of peace. The willingness to struggle that filled the past year has given us a new appreciation of peace that we have earned at the dawn of the New Year; but we know that this peace is only a mirage. We are still on the road to true peace, even if we are still distant from that final victory. It is only through these struggles that we can obtain a lasting peace and victory: to fight without rest, to combat till the end, these are our orders.

When youth becomes aware of a high ideal and is animated by love, it is the Cross that feeds that love; on the road to victory, there will always be a trail of blood, and there are tears that wash the fruits of victory. Repeated combat strengthens courage, and one victory sustains one until glory. Soldiers experience moments of rest, and it is the profitable use of those calm moments that can mean defeat or victory. We are now at the point during which to prepare for hard combat; it is during this time that we can make certain a glorious victory for the future. This is our mission. This is the direction of our efforts for the year 1953. The glorious battle of 1952 continues to shine on the year just begun. It is sublime to live for battle; but the grandeur of this life depends upon the desires of the Bishop and the Will of God.

May Your Excellency be blessed by the vision of the Heavenly Jerusalem. After these days of life, may Your Excellency see Christians embrace the world in divine love; that the world might be conquered; may the intercession of Our Lady of Fatima realize the hopes of Your Excellency; may Peace come upon us; may sinners convert; may the Reign of God arrive on earth.

Appendix 9

Pope Pius XII's Encyclical *Ad Sinarum Gentem,*
On the Supra nationality of the Church, October 7, 1954. [241]

To the Venerable Brethren and Beloved Sons, the Archbishops, Bishops, and other local Ordinaries and other members of the Clergy and People of China in Peace and Communion with the Apostolic See.

Venerable Brothers and Beloved Sons, Greetings and Apostolic Benediction.

About three years ago We issued the apostolic letter *Cupimus Imprimis* to Our dear Chinese people, and in special manner to you, Venerable Catholic Brothers and beloved sons. We issued it not only to express to you Our sympathy in your afflictions, but also to exhort you paternally to fulfill all the duties of the Christian religion with that resolute fidelity that sometimes demands heroic strength. At the present moment, We once more send up Our prayers, together with yours, to Almighty God, Father of mercy, that "as the sun shines forth again after the tempest and the storm, so, too, after so much distress, disturbances and suffering, there will, with God's help, shine forth upon your Church peace, tranquility and freedom".

In recent years, however, the conditions of the Catholic Church in your midst have not improved in the least. The accusations and calumnies against the Apostolic See and those who keep themselves faithful to it have increased. The Apostolic Nuncio, who represented Our person among you has been expelled. The snares to deceive those less instructed in the truth have been intensified.

However—as I wrote to you—"you are opposing with a firm will all forms of insidious attack, whether subtle, hidden, or masked under a false appearance of truth". We know that these words of Our previous Apostolic Letter were not able to reach you. So We willingly repeat them for you by means of this Encyclical. We also know, to Our great mental comfort, that you have persevered in your firm and holy resolve, and that no force has succeeded in separating you from the unity of the Church. For this We heartily congratulate you and give you deserved praise.

But as We must be solicitous for the eternal salvation of each person, We cannot hide the sadness and affliction of Our soul in learning that, although the great majority of Catholics have remained steadfast in the Faith, still there are

---

[241] Claudia Carlen, *The Papal Encyclicals, 1939-1958,* pp. 265-269.

some in your midst who, either deceived in their good faith, or overcome by fear, or misled by new and false doctrines, have adhered, even recently, to dangerous movements being promoted by the enemies of all religion, especially of the religion divinely revealed by Jesus Christ.

The consciousness of Our duty demands that We once more direct Our words to you through this Encyclical Letter, with the hope that it can become known to you. May it be of some comfort and encouragement for those who persevere staunchly and bravely in truth and virtue. To the others may it bring the light of Our paternal admonitions.

First of all today as in the past, the persecutors of the Christians falsely accused them of not loving their country and of not being good citizens. We wish once more to proclaim—what cannot fail to be recognized by anyone guided by right reason—that the Chinese Catholics are second to no one in their ardent love and ready loyalty to their most noble fatherland. The Chinese people—We want to repeat what We wrote in its praise in the Apostolic Letter cited above—"from the most remote times has been eminent among the other people of Asia for its achievements, its literature and the splendor of its civilization, and once it had been illuminated by the light of the Gospel that greatly excels the wisdom of this world, drew from it still finer qualities of soul, namely the Christian virtues which perfect and strengthen natural virtues".

We see that you are also worthy of praise for this reason. In the daily and prolonged trials in which you find yourselves, you follow only the just way when you give, as become Christians, respectful homage to your public authorities in the field of their competency. Moved by love of your country, you are ready to fulfill all your duties as citizens. But it is also a great consolation for Us to know that when the occasion has arisen, you have openly affirmed, and still affirm, that you can in no way stray from the precepts of the Catholic religion and that you can in no way deny your Creator and Redeemer, for Whose love many of you have faced torture and prison.

As We have already written to you in the previous Letter, this Apostolic See, especially in these recent times, has exercised the greatest solicitude that as many priests and Bishops of your own noble race as possible be correctly instructed and trained. And so Our immediate predecessor of happy memory, Pius XI, personally consecrated in the majestic Basilica of St. Peter the first six Bishops chosen from among your people. We ourselves, having nothing dearer to Our heart than the daily advancement of your Church, have been happy to establish the Sacred Hierarchy in China and for the first time in history have conferred the dignity of the Roman Purple on one of your citizens.

We desire, then, that the day may soon come—for this We send up to God most ardent petitions and suppliant prayers—when Bishops and priests of your own nation and in sufficient number can govern the Catholic Church in your immense country, and whom there will no longer be need of help from foreign missionaries in your apostolate.

But the truth itself and the knowledge of Our duty demand that We propose for your careful attention the following points: First, these preachers of the Gospel, who left their own beloved countries to cultivate among you the Master's field, with their labor and sweat, are not moved by earthly motives. They seek only, and desire nothing more than, to illumine your people with the light of Christianity, to teach them Christian customs and to help them with a supernatural charity. In the second place, even when the increased number of Chinese clergy will no longer need the aid of foreign missionaries, the Catholic Church in your nation, as in all the others, will not be able to be ruled with "autonomy of government," as they say today.

In fact, even then, as you well know, it will be entirely necessary for your Christian community, if it wishes to be part of the society divinely founded by our Redeemer, to be completely subject to the Supreme Pontiff, Vicar of Jesus Christ on earth, and be strictly united with him in regard to religious faith and morals. With these words—and it is well to note them—is embraced the whole life and work of the Church, and also its constitution, its government, its discipline. All of these things depend certainly on the will of Jesus Christ, Founder of the Church.

By virtue of God's Will, the faithful are divided into two classes: the clergy and the laity. By virtue of the same Will is established the twofold sacred hierarchy, namely of orders and jurisdiction. Besides—as has also been divinely established—the power of orders (through which the ecclesiastical hierarchy is composed of Bishops, priests, and ministers) comes from receiving the Sacrament of Holy Orders. But the power of jurisdiction, which is conferred upon the Supreme Pontiff directly by divine right, flows to the Bishops by the same right, but only through the Successor of St. Peter, to whom not only the simple faithful, but even all the Bishops must be constantly subject, and to whom they must be bound by obedience and with the bond of unity.

Finally by the same Divine Will, the people or the civil authority must not invade the rights and the constitution of the ecclesiastical hierarchy [cf. Council of Trent, Sess. XXIII; *De Ordine*, Cann. 2-7; Vatican Council I, Sess. IV; Canons 108-109].

All ought to note—what to you, Venerable brothers and beloved sons, is evident—that We intensely desire that the time will soon come when the financial means furnished by the Chinese people will suffice for the needs of the Church in China. However, as you well know, the offerings received for this from the other nations have their origin in that Christian charity through which all those who have been redeemed by the sacred blood of Jesus Christ are necessarily united to one another in fraternal alliance and are spurred by Divine Love to spread everywhere, according to their strength, the Kingdom of our Redeemer. And this not for political or any profane ends, but only to put into useful practice the precept of charity that Jesus Christ gave to us all, and through which we are recognized as His true disciples [cf. *John* 13, 35]. Thus have the Christians of all ages voluntarily done, as the Apostle of the Gentiles related to the faithful of Macedonia and Achaia, who willingly sent their offerings "for the poor among the saints at Jerusalem" [*Rom* 15, 26], and as the Apostle exhorted his children in Christ who lived in Corinth and Galatia to do the same thing [cf. *I Cor* 16, 1-2].

Lastly, there are some among you who would wish that your Church would be completely independent, not only, as We have said, in regard to its government and finances, but also in regard to the teaching of Christian doctrine and sacred preaching, in which they try to claim "autonomy".

We do not at all deny that the manner of preaching and teaching ought to differ according to place and therefore ought to conform, when possible, to the nature and particular character of the Chinese people, as also to its ancient traditional customs. If this is properly done, certainly greater fruits will be gathered among you.

But—and it is absurd merely to think of it—by what right can men arbitrarily and diversely in different nations, interpret the Gospel of Jesus Christ?

Bishops, who are the successors of the Apostles, and priests, who according to their proper office cooperate with the Bishops, have been charged with announcing and teaching that Gospel which Jesus and His Apostles first announced and taught, and which this Holy See and all the Bishops united to it have preserved and transmitted pure and inviolate through the centuries. The holy pastors, therefore, are not the inventors and the composers of this Gospel, but only its authorized custodians and its divinely constituted heralds. Wherefore, We Ourselves, and the bishops together with Us, can and ought to repeat the words of Jesus Christ: "My teaching is not my own, but his who sent me" [*John* 7, 16]. And to all the Bishops, in every age, can be directed the exhortation of St. Paul: "O Timothy, guard the trust and keep free from profane novelties in speech and the contradictions of so-called knowledge" [*I Tim* 6, 20]. And so also these words of the same Apostle: "Guard the good trust through the Holy Spirit, who dwells in us" [*2 Tim* 1, 14]. We are not teachers of a doctrine invented by the human mind. But our conscience obliges us to embrace and follow what Jesus Christ Himself taught, and what He solemnly commanded His Apostles and their successors to teach [cf. *Matt* 28, 19-20].

A Bishop, or a priest of the true Church of Christ, ought time and again to meditate on what the Apostle Paul said of his preaching of the Gospel: "For I give you to understand, brethren, that the Gospel which was preached by me is not of man. For I did not receive it from man, nor was I taught it; but I received it by a revelation of Jesus Christ" [*Gal* 1, 11-12].

Being most certain that this doctrine (whose integrity We must defend with the help of the Holy Ghost) has been divinely revealed, We repeat these words of the Apostle to the Gentiles: "But even if we or an angel from heaven should preach a Gospel to you other than that which we have preached to you, let him be anathema" [*Gal* 1, 8].

One can easily see, Venerable Brothers and beloved sons, why he cannot be considered a Catholic or bear the name of Catholic who professes or teaches differently from what We have up to this point briefly explained. This includes those persons who have adhered to the dangerous principles underlying the movement of the "Three Autonomies," or to other similar principles.

The promoters of such movements with the greatest cunning seek to deceive the simple or the timid, or to draw them away from the right path. For this purpose they falsely affirm that the only true patriots are those who adhere to the church thought up by them, that is, to that which has the "Three Autonomies." But, in reality they seek, in a word, to establish finally among you a "national" church, which no longer could be Catholic because it would be the negation of that universality or rather "catholicity" by which the society truly founded by Jesus Christ is above all nations and embraces them one and all.

We want to repeat here the words that We have written on the same argument in the letter already cited: "The Church does not single out a particular people, an individual nation, but loves all men, whatever be their nation or race, with that supernatural charity of Christ, which should necessarily unite all as brothers, one to the other.

Hence it cannot be affirmed that she serves the interests of any particular power. Nor likewise can she be expected to countenance that particular churches be set up in each nation, thus destroying that unity established by the Divine Founder, and unhappily separating them from this Apostolic See where Peter, the Vicar of Jesus Christ, continues to live in his successors until the end of time.

Whatever Christian community were to do this, would lose its vitality as the branch cut from the vine [cf. *John* 15, 6] and could not bring fourth salutary fruit".

We earnestly exhort "in the heart of Christ" [*Phil* 1, 8] those faithful of whom We have mournfully written above to come back to the path of repentance and salvation. Let them remember that, when it is necessary, one must render to Caesar what is Caesar's, and with greater reason, one must render to God what is

God's [cf. *Luke* 20, 25]. When men demand things contrary to the Divine Will, then it is necessary to put into practice the maxim of St. Peter: "We must obey God rather than men" [*Acts* 5, 29]. Let them also remember that it is impossible to serve two masters, if these orders of things are opposed to one another [cf. *Matt* 6, 24]. Also at times it is impossible to please both Jesus Christ and men [cf. *Gal* 1, 10]. But if it sometimes happens that he who wishes to remain faithful to the Divine Redeemer even unto death must suffer great harm, let him bear it with a strong and serene soul.

On the other hand, We wish to congratulate repeatedly those who, suffering severe difficulties, have been outstanding in their loyalty to God and to the Catholic Church, and so have been "counted worthy to suffer disgrace for the name of Jesus" [*Acts* 5, 41]. With a paternal heart We encourage them to continue brave and intrepid along the road they have taken, keeping in mind the words of Jesus Christ: "And do not be afraid of those who kill the body but cannot kill the soul. But rather be afraid of him who is able to destroy both soul and body in hell . . . But as for you, the very hairs of your head are all numbered. Therefore do not be afraid. . . for everyone who acknowledges me before men, I will also acknowledge him before my Father in heaven" [*Matt* 10, 28; 30-33].

Certainly, O Venerable Brothers and beloved sons, the struggle imposed on you by divine law is not a light one. But Christ the Lord, Who has declared blessed those who suffer persecution for justice sake, has commanded them to be glad and rejoice, for their reward in heaven will be very great [cf. *Matt* 5, 10-12].

He Himself will benignly assist you from Heaven with His powerful aid, so that you can fight the good fight and keep the faith [cf. *2 Tim* 4, 7]. Then too, the Mother of God, the Virgin Mary, who is also the most loving mother of all, will assist all of you with her most efficacious protection. May she, the Queen of China, defend and help you in a particular way in this Marian Year, so that you may persevere with constancy in your resolutions. May you be aided by the Holy Martyrs of China, who serenely faced death for love of their fatherland, and above all for their loyalty to the Divine Redeemer and His Church.

Meanwhile may the Apostolic Benediction be for you an omen of heavenly graces, which in testimony of Our most special benevolence, We impart with much affection in the Lord both to you, Venerable Brothers and beloved sons, and to the whole and dearest Chinese nation.

Given at Rome, at St. Peter's, October 7, Feast of the Most Holy Rosary of the Blessed Virgin Mary, 1954, in the sixteenth year of Our Pontificate.

PIO PP. XII

Appendix 10

Pope Pius XII's Encyclical *Ad Apostolorum Principis,* On Communism and the Church in China, June 29, 1958. [242]

To Our Venerable Brethren and Beloved Children, the Archbishops, Bishops, and other Local Ordinaries, and Clergy and People of China in Peace and Communion with the Apostolic See.

Venerable Brethren and Beloved Children, Greetings and Apostolic Benediction.

At the tomb of the Prince of the Apostles, in the majestic Vatican Basilica, Our immediate Predecessor of deathless memory, Pius XI, duly consecrated and raised to the fullness of the priesthood, as you well know, "the flowers and . . . latest buds of the Chinese episcopate" [*Acta Apostolicae Sedis*, 18 (1926), 432].

On that solemn occasion he added these words: "You have come, Venerable Brethren, to visit Peter, and you have received from him the shepherd's staff, with which to undertake your apostolic journeys and to gather together your sheep. It is Peter who with great love has embraced you who are in great part Our hope for the spread of the truth of the Gospel among your people" [*Acta Apostolicae Sedis*, 18 (1926), 432].

The memory of that allocution comes to Our mind today, Venerable Brethren and dear children, as the Catholic Church in your fatherland is experiencing great suffering and loss. But the hope of our great Predecessor was not in vain, nor did it prove without effect, for new bands of shepherds and heralds of the Gospel have been joined to the first group of bishops whom Peter, living in his Successor, sent to feed those chosen flocks of the Lord.

New works and religious undertakings prospered among you despite many obstacles. We too shared that hope when later We had the pleasure of establishing the hierarchy in China and saw yet wider paths opening up for the spread of the Kingdom of Jesus Christ.

But, alas, after a few years the sky was overcast by storm clouds. On your Christian communities, many of which had been flourishing from times long past, there fell sad and sorrowful times. Missionaries, among whom were many archbishops and bishops noted for their apostolic zeal, and Our own Internuncio were driven from China, while bishops, priests, and religious men and women,

---

[242] Claudia Carlen, *The Papal Encyclicals, 1939-1958,* pp. 365-371.

together with many of the faithful, were cast into prison or incurred every kind of restraint and suffering.

On that occasion We raised Our voice in sorrow, and, in Our Encyclical of January 18, 1952, *Cupimus imprimis* [*Acta Apostolicae Sedis*, 44 (1952), 153ff], rebuked the unjust attack. In that letter, for the sake of truth and conscious of Our duty, We declared that the Catholic Church is a stranger to no people on earth, much less hostile to any. With a mother's anxiety, she embraces all peoples in impartial charity. She seeks no earthly advantage but employs what powers she possesses to attract the souls of all men to seek what is eternal. We also stated that missionaries promote the interest of no particular nation; they come from every quarter of the earth and are united by a single love, God, and thus they seek and hope for nothing else save the spread of God's Kingdom. Thus, it is clear that their work is neither without purpose nor harmful, but beneficent and necessary since it aids Chinese priests in their Christian apostolate.

And some two years later, October 7, 1954, another Encyclical Letter was addressed to you, beginning *Ad Sinarum gentem* [*Acta Apostolicae Sedis*, 47 (1955), 5 ff], in which We refuted accusations made against Catholics in China. We openly declared that Catholics yielded to none (nor could they do so) in their true loyalty and love of their native country. Seeing also that there was being spread among you the doctrine of the so-called "Three Autonomies," We warned—by virtue of that universal teaching authority which We exercise by divine command—that this same doctrine as understood by its authors, whether in theory or in its consequences, cannot receive the approval of a Catholic, since it turns minds away from the essential unity of the Church.

In these days, however, We have to draw attention to the fact that the Church in your lands in recent years has been brought to still worse straits. In the midst of so many great sorrows it brings Us great comfort to note that in the daily attacks which you have met, neither unflinching faith nor the most ardent love of the Divine Redeemer and of His Church has been wanting. You have borne witness to this faith and love in innumerable ways, of which only a small part is known to men, but for all of which you will someday receive an eternal reward from God.

Nevertheless, We regard it as Our duty to declare openly, with a heart filled to its depths with sorrow and anxiety, that affairs in China are, by deceit and cunning endeavor, changing so much for the worse that the false doctrine already condemned by Us seems to be approaching its final stages and to be causing its most serious damage.

For by particularly subtle activity an association has been created among you to which has been attached the title of "patriotic," and Catholics are being forced by every means to take part in it.

This association—as has often been proclaimed—was formed ostensibly to join the clergy and the faithful in love of their religion and their country, with these objectives in view: that they might foster patriotic sentiments; that they might advance the cause of international peace; that they might accept that species of socialism which has been introduced among you and, having accepted it, support and spread it; that, finally, they might actively cooperate with civil authorities in defending what they describe as political and religious freedom. And yet—despite these sweeping generalizations about defense of peace and the fatherland, which can certainly deceive the unsuspecting—it is perfectly clear that this association is simply an attempt to execute certain well defined and ruinous policies.

For under an appearance of patriotism, which in reality is just a fraud, this association aims primarily at making Catholics gradually embrace the tenets of atheistic materialism, by which God Himself is denied and religious principles are rejected.

Under the guise of defending peace the same association receives and spreads false rumors and accusations by which many of the clergy, including venerable bishops and even the Holy See itself, are claimed to admit to and promote schemes for earthly domination or to give ready and willing consent to exploitation of the people, as if they, with preconceived opinions, are acting with hostile intent against the Chinese nation.

While they declare that it is essential that every kind of freedom exist in religious matters and that this makes mutual relations between ecclesiastical and civil powers easier, this association in reality aims at setting aside and neglecting the rights of the Church and effecting its complete subjection to civil authorities.

Hence all its members are forced to approve those unjust prescriptions by which missionaries are cast into exile, and by which bishops, priests, religious men, nuns, and the faithful in considerable numbers are thrust into prison; to consent to those measures by which the jurisdiction of many legitimate pastors is persistently obstructed; to defend wicked principles totally opposed to the unity, universality, and hierarchical constitution of the Church; to admit those first steps by which the clergy and faithful are undermined in the obedience due to legitimate bishops; and to separate Catholic communities from the Apostolic See.

In order to spread these wicked principles more efficiently and to fix them in everyone's mind, this association—which, as We have said, boasts of its patriotism—uses a variety of means including violence and oppression, numerous lengthy publications, and group meetings and congresses.

In these meetings, the unwilling are forced to take part by incitement, threats, and deceit. If any bold spirit strives to defend truth, his voice is easily smothered and overcome and he is branded with a mark of infamy as an enemy of his native land and of the new society.

There should also be noted those courses of instruction by which pupils are forced to imbibe and embrace this false doctrine. Priests, religious men and women, ecclesiastical students, and faithful of all ages are forced to attend these courses. An almost endless series of lectures and discussions, lasting for weeks and months, so weaken and benumb the strength of mind and will that by a kind of psychic coercion an assent is extracted which contains almost no human element, an assent which is not freely asked for as should be the case.

In addition to these there are the methods by which minds are upset—by every device, in private and in public, by traps, deceits, grave fear, by so-called forced confessions, by custody in a place where citizens are forcibly "re-educated", and those "Peoples' Courts" to which even venerable bishops are ignominiously dragged for trial.

Against methods of acting such as these, which violate the principal rights of the human person and trample on the sacred liberty of the sons of God, all Christians from every part of the world, indeed all men of good sense cannot refrain from raising their voices with Us in real horror and from uttering a protest deploring the deranged conscience of their fellow men.

And since these crimes are being committed under the guise of patriotism, We consider it Our duty to remind everyone once again of the Church's teaching on this subject.

For the Church exhorts and encourages Catholics to love their country with sincere and strong love, to give due obedience in accord with natural and positive divine law to those who hold public office, to give them active and ready assistance for the promotion of those undertakings by which their native land can in peace and order daily achieve greater prosperity and further true development.

The Church has always impressed on the minds of her children that declaration of the Divine Redeemer: "Render therefore to Caesar the things that are Caesar's and to God the things that are God's" [*Luke* 20. 25]. We call it a declaration because these words make certain and incontestable the principle that Christianity never opposes or obstructs what is truly useful or advantageous to a country.

However, if Christians are bound in conscience to render to Caesar (that is, to human authority) what belongs to Caesar, then Caesar likewise, or those who control the state, cannot exact obedience when they would be usurping God's rights or forcing Christians either to act at variance with their religious duties or to sever themselves from the unity of the Church and its lawful hierarchy.

Under such circumstances, every Christian should cast aside all doubt and calmly and firmly repeat the words with which Peter and the other Apostles answered the first persecutors of the Church: "We must obey God rather than men" [*Acts* 9, 6].

With emphatic insistence, those who promote the interests of this association which claims a monopoly on patriotism, speak over and over again of peace and admonish Catholics earnestly to exert all their efforts to establish it. On the surface these words are excellent and righteous, for who deserves greater praise than the man who prepares the way to introduce and establish peace?

But peace—as you well know, Venerable Brethren and beloved sons—does not consist of words alone and does not rely on changing formulas which are suitable for the moment but contradict one's real plans and practices, which do not conform with the meaning and way of true peace but with hatred, discord, and deceit.

Peace worthy of the name must be founded on the principles of charity and justice which He taught who is the "Prince of Peace" [*Isaiah* 9,6], and who adopted this title as a kind of royal standard for Himself. True peace is that which the Church desires to be established: one that is stable, just, fair, and founded on right order; one which binds all together—citizens, families, and peoples—by the firm ties of the rights of the Supreme Lawgiver, and by the bonds of mutual fraternal love and cooperation.

As she looks forward to and hopes for this peaceful dwelling together of nations, the Church expects each nation to preserve that degree of dignity which becomes it. For the Church, which has ever kept a friendly attitude toward the various events in your country, long ago spoke through Our late Predecessor of happy memory and expressed the desire that "full recognition be given to the legitimate aspirations and rights of the nation, which is more populous than any other, whose civilization and culture go back to the earliest times, which has, in past ages, with the development of its resources, had periods of great prosperity, and which—it may be reasonably conjectured—will become even greater in the future ages, provided it pursues justice and honor" [Message of Pius XI to the Apostolic Delegate to China, August 1, 1928: *Acta Apostolicae Sedis*, 20 (1928), 245].

On the other hand, as has been made known by radio and by the press, there are some—even among the ranks of the clergy—who do not shrink from casting suspicion on the Apostolic See and hint that it has evil designs toward your country.

Assuming false and unjust premises, they are not afraid to take a position which would confine within a narrow scope the supreme teaching authority of the Church, claiming that there are certain questions—such as those which concern social and economic matters—in which Catholics may ignore the teachings and the directives of this Apostolic See.

This opinion—it seems entirely unnecessary to demonstrate its existence—is utterly false and full of error because, as We declared a few years ago to a special meeting of Our Venerable Brethren in the episcopacy:

"The power of the Church is in no sense limited to so-called 'strictly religious matters'; but the whole matter of the natural law, its institution, interpretation and application, in so far as the moral aspect is concerned, are within its power.

"By God's appointment the observance of the natural law concerns the way by which man must strive toward his supernatural end. The Church shows the way and is the guide and guardian of men with respect to their supernatural end" [*Address to Cardinals and Bishops*, November 2, 1954: *Acta Apostolicae Sedis*, 46 (1954), 671-672].

This truth had already been wisely explained by Our Predecessor St. Pius X in his Encyclical Letter *Singulari quadam* of September 24, 1912, in which he made this statement: "All actions of a Christian man so far as they are morally either good or bad—that is, so far as they agree with or are contrary to the natural and divine law—fall under the judgment and jurisdiction of the Church" [*Acta Apostolicae Sedis*, 4 (1912), 658].

Moreover, even when those who arbitrarily set and defend these narrow limits profess a desire to obey the Roman Pontiff with regard to truths to be believed, and to observe what they call ecclesiastical directives, they proceed with such boldness that they refuse to obey the precise and definite prescriptions of the Holy See. They protest that these refer to political affairs because of a hidden meaning by the author, as if these prescriptions took their origin from some secret conspiracy against their own nation.

Here We must mention a symptom of this falling away from the Church. It is a very serious matter and fills Our heart—the heart of a Father and universal Pastor of the faithful—with a grief that defies description. For those who profess themselves most interested in the welfare of their country have for some considerable time been striving to disseminate among the people the position, devoid of all truth, that Catholics have the power of directly electing their bishops. To excuse this kind of election they allege a need to look after the good souls with all possible speed and to entrust the administration of dioceses to those pastors who, because they do not oppose the Communist desires and political methods, are acceptable by the civil power.

We have heard that many such elections have been held contrary to all right and law and that, in addition, certain ecclesiastics have rashly dared to receive Episcopal consecration, despite the public and severe warning which this Apostolic See gave those involved.

Since, therefore, such serious offenses against the discipline and unity of the Church are being committed, We must in conscience warn all that this is completely at variance with the teachings and principles on which rests the right order of the society divinely instituted by Jesus Christ our Lord.

For it has been clearly and expressly laid down in the canons that it pertains to the one Apostolic See to judge whether a person is fit for the dignity and burden of the episcopacy [Canon 331, sect. 3], and that complete freedom in the nomination of bishops is the right of the Roman Pontiff [Canon 329, sect. 2]. But if, as happens at times, some persons or groups are permitted to participate in the selection of an Episcopal candidate, this is lawful only if the Apostolic See has allowed it in express terms and in each particular case for clearly defined persons or groups, the conditions and circumstances being very plainly determined.

Granted this exception, it follows that bishops who have been neither named nor confirmed by the Apostolic See, but who, on the contrary, have been elected and consecrated in defiance of its express orders, enjoy no powers of teaching or of jurisdiction since jurisdiction passes to bishops only through the Roman Pontiff as We admonished in the Encyclical Letter *Mystici Corporis* in the following words:

". . . As far as his own diocese is concerned each (bishop) feeds the flock entrusted to him as a true shepherd and rules it in the name of Christ. Yet in exercising this office they are not altogether independent but are subordinate to the lawful authority of the Roman Pontiff, although enjoying ordinary power of jurisdiction, which they receive directly from the same Roman Pontiff" [*Acta Apostolicae Sedi*, 35 (1943), 211-212].

And when We later addressed to you the letter *Ad Sinarum gentem*, We again referred to this teaching in these words: "The power of jurisdiction which is conferred directly by divine right on the Supreme Pontiff comes to bishops by that same right, but only through the successor of Peter, to whom not only the faithful but also all bishops are bound to be constantly subject and to adhere both by the reverence of obedience and by the bond of unity" [*Acta Apostolicae Sedis*, 47 (1955), 9].

Acts requiring the power of Holy Orders which are performed by ecclesiastics of this kind, though they are valid as long as the consecration conferred on them was valid, are yet gravely illicit, that is, criminal and sacrilegious.

To such conduct the warning words of the Divine Teacher fittingly apply: "He who enters not by the door into the sheepfold, but climbs up another way, is a thief and a robber" [*John* 10. 1]. The sheep indeed know the true shepherd's voice. "But a stranger they will not follow, but will flee from him, because they do not know the voice of strangers" [*John* 10. 4-5].

We are aware that those who thus belittle obedience in order to justify themselves with regard to those functions which they have unrighteously assumed, defend their position by recalling a usage which prevailed in ages past. Yet everyone sees that all ecclesiastical discipline is overthrown if it is in any way lawful for one to restore arrangements which are no longer valid because the supreme authority of the Church long ago decreed otherwise. In no sense do they excuse their way of acting by appealing to another custom, and they indisputably prove that they follow this line deliberately in order to escape from the discipline which now prevails and which they ought to be obeying.

We mean that discipline which has been established not only for China and the regions recently enlightened by the light of the Gospel, but for the whole Church, a discipline which takes its sanction from that universal and supreme power of caring for, ruling, and governing which our Lord granted to the successors in the office of St. Peter the Apostle.

Well known are the terms of the [First] Vatican Council's solemn definition: "Relying on the open testimony of the Scriptures and abiding by the wise and clear decrees both of our predecessors, the Roman Pontiffs, and the general Councils, We renew the definition of the Ecumenical Council of Florence, by virtue of which all the faithful must believe that 'the Holy Apostolic See and the Roman Pontiff hold primacy over the whole world, and the Roman Pontiff himself is the Successor of the blessed Peter and continues to be the true Vicar of Christ and head of the whole Church, the father and teacher of all Christians, and to him has the blessed Peter and our Lord Jesus Christ committed the full power of caring for, ruling and governing the Universal Church. . ."

"We teach, . . . We declare that the Roman Church by the Providence of God holds the primacy of ordinary power over all others, and that this power of jurisdiction of the Roman Pontiff, which is truly Episcopal, is immediate. Toward it, the pastors and the faithful of whatever rite and dignity, both individually and collectively, are bound by the duty of hierarchical subordination and true obedience, not only in matters which pertain to faith and morals, but also in those which concern the discipline and government of the Church spread throughout the whole world, in such a way that once the unity of communion and the profession of the same Faith has been preserved with the Roman Pontiff, there is one flock of the Church of Christ under one supreme shepherd. This is the teaching of the Catholic truth from which no one can depart without loss of faith and salvation" [Vatican Council I, session IV, chap. 3; *Coll. Lac.*, VII, p. 484].

From what We have said, it follows that no authority whatsoever, save that which is proper to the Supreme Pastor, can render void the canonical appointment granted to any bishop; that no person or group, whether of priests or of laymen, can claim the right of nominating bishops; that no one can lawfully confer Episcopal consecration unless he has received the mandate of the Apostolic See [Canon 953].

Consequently, if consecration of this kind is being done contrary to all right and law, and by this crime the unity of the Church is being seriously attacked, an excommunication reserved *specialissimo modo* to the Apostolic See has been established which is automatically incurred by the consecrator and by anyone who has received consecration irresponsibly conferred [Decree of the Sacred Congregation of the Holy Office, April 9, 1951: *Acta Apostolicae Sedis*, 43 (1951), 217-218].

What then is to be the opinion concerning the excuse added by members of the association promoting false patriotism that they had to act as they alleged because of the need to tend to the souls in those dioceses which were then without a bishop?

It is obvious that no thought is being taken of the spiritual good of the faithful if the Church's laws are being violated, and further, there is no question of vacant sees, as they wish to argue in defense, but of Episcopal sees whose legitimate rulers have been driven out or now languish in prison or are being obstructed in various ways from the free exercise of their power of jurisdiction. It must likewise be added that those clerics have been cast into prison, exiled, or removed by other means, whom the lawful ecclesiastical superiors had designated in accordance with canon law and the special powers received from the Apostolic See to act in their place in the government of the dioceses.

It is surely a matter for grief that while holy bishops noted for their zeal for souls are enduring so many trials, advantage is taken of their difficulties to establish false shepherds in their place so that the hierarchical order of the Church is overthrown and the authority of the Roman Pontiff is treacherously resisted.

And some have even become so arrogant that they blame the Apostolic See for these terrible and tragic events (which have certainly been deliberate accomplishments of the Church's persecutors) even though everyone knows that the Church has been unable, in the past and at present, when such information has been needed, to obtain requisite data about qualified candidates for the episcopacy simply because she was prevented from communicating freely and safely with the dioceses of China.

Venerable brethren and dear children, thus far We have told you of the anxiety with which we are moved by the errors which certain men are trying to sow among you, and by the dissensions which are being aroused. Our intention is that, enlightened and strengthened by the encouragement of your common Father, you may remain steadfast and without blemish in that faith by which We are united and by which alone We shall obtain salvation.

But now, following the ardent dictates of Our heart, We must tell you of the close and particular feelings of intimacy which draw Us near to you. To Our mind come those torments which rend asunder your bodies or your minds, particularly those which the most valiant witnesses of Christ are enduring, among whose number are several of Our Venerable Brethren in the episcopate. Daily at the altar We offer to the Divine Redeemer the trials of all of them, together with the prayers and sufferings of the whole Church. Be constant then and put your trust in Him according to the words: "Cast all your anxiety upon Him, because He cares for you" [*I Peter* 5.7].

He sees clearly your anguish and your torments. He particularly finds acceptable the grief of soul and the tears which many of you, bishops and priests, religious and laymen, pour forth in secret when they behold the efforts of those who are striving to subvert the Christians among you. These tears, these bodily pains and tortures, the blood of the martyrs of past and present—all will bring it about that, through the powerful intervention of Mary, the Virgin Mother of God, Queen of China, the Church in your native land will at long last regain its strength and in a calmer age, happier days will shine upon it.

Relying on this hope, to you and to the flocks committed to your care We most lovingly grant in the Lord, as a token of divine gifts and a sign of Our special good will, Our Apostolic Benediction.

Given at St. Peter's, in Rome, June 29th, the Feast of the Holy Apostles Peter and Paul, in the year 1958, the 20th of Our Pontificate.

PIO PP. XII

Appendix 11

Letter of Pope Paul VI to Bishop Ignatius Kung Pin-Mei, October 7, 1974. [243]

To Our Venerable Brother

Ignatius Kung Pin-Mei

Bishop of Shanghai

Through these words which We send to you, Venerable Brother, where in your present habitation, in a hidden serenity, you recollect the 25th anniversary of your episcopal ordination, We wish to manifest an earnest pledge of Our solicitude towards you, as well as to accomplish a duty of veneration and gratitude. With this in mind it is Our most earnest desire that Our words may indeed serve to convey healing consolation to you in your endurance of sorrow.

It is in no way hidden from Us how much you have achieved from the very outset of your episcopacy, nor are We unaware that your outstanding merits of life and rectitude of conscience presently endure intense sorrow. It is evident to those who have observed and studied your years passed in China, first as spiritual shepherd of Suchou and later as spiritual ruler of the Church of Shanghai, that you brought to your labors a greatness of spirit equal to your episcopal call. In you, as dispenser and faithful minister of the divine mysteries, outstanding intellectual talent, prudent judgment, diligent care, and force of natural talent made extend the wealth of charity to all parts and to all needs of the flock entrusted to you; you endeavored and constantly sought to achieve and reach to that perfect peace which is the bond and noblest good of our human communities.

However, difficult and arduous concerns became your lot; they were a burden of affliction which in no wise perverted your constancy in vocation, your safeguarding of the Catholic Faith, or your love of your naive land. What can be Our words of counsel, what Our exhortations to strengthen you against evils and to endow you with increased fortitude? "Take heart, keep high your courage, all you that wait patiently for the Lord" (cf. *Ps.* 30, 25). Jesus Christ, who is truly Emmanuel, that is, God with us, indeed does stand looking upon His just ones who endure bitter sufferings as do athletes their trial on the path to victory. He is there

---

[243] Vatican October 7, 1974, Pope Paul VI to Bishop Ignatius Kung Pin-Mei, Vatican Archives, Secretary of State, Archives of Paul VI, Prot. 266/060. And in the Cardinal Kung Foundation.

gazing upon them, giving them strength and making ready the rewards which accompany immortal glory. For this reason Job spoke his words: "Lord, would you but vindicate me, and set me right with you! I care not who else is for or against me" (*Job* 17, 3). It is fire that tests gold, tribulation that proves saints; trials endured for Christ's sake bring virtue to a summit of perfection, where like the Apostles, innocent of all malice, it endures wrongdoing while forgiving the malefactors. What has been laid upon us as penalty, thus turns into honor splendidly serving the public good by example and merit; unshaken possession of peace of soul endures in him who suffers his pains for the glory of the Gospel and for the triumph of the Cross; imprisoned though he may be, his dwelling is already assured in heaven.

It is with these thoughts in mind that unceasingly we pray to our God of peace and all consolation that soon the dawn of peace may shine upon our beloved land of China, and that you may early be restored to the liberty fitting to your sacred position. May the most Blessed Virgin Mary, Consoler of the afflicted, Mother of hope and saintly joy, bestow still more plentifully upon you of her treasures of help and solace.

To this expression of reverence which We extend to you, Venerable Brother, on the 25th anniversary of your episcopal office we join Our Apostolic Blessing and wish it to be enjoyed by all, near or far, who in any degree share in this religious remembrance.

Given from the Vatican, the seventh day of October, in the year 1974, the twelfth of Our Pontificate.

PAULUS PP. VI

Appendix 12

Bishop Kung's Appeal Letter, 1979. [244]

A Letter of Appeal

To: The Supreme People's Court in Beijing

I, Kung Pin Mei, the undersigned, Bishop of the Catholic Diocese of Shanghai as well as the Apostolic Administrator of the Suzhou Diocese and the Nanjing Archdiocese, was sentenced to life imprisonment on the 17th of March 1960.

I hereby set forth the following analysis of and an appeal against the judgement made by Shanghai Intermediate People's Court in 1960, Shanghai Criminal Case No. 162. I request that the People's Government handle this appeal with impartiality to the end that it will honor the factual evidence by nullifying the false accusations.

A. Brief biography

The appellant, Kung Pin Mei, was born into a landlord's family at West Sacred Heart Church, Tangmuqiao Village, Chuansha County, Jiangsu Province on the 2nd of August 1901 (i.e. the 27th year of Emperor Guangxu's reign in the Qing dynasty). [245] My family has been Catholic for many generations. I am the eldest of four children. From the age of six, I received my education at home, studying Chinese classics, namely the Four Books, and the Confucian Classics. At the age of twelve, I entered the Church-run Dayi Primary School in my home town. In the following year, I entered Xuhui College (St Ignatius High School) in Shanghai. At the age of nineteen, when the "May the Fourth" Movement took place, I graduated from the high school, and left my family, abandoning the worldly life voluntarily. I chose to study at Xujiahui Seminary in preparation for receiving the Sacrament

---

[244] This English translation of the complete text from the original Chinese was provided by the Cardinal Kung Foundation.

[245] The West Sacred Heart Church was a family "chapel" built into the family home. It was a very large structure that was open to the public occasionally for Masses. Bishop Kung was not baptized here, but in the local parish church of Our Lady of Lourdes. Stamford April 17, 2013 Joseph Kung to Msgr. Stephen M. DiGiovanni, Basilica Archives.

of Holy Orders for evangelization. While there I studied Literature for three years, Theology and Philosophy for six years, and underwent a parish internship for two years. Finally, in May 1930, I was ordained a priest. On the 7th of October 1949. I was consecrated as the Bishop of Suzhou. During this period of nineteen years, with the exception of parish work at Gaoqiao, Fengxian from 1934 to 1936, I successively held the posts of headmaster and director at various primary and middle schools. These are Yaochan Primary School in Nanqiao, Zhengxin Middle School and Guangqi Middle School, both in Songjiang, Aurora Middle School in Shanghai, and Gonzaga Primary and Middle Schools. On the 8th of August 1950, I was transferred from Suzhou to serve as the Bishop of Shanghai, and as the Apostolic Administrator of the Suzhou diocese and the Nanjing archdiocese. At midnight on the 8th of September 1955, having served my tenure of office for five years and one month, I was arrested and sent to prison. I was finally sentenced to life imprisonment on the 17th of March 1960. I have so far been imprisoned for reform for twenty-four years and two months.

B. The first appeal

It has been twenty years since I was sentenced. I felt that it would be better for me not to make an appeal or to file a complaint until now for the following two reasons: firstly, I could not stand reminiscing the events of the past; secondly, before Chairman Hua promulgated the policy of governing the country by law, there was a practice in the prison that those who attempted to make an appeal became the targets of criticism for refusing to plead guilty or for opposing being reformed. Therefore, as there was in fact no place for me to appeal the injustice, nor did I dare to expose the mistakes that had been made by the authority, it was better for me not to appeal.

Since this spring, government officials have repeatedly come to review my case, explicitly allowing me to make an appeal and to expose the mistakes. This is a concrete manifestation that the government is ruling the country by a legal system. I should have definitely been criticized if I had not taken this God-given opportunity. In this letter of appeal, I hereby expound the points in the judgment that run contrary to the facts. By submitting this letter of appeal, I hope that the government can clearly distinguish the rights from wrongs in order to demonstrate the solemn spirit of the legal system upheld by the government and to re-establish the rightful reputation of the Church.

Personal merit or misfortune does not matter much to the appellant. The most important goal that I am looking for is rather that the Chinese citizens in our country should be able to enjoy the human rights and freedom of religion and belief as given in the constitution. The questions are: Does the Church have the right to safeguard the integrity of its own basic faith? Does the State have the right to force the Church whether or not to believe in its basic faith?

C. The Three-Self Reform Movement:
Protecting our religion and safeguarding Church doctrine

During my tenure of the first five years, the most important focus of conflict between the Catholic Church and the State was when the government tried to create a schism in the Church by promoting the Three-Self Reform Movement which forced the Catholics to sever their religious communion with the Roman Pontiff. In opposition to this forced schism, the Church fought to protect the Catholic religion and to safeguard its doctrine by maintaining its communion with the Roman Pontiff. The following sets forth a brief account:

When I took over the helm of the Shanghai diocese in August, 1950, Yang Shida, Hu Wenyao and others (all of them resided in Shanghai) had already acted as leaders to start promoting among the faithful in Shanghai the Three-Self Reform Movement as advocated by the government; namely, self-government, self-propagation, and self-support. In other words, the three points are that Chinese bishops should govern the Church by themselves; Chinese clergy should preach and evangelize by themselves; Chinese citizens should raise funds by themselves for apostolic work without foreign support. These ideas not only had met our faithful's wishes; but also are the three basic principles adopted by our Popes of past ages when developing missions across the world. Moreover, over forty dioceses governed by Chinese bishops had already implemented and accomplished these Three-Self Reform principles. Our Shanghai diocese also already had the manpower and material resources to fully accomplish these three principles. Why do we need to promote the Three-Self Reform Movement again? If the government wanted to promote the movement again, what is its ulterior motive? It only wants to force the faithful to server their communion with the Roman Pontiff, thereby joining the Three-Self Reform Movement in order to affect a schism. As expected, the widely-known new Three-Self Reform Movement at that time, after the big "anti-imperialist patriotic" movement, expelled all the foreign clergy. In August 1957, after the Catholic Patriotic Association came into being, its first

President, Bishop Pi Shushi of Shenyang and others directly telegraphed the Roman Pontiff, declaring their severance of religious communion from him and that they would self-consecrate bishops without a mandate, self-administer the Church, and initiate schism in China. These pieces of evidence, as predicted by the faithful, proved the true nature of the falsehood of this Three-Self Reform Movement.

It was said, "Isn't it divinely wonderful if we can understand minute signs when something germinates?" "In the formation of sleet, ice crystals need to be amassed first." From small clues we can see how things will develop – like the diocese of Shanghai. Yao Zantang, Diocesan Administrator of Shanghai, had already, to serve as a warning, excommunicated Yang Shida, a former member of the "Young People's Three Principles of Mankind Association" who had made himself successful by committing sinful acts. In the spring of 1951, as the faithful were dissatisfied with the titular President of Aurora University, Hu Guangyao, whose words and deeds are characteristic of revolutionized and apostatized anti-faith rhetoric, I requested him to make a profession of faith in order to show his integrity and to relieve the doubts about his stand in the minds of the faithful. Hu refused. Prior to his failure to make the profession of faith, according to canon law, he had already been temporarily suspended from receiving Holy Communion. At the same time, I re-emphasized to the faithful the important canon law that they must not participate in the Three-Self Reform and schismatic Movement, because this is tantamount to severing oneself from the Church. Therefore, those who knowingly violated the canon law by participating in this schismatic movement must face the penalty of being excommunicated and forbidden to receive the Sacraments. Moreover, I gave the warning again to those Catholics who joined the Communist Party, the Communist Youth League, and the Young Pioneers that they would receive the same punishment as stated in the canon law and be forbidden from receiving the Sacraments. This was a life-or-death conflict between the Church and the State. This is also the reason why I was arrested and sentenced.

D. Refusing to make a deal

During my tenure of office, the government urged me to reform and sever my religious ties with the Pope. Unfortunately, the day before the sentence, the Chief Prosecutor of the Shanghai city, Lu Ming, came to the prison to urge me to consider gaining freedom and happiness in my old age in return for severing my religious relations with the Pope as well as breaking off political and economic ties from him. I replied: I absolutely will not consider this deal of momentary comforts of life by apostatizing my religion.

By human nature, we prefer to live rather than to die. However, there is something that is even more preferable to life. To a man of virtue, they are integrity, righteousness and morals. To the faithful, it is the integrity of faith. There is something even more detestable than death. To a loyal patriot, it is the betrayal of the ruler and the nation. To a Christian, it is the betrayal of God and Jesus. To separate from the sole representative of Jesus Christ on earth, the Roman Pontiff, is to make myself lose the most basic Catholic faith, becoming a heretic without the Pope, a headless corpse, a rootless log, water without source, and a religious corpse without a transcendent life. This is a serious issue in the history of the Holy Catholic Church for which millions of people have fought by shedding their blood and sacrificing their lives. Therefore, in the spring of 1950, at the religious meeting in Beijing, Premier Zhou said, "It is a wise and reasonable promise that Catholics, on the basis of severing their political and economic ties with the Roman Pontiff, can maintain their pure religious communion with the Pontiff." Unfortunately this has not happened. With regard to these important issues, I frankly and openly replied to the Chief Prosecutor that I absolutely will not sever my communion with the Roman Pontiff: today or ever. Therefore, on the 17th of March 1960, I was sentenced to life imprisonment. My refusal to sever my religious communion with the Pontiff was the main reason for the punishment inflicted on me.

E. Protecting the law with sincerity

Under the great policy of holding the guiding principle of managing the nation, and of governing the whole country according to law as advocated by the current leader, Chairman Hua, I hope that the government will examine international rules and the Chinese national code of law. For those countries having in their constitution the freedom of religion and belief, does the state regime of those countries have the power to reform the basic tenets of the dogma of a Church believed in by its followers in order to make them schismatic from that original Church? For an example, does the Chinese regime have the right to force the Catholics to sever their religious communion with the Roman Pontiff so as to make them become like the schismatic Greek Church in Eastern Europe or the Reformed Protestants in Western Europe?

Answer: No such right.

Below is the evidence:

E/I. Examining international rules on the freedom of religion and belief

During the Reformation period, religious believers were often forced by the authority of Western European's feudalism to renounce and change their Church's doctrines, resulting in brutal religious warfare. In order to stop this warfare, many civilized countries in today's world signed "Concordats". Out of these the current constitution of freedom of religion and belief was born on an international scale. Under the spirit of this constitution, the freedom of religious belief and of protecting the dogma of one's Church was assured. One is no longer under a government's mandate to change the dogma of one's religion, nor has a government authority to infringe on one's religious freedom. This being so, one no longer has to endure the burden of the fear of being forced to become schismatic by altering the Church's basic dogma. Therefore, if a state regime does not relinquish its own constitution, it does not have the legal power to recklessly alter the basic beliefs of individual churches within its territory.

E/II. Questioning the State code of law

In 1956, the Preamble of the First Draft Constitution contained the phrase "the State has the power to reform religion ...". Thanks to the submission made by the representatives of religion, including Dalai Panchen, who were involved with drafting the Constitution at that time, that phrase "the State has the power to reform religion ..." did not appear in the Preambles of the official edition of the First, Second and the Third Constitutions. According to the teaching bequeathed by Chairman Mao, ... we cannot use administrative order to abolish religion, nor can we coerce people into not believing a religion. Therefore, based on the legal system of the State and the teaching of Chairman Mao, one is unable to locate the basis on which the State has the power to reform religion. Hasn't the State violated its constitution by forcibly reforming the basic tenets and doctrine of a religion when the State has no such authority to do so?

I hope that the government will carry out a thorough investigation and make rectification in order to fulfill the State's spirit of "rule by law", thereby restoring the international reputation that China really does have freedom of religion and belief. This rectification can certainly win the sympathy and support of over one billion faithful believing in God and Jesus Christ, and over three billion believers in God.

F. The three main charges

Knowing that the State has a constitution respecting the freedom of religion and belief, the government reflected in its own judgment that it has no legal power to impose reform and create schism in a religion. Therefore, the judgment did not contain a single word about the fact that I had led the clergy and the faithful to oppose the Three-Self Reform schismatic movement. Instead, it stated the following three main charges:

(1)   I was a leader organizing and leading an anti-revolutionary clique.

(2)   I was in collusion with imperialism.

(3)   I had betrayed the motherland.

This was meant to show conspicuously that I had committed the most heinous crimes, and to exaggerate the legitimacy and flawlessness of the judgment.

Below is my analysis:

(F1)   As the leader organizing and leading an anti-revolutionary clique: Firstly, please state the name, constitution and membership of the clique that I was accused to have organized. I believe that no additional information about the organization can be provided by the government other than the fifteen serving bishops and priests of the so-called counter-revolutionary clique. Bishops and priests are affiliated only to the Church organization, not to anything else. The Church also does not allow us to belong to any extra-judicial organizations and I have never joined any extra-judicial organizations. Moreover, among the fifteen names mentioned, only five were diocesan clergy and the rest were not diocesan staff and were not subject to the jurisdiction of my diocese. How could these visiting staff from other dioceses be grouped into the organization of my diocese?

(F2)   With regard to the collusion with imperialism: This is astounding. I examined my conscience to ask myself: What kind of persons could I have colluded with?

(F2a) If you were referring to the colonial invasion of the European and American powers, then the government should have known that I started to serve as Bishop of Shanghai in August 1950, one year after the "Liberation". By that time, the colonial imperialists had already retreated to their own countries. Or, if referring to the period after their retreat, I had no connection to collude with them. I did not even have an iota of relationship with them. How could I secretly collude with them to cause grave harm to the Chinese nation and the people?

(F2b) If the government was referring to the foreign ecclesiastics who had transferred the diocesan staff to me, or even the Holy See that had religious ties with them, the judgment, in order to demonstrate the rule of law, should have frankly and openly stated their full names, and clearly pointed out what sort of betrayal and collusion I was involved in with them.

(F3)   With regard to betraying my motherland, this made me fume with indignation and become deeply grieved. I was born and brought up here. How could I have the heart to betray my motherland? Therefore, if I ever committed the crimes of jeopardizing the sovereignty of the motherland, conspiring to subvert and divide the country, and betraying the motherland, please state the specific criminal acts concretely in order to expose them. The government should not put any false label on me.

G. Fabrication

Even worse, the judgment indulged in its wildest fantasy, fabricating that the Bishop's House, and the seminaries which were under my management, had secretly kept guns, ammunition and radio stations. I once assured the authorities that of our fifteen people who were collectively sentenced, none of them secretly possessed the above-mentioned prohibited items. I also knew that there was a wooden gun butt without a barrel and a bolt buried inside the Bishop's House. In early August of 1952, when I was living at the Bishop's House in Shanghai, at 36 Sichuan South Road, the financial director of the accountant's office, Father Georges Germain, told me that he had already instructed people to destroy the wooden gun butt and other old, worn-out items found in the store room of the Bishop's House. The place would then have nothing that could be used by people to cause harm.

In September 1955, the arraigner told me that the public security officers had picked up a wooden gun butt from the Bishop's House which was too late to have buried in the soil and had been thrown into a well. Then he showed me an article published in the "Liberation Daily", stating that in the ground of the garden of the Bishop's House, the public security officers, in front of Father Zhu Dayi, dug out a wooden gun butt without a barrel and a bolt. We were accused of intending to use this as a secretly possessed weapon. I replied that this must be the above-mentioned wooden gun butt that was due to be destroyed and buried in the soil by a person who was entrusted to do so, and that it had neither a barrel nor a bolt and could not become a harmful weapon. The judgment stated that this was the gun secretly kept inside the Bishop's House! With regard to the alleged guns and ammunition hidden inside other churches, seminaries and schools, the government had neither specified the locations and the names of the churches nor showed me the photographs in the newspaper. Presumably they could not find the things they needed and thus could not name the places or take any photographs for newspapers. Inasmuch as a trivial thing like a gun butt was reported in the newspaper with its photograph taken, one can imagine what would have happened if these were real guns and ammunition. Hence, this was counter-evidence proving that the guns and ammunition had not existed!

The secret possession of the so-called two radio stations is not even worth laughing about! How could a radio station be privately set up and secretly possessed? If it is called a radio station, it must require transmission engineering techniques, broadcasting staff, broadcasting materials …. These things cannot be hidden inside a box. A radio station needs listeners as well. Can the government display the components of these radio stations launched by me in order to prove their existence? It is impossible to make something out of nothing. Otherwise, the government would have boasted about it. I hope that the government can set these wrongs right to show the public that the rule by law comes first.

H. An analysis of the accusation of sabotaging the three major Movements

The judgment stated that I had engaged in sabotaging the following three major Movements, namely:

    (1)   To Resist U.S. Aggression and To Resist Aiding Korea,

    (2)   The Land Reform Movement, and

(3)   Socialist Construction.

I hereby set forth my appeal in the following:

H/I. Regarding the Movement to Resist U.S. Aggression and to Resist Aiding Korea

The government had seized, among my correspondence, a memorandum in French sent by the Diocesan Legal Advisor and the Superior of the Society of Jesus, a French priest Father Fernand Lacretelle, and signed by him on the 27th of April 1951. It contains six points, describing his evaluation of the political campaigns regarding Church doctrine within and outside the country over the past year, and the concrete actions needed to address them. One of the points was a notice by Father Lacretelle to inform the Jesuits who were working in the city area. He instructed them to urge parents and teachers to teach the young Catholics wishing to join the army or the cadre voluntarily to consider the risk of losing the Catholic faith after their stint in the military, because they would be learning Marxist-Leninist atheism and materialism during the stint. In this way, Father Lacretelle's aim was to urge the young Catholics to think carefully so as to avoid the risk of losing their faith. It had the effect of making the young Catholics less inclined to join the army and the cadre. Father Lacretelle himself should bear this responsibility. As I took the laissez-faire attitude of letting Father Lacretelle to do whatever he wants, I should also bear some of the responsibility.

In the memorandum, Superior Lacretelle commented that the War to Resist US Aggression and to Resist Aiding Korea was "not absolutely a just war". However, the judgement, based on the arbitrary distortion made by the arraigner, altered it to "an absolutely unjust war". This was definitely an unjust slander. With regard to this distortion, a copy is available in the court for inspection. The original text in French was: *La guerre de Corée n'est pas absolument juste*, which should be translated into: The Korean War is not absolutely just. The judgment wrote this as "absolutely is an unjust war". Everyone knows that these two translations are completely different in their meaning.

Father Fernand Lacretelle closed Xujiahui Jesuit House at midnight on the 15th of June, 1953, and was arrested when foreign priests, brothers and nuns were expelled from China. After being detained for fourteen months, he was expelled from China as the result of what he was accused to have done. However, the judgment made me shoulder the heavier burden of being solely responsible for ordering clergy and faithful to engage in sabotaging the Movement of Resisting the US Aggression and of Resisting to Aid Korea. This was an unjust statement, an unjust exaggeration.

H/II. Regarding the Land Reform Law

In the autumn of 1950, the government implemented land reforms. In mid-October, while visiting the Jinshan district, Songjiang for Church matters, I saw land-division signs erected all over the land, which indicated the completion of the land distribution. Father Fernand Lacretelle had conducted an academic talk on the Church's views on land reforms, a hot topic in the world, at Aurora University. In order to enable the missionaries in suburban areas to have an understanding of the Church's views on this issue, I had invited Father Lacretelle to conduct the talk on the Church's views on the land reform issue again when the missionaries had their regular academic talks during the retreat at Dongjiadu clergy house.

For many years, because the clergy house had only about forty rooms, the clergy retreat, which was held in the first two months of every year (i.e. before or after the Chinese New Year) was conducted in two groups. Each group had about forty people and lasted for six full days. With regard to that retreat held in 1951, as the priests of the two dioceses of Suzhou and Haimen also wished to join the retreat at Dongjiadu, we added one more group to meet their needs in mid-December of 1950. This made a total of three rounds of retreats. This was meant to adapt to the needs of the neighboring dioceses and was absolutely not intended to pioneer three rounds of retreats in order to "convene and instruct one hundred and twenty priests from the three dioceses to sabotage the Land Reform Law". According to our old practice, we had a break in summer and a retreat in winter. When the missionary priests had two gatherings at Dongjiadu, there were normally two occasions when professors of theology and canon law experts came to Dongjiadu to conduct academic talks on theological theories and canon law. After the talks, the priests raised questions and the speakers gave explanations and answered their questions, as in the classroom discussions.

That year, the conversations during the talks on the new issues of land reforms inevitably involved comments that could be criticized by the government if we violated the spirit of land reforms. However, they were definitely not criminal rallies designed to sabotage the land reforms by following what the authority erroneously called "reactionary" instructions of the Holy See as conveyed by James Edward Walsh, and the "reactionary" orders made by Fernand Lacretelle.

Furthermore, when the implementation of land reforms commenced in early 1950, the diocese had already asked all the pastors and parish priests to come and collect the land deeds and farmland documents, which totaled about ten thousand *mu* (unit of one Chinese acre) of land in the outlying counties. These deeds and documents were kept in the Bishop's House. They were all submitted to the peasant association for processing and destruction, in order to show that we abided by the law. How could I be so stupid as to make unreasonable and unbeneficial criminal opposition to the "Land Reform" again in December 1950, January and February 1951, after all the land had been returned to the peasants? Moreover, I was alleged to have ordered the clergy, during the talks at the three rounds of retreats between December 1950 and 1951, to sabotage the land reform work, which had already been completed by mid-November 1950. Was it not an illogical lie that had distorted the time sequence? Therefore, the case compiled in the judgment was a false charge which ran contrary to the facts and the details.

H/III. Regarding the General Line for Socialist Construction Movement

In 1953, the Holy See declared 1954 as the Marian Year to mark the celebration of the 100th anniversary of the dogma of the Immaculate Conception proclaimed on the 8th of December 1854. I subsequently issued to the faithful a "pastoral letter" (an open letter addressed by a bishop to the faithful), encouraging the faithful to observe the rules, receive Holy Communion as often as possible, take worldly blessings lightly, walk firmly on "the way to Heaven" and offer their love to Mary Immaculate. The writer of the pastoral letter, Zhou Shiliang, inspired by the wording of the widely-known General Line at that time, changed the old saying "the way to Heaven" into "the line to the Kingdom of Heaven" in order to keep up with the current trend. With regard to this change of wording, the verdict judged that the use of "the line to the Kingdom of Heaven" was against the line of the nation during the transitional period. In view of this, I believe that the sharp-sighted government may not support this kind of literary inquisition during a democratic era.

With regard to the three above-mentioned points, I should admit without reservation and be willing to do penance if any of these crimes were committed by me. Regarding the frame-ups and erroneous accusations, I hereby hope that the government will rectify and redress them to accomplish the rule by law.

I. Unfortunate illusion

In September 1955, soon after my arrest, I admitted to the arraigner that, as described in Section C, I had led clergy and faithful to oppose the schismatic Three-Self Reform Movement in order to maintain the fundamental beliefs of the Holy Catholic Church, and had encouraged the faithful to be martyrs and to sacrifice their lives in the pursuit of virtue, rather than, under any circumstances, to seek life at the expense of virtue. I encouraged them that it was better to die proudly than to live in disgrace so as to maintain the loyalty and purity of their spirits. However, I did not plead guilty to fulfilling my duty: Protecting my religion and safeguarding the doctrine are the duties of bishops and priests. Whoever holds this post will perform the duties thereof until their death. All bishops and priests in the world must fulfill their duties with their lives even unto death. Then, I ask, what crimes had I committed by protecting my religion and safeguarding its doctrine in a country which had freedom of religion and belief?

In the spring of 1956, I read an article in the *People's Daily* reporting that the then Vicar Capitular of Shanghai, Father Zhang Shilang, made a speech at the National People's Congress in Beijing. He said that the government had returned one hundred and forty-four churches to the Church over the past six months, specially offered some preferential treatment such as education for our young Catholics and employment for our strong Catholics, and also did not forcibly implement the schismatic Movements including the Three-Self Reform Movement. After reading this news article, I mistakenly believed that the government was taking a serious and trustworthy approach in the implementation of the constitution for the freedom of religion and belief and thus regretted my past when I thought that the government had implemented the policy to exterminate religion and, consequently, had strongly resisted this. Thus, I created illogical sophistries, arguing that "whoever is against the reactionary government is a reactionary", and considered myself as a reactionary, bringing pain and sorrow to my friends and the faithful. This was the unfortunate illusion that caused me to grieve deeply all the time. Indeed, the facts speak for themselves. Good times do not last long. In August of the following year (1957), when the Catholic Patriotic Association was established in Beijing, the first President, Pi Shushi, and others telegraphed the Roman Pontiff directly to sever their religious communion with him, self-consecrating bishops, self-managing the Church, creating the first schismatic Church in China, and accomplishing the aim of the Three-Self Reform Movement.

In the beginning of the Cultural Revolution in 1965, under the fanatic zeal of the Gang of Four, churches and cathedrals in Shanghai and other places were closed and damaged. Bibles, holy statues, altars, and sacred vestments were burnt and destroyed. Clergy were detained. The support of the constitution for the freedom of religion and belief had been swept away without a trace altogether. The only thing in the Catholic Church across the country that had survived was just the invisible church of the sacred love of Jesus Christ cherished deep in the hearts of the faithful. Alas, what a disastrous illusion!

J. Betraying the trust

I recall that in the spring of 1956, I felt remorseful and sorrowful (for my action of resisting the government under the belief that the government had implemented the policy of exterminating religion); because, at that time, I sincerely, but mistakenly, believed that the government was making a serious attempt to implement the constitution of freedom of religion and beliefs. Under this excitement, in late March, with my heart-felt sincerity, I clearly disclosed to the government that there were 1,830 taels (unit of one Chinese ounce) of gold buried on my property. This gold was bequeathed by former Bishop Auguste Haouissée from the evangelization fund. On the 4th of April, the government told me that the buried valuables had been unearthed in full. Therefore, from the 12th of June onwards, I was given fifty cents per day for medium-rank meals, which was alleged to be stipulated by the court. Later, the government wanted me to admit that this amount of buried gold belonged to the former financial director, Father Georges Germain, for use of reactionary movement. I refuted it resolutely. It was right and proper for the former financial director, prior to his departure of duty, to transfer to the diocese the cash, and assets, along with more than two thousand acres of land and three thousand houses in the city. How could it be said to be reactionary funds privately given by him? However, the government staff betrayed my trust towards the government and fabricated the details for the purpose of confiscation. I hereby set forth an appeal to the government and request that the government handle this appeal with impartiality to the end.

A summary reiterating the whole story

A Letter of Appeal

Dear Mr. Jiang Hua, President of the Supreme People's Court in Beijing,

The appellant, Kung Pin-Mei, was the Bishop of the Shanghai diocese as well as the Apostolic Administrator of the Suzhou diocese and the Nanjing archdiocese from 1949 to 1955.

On the 8th of September 1955, I was arrested by the Public Security Bureau of Shanghai City. On the 17th of March 1960, I was sentenced to life imprisonment by the Shanghai Intermediate People's Court.

On the 13th of November 1979, I submitted to the Supreme People's Court a letter of over 8,000 words concerning the judgment of Shanghai Criminal Case No. 162 made in 1960. In the letter, I set forth an analysis of, and an appeal against, the judgment and requested that you handle the appeal with impartiality to the end, and to discover right from wrong.

The letter, which was submitted to you by the City Prison in an official envelope through the internal postal system, should have reached you safely without delay. However, it has already been two years that I have not received any word from you. Therefore, instead of venturing to write another lengthy letter, I hereby sincerely request that you handle my first letter of appeal, and my follow-up letter, which requested that you handle my appeal as soon as possible, in order to implement a fair policy which shows that the nation is governed by the rule of law.

Yours truly,

Kung Pin-Mei

Appellant

17th November, 1981

In the following three to four years, I made the same request to the Supreme Court. However, I have not received a single word of reply. In 1985, the Section Chief, Mr. Ding, came to understand my case. I thought that he was an honest person and trustingly gave Mr. Ding the original copy of my letter of appeal and the manuscript of the second letter. However, he not only did not verify with the City Prison regarding my letter of appeal to the Supreme Court, but even deceived me that I would be granted parole on the 3rd of July 1985, and then would be released as soon as possible. Until today the 18th of January 1987, I am still in detention because, with determination, I will not agree to sever my religious communion with the Roman Pontiff.

I hereby make my appeal again to the government according to the factual evidence.

Handwritten by Kung Pin-Mei

18th January, 1987

Appendix 13

The Stations of the Cross composed by Bishop Kung during his imprisonment.[246]

Introduction

The Holy City Spattered with Blood: Fourteen Stations of the Cross

The distance from the hall of the Roman Governor Pontius Pilate to Mount Calvary measured only 4 to 5 miles, but it was rugged and treacherous—sloping as it descended to exit the Western Gate, then through the valley and finally climbing Mount Calvary. Walking to complete this journey with serious wounds all over His body and carrying a heavy wooden Cross on His shoulder, Jesus' agony truly defies our imagination!

As an act of reparation and gratitude, early Christians frequently assembled to retrace Jesus' steps to His crucifixion, venerating and reflecting on the fourteen stations. Passing down from generations to the present days, Catholics all over the

---

[246] Cardinal Kung Foundation Archives. Stamford October 5, 2012, Joseph Kung to Monsignor Stephen DiGiovanni, Basilica Archives. These Stations of the Cross were written in Chinese by Bishop Kung in 1985 while under house arrest under the watch of the Patriotic Association Bishop of Shanghai. After their completion, Bishop Kung entrusted them to Father Ai, the parochial vicar at the Cathedral of Shanghai, who had been ordained by Bishop Kung years earlier. The priest gave the manuscript of the Stations of the Cross to an American-Chinese lady visiting Shanghai, asking that she bring them out of the country. Fearful that her luggage and hotel might be searched, she hand-copied the Stations of the Cross and mailed them to Hong Kong, then destroyed the originals. She was subsequently searched and detained, and warned that if she published any documents about Bishop Kung after her return to the United States, her relatives in China and Fr. Ai would be punished. When Bishop Kung arrived in Connecticut, the lady returned her copy of the Stations to him, explaining that she had destroyed the original. Bishop Kung reviewed the copy she had made and wrote a few corrections, since the lady had miscopied some of the Chinese characters. The meditations are truly of Bishop Kung's composition. The present translation was completed by Agnes Kung and her sister Magdalene Lie. While Cardinal Kung lived at the Queen of Clergy Retirement Home at Saint Joseph Hospital in Stamford, Connecticut, he daily prayed these Stations of the Cross in the hospital chapel at 3:00 pm, followed by twenty minutes of meditation before the Blessed Sacrament. This became well known. Even the homeless knew his schedule. On two occasions, a man asked for money for train fare, and another asked for food. The Cardinal left the chapel, went upstairs to his room, and returned with $5.00 for each man. When the hospital superior, Sister Daniel Marie, heard of this, she was alarmed. "The Bishop survived in jail for 30 years", she is reported to have said. "The last thing I want is for him to be hurt in the hospital." She alerted the hospital security guards to be more attentive to the homeless when the Cardinal was nearby. But the good Cardinal did not mind in the least.

world often make the Way of the Cross as devotion in thanksgiving for our redemption and to show our deep love for Jesus.

The First Station:

Condemning the Innocent One to Death—An Unjust Verdict

A crowd of Jews intimidated the cowardly Pilate with a fanatic demonstration and secured from him an unjust verdict. The Roman soldiers then tore off the blood stained scarlet cloak from Jesus' sacred body, and they clothed Him in His own garment. They immediately brought forth an already prepared big, heavy wooden cross, forcibly put it on His shoulder, and started him towards the West Gate of the Holy City to Calvary, the execution site, to be crucified. Thus a grievous crime of injustice against an Innocent was committed!

We adore You, O Christ, and we praise You;

Because by Your Holy Cross You have redeemed the world.

The Second Station:

Embrace the Cross and Follow Christ

Jesus viewed the Cross as the instrument of salvation for mankind and as the Divine will of His Father. In total obedience, Jesus accepted the Holy Cross willingly and climbed Calvary to complete the redemption of mankind with the sacrifice of His own blood. Oh, we venerate the Holy Cross—for sinners you unlock the gate of heaven and shut the gate of hell; you are the ardent hope of mankind and peace to the sorrowful; to the persons of goodwill, you give them spiritual strength to overcome temptations, to conquer the three enemies: the devil, the world and the flesh, and to secure the promise of heaven.

But we are fearful of suffering and death, and live lives of dreams. Rarely do we dare to ask for the grace of your Cross to follow You up Calvary. Therefore, though we dare not ask for Your Cross, we implore You to grant us the grace to embrace the Cross in our lives and not to run away from its burden.

We adore You, O Christ, and we praise You;

Because by Your Holy Cross You have redeemed the world.

The Third Station:

Jesus Falls the First Time

Toward noon, Jesus succumbed to hunger and injury. Suffering from extreme fatigue and with the weight of the heavy Cross crushing down His injured back, His sacred body stumbled to the ground. But, Jesus endured patiently and pressed forward without complaint or resentment in order to fulfill the will of His Father.

Jesus, grant me grace to see myself clearly, not to commit sins and wicked deeds that were the cause of Your falls and great suffering. Let me resolve not to sin again, or at least to be less sinful that I might reduce Your burden. I beg You to grant me endurance to bear insults and suffering as penance for my sins; grant me perseverance and courage to walk the rugged road of life, full of obstacles, and not to be afraid to rise from every fall, to follow You, My Lord, closely, never to falter or lag behind.

We adore You, O Christ, and we praise You;

Because by Your Holy Cross You have redeemed the world.

The Fourth Station:

Meeting on the Way to Calvary

Along the winding road stood the Blessed Mother and John, waiting to bid Jesus farewell. What a heart-wrenching meeting between a mother and a son—the heart of the Blessed Mother cradling the sorrowful Jesus while Jesus' heart holding His weeping Mother. Both hearts were pierced, suffering extreme sorrow in silence.

Most Holy and Sorrowful Virgin Mary, pray for us so that we can benefit from the promises of Jesus Christ. O Blessed Mother, I am the cause of your son's suffering, my sins are grave—they are the swords piercing through your heart. I do not deserve your mercy. However, knowing Your boundless kindness, please intercede for me with Jesus Christ, Your Son, that He might forgive my sins. At the hour of my death, let me see Jesus who will take me to enjoy eternal happiness in heaven. Amen.

We adore You, O Christ, and we praise You;

Because by Your Holy Cross You have redeemed the world.

The Fifth Station:

Embrace the Cross

The mob feared that Jesus might die of serious wounds before reaching Mount Calvary to be crucified. They forced a passer-by, Simon, to help Jesus carry His heavy Cross to the execution site. Simon was blessed to perform this act, an act that the apostles were not given the opportunity to perform in their filial love for Jesus. If you are envious of Simon, you only need to endure patiently all kinds of hardships in your life: poverty, sickness, trials and tribulations in carrying out your daily duties. This is the way of carrying the Cross given to you by God. If you can actively preach the Gospel, save more souls, and share in Jesus' work of salvation, you will be helping Jesus in carrying His Cross as Simon had done.

We adore You, O Christ, and we praise You;

Because by Your Holy Cross You have redeemed the world.

The Sixth Station:

Adoration of His Sacred Image

Veronica, a brave holy woman, was moved by Jesus' soiled, bloodstained face. She braved the cruel ferocious mobs, rushed directly to Jesus and offered her veil to wipe His holy face. To reward Veronica's righteous courage, Jesus imprinted His sacred image on her veil.

O my Jesus, grant me the grace to always see You—mankind's most beautiful image! Please preserve my fidelity to You. Let me not be stained with sins lest I would be ashamed to venerate Your Holy Face. Grant me courage not to recoil from my duties due to suffering or even death. Grant me prudence to clearly recognize false belief by focusing on the vision of Your Holy Face.

We adore You, O Christ, and we praise You;

Because by Your Holy Cross, you have redeemed the world.

The Seventh Station:

Jesus Falls Again

Jesus carried the Cross through the West gate. Overcome by exhaustion, He fell again at the feet of sinners, subjected to trampling and ridicule.

O my meek and kind Savior, You got up and pushed on for my redemption without any complaint. From dust I came, but my sins cast me even lower. I was arrogant and conceited, putting myself above others. With this attitude I not only deceived others, I also fooled myself. Shamefully I committed the serious sin of pride. I now repent with humility. I beg my Lord to forgive me all my past sins and grant me the virtue of charity and humility.

We adore You, O Christ, and we praise you;

Because by Your Holy Cross, You have redeemed the world.

The Eighth Station:

Weep for Your Sins

As Jesus exited the gate, some women who were following Jesus were weeping with great compassion. Jesus consoled them and said, "Women of Jerusalem, weep not for my suffering, but weep for the sins that caused my suffering. Weep also for the future disaster that shall befall you and your children. There shall be fire and destruction of the temple and the holy city, the killing and enslavement of the people, and the great suffering of the end of a nation."

O Jesus, I implore You to give me tears to cleanse my soul and the resolve to sin no more so that I can avoid the heavy punishment due for my sins.

We adore You, O Christ, and we praise you;

Because by Your Holy Cross, You have redeemed the world.

The Ninth Station:

The Third Fall and Rise of Jesus

Jesus descended a hilly slope from the East Hill of the Holy City before climbing Mount Calvary again. Under the crushing weight of the wooden Cross, Jesus fell to the ground for the third time. This fall caused him the most intense pain which cut His mouth and teeth and opened wide His sacred wounds. Eager to redeem the world, three times Jesus fell and rose again; each time He fell heavily but each time He struggled quickly to His feet, bravely pushing forward to His execution site to complete His great act of redemption.

O Jesus, give me spiritual strength and fortitude. Grant me not only wisdom to discern temptations, but also an unshakable will not to commit sin. If I should fall, let me not be afraid to get up and try again, to follow Your footsteps and never succumb to fear or despair.

We adore You, O Christ, and we praise you;

Because by Your Holy Cross, You have redeemed the world.

The Tenth Station:

Nailing My own Desire to the Cross

His back hunched, Jesus stumbled along, forcing Himself forward, muscles contorted, limbs almost paralyzed with fatigue. He collapsed on the edge of the crucifixion site. A soldier moved Him to the center of the site and tore off His blood-soaked garments taking with it His skin and flesh. This exposed Jesus' naked mangled body, subjecting Him to unspeakable humiliation and pain. They further forced Jesus to drink some sour wine to increase His pain.

Jesus, I indulged sinfully in sumptuous food, fashion, and sexual pleasure, thus causing You this humiliation and suffering. I resolve to renounce all sins related to gluttony, seductive clothing, and passions of the flesh, so that I may show my gratitude to You for Your suffering caused by me.

We adore You, O Christ, and we praise you;

Because by Your Holy Cross, You have redeemed the world.

The Eleventh Station:

You Pierced My Hands and My Feet, and Counted My Bones

Taking a hammer, the soldiers pounded three large nails into Jesus' hands and feet. Then, they tied His sacred body to the Cross. Imagine the big iron nails piercing Jesus' flesh, slicing tendons, and being forced between the bones of His limbs. What horrific pain! What cruelty! This was a torturous punishment designed for the worst criminals and slaves—never for a Roman citizen. Lying on the Cross with outstretched arms and legs, Jesus suffered the crucifixion to redeem my sins of succumbing to worldly pleasures and uncontrolled desires.

From now on, I resolve to nail my passions and desires to the Cross with Jesus, in order to eliminate the root cause of my sins.

We adore You, O Christ, and we praise You;

Because by Your Holy Cross, You have redeemed the world.

The Twelfth Station:

All Generations Venerate the Holy Cross

At noon, the soldiers elevated the Cross and placed it between two crucified criminals one of whom was cynical and insulting to Jesus Christ. With every movement of the Cross, Jesus' wounds were further split apart. O Holy Son of God, what suffering! What humiliation!

Behold, hanging high on the Cross was the sacred body of Jesus, all naked, broken and racked!

Jesus Christ, we adore You and we praise You. I kneel before You and humbly confess my sins. I know that it was my sins that pierced Your hands and feet, caused You to shed your Holy Blood, crowned Your head with thorns and smeared Your face with spittle and dirt. It was my sins that pierced Your chest and heart. My sins caused Your most perfect body to be trampled upon like worthless creatures in the mud. Jesus, it was the sins of my life that were the cause of Your suffering. I am not worthy of looking at Your Holy Face. I implore You to forgive all my sins. I will not sin against You again.

We adore You, O Christ, and we praise You;

Because by Your Holy Cross, You have redeemed the world.

Jesus Bowed His Head and Died

It was the day before Passover (Saturday, 14th of Nisan]. Jesus' body had been hanging on the Cross since noon—His entire body weight suspended by three nails. His crown of thorns prevented Him from looking up towards heaven; He could only look at the jeering, abusing crowd below. O what unspeakable heart-wrenching torture! He had remained in this state for three hours when He cried in a loud voice: "It is finished." Jesus then bowed His head and gave up His spirit.

At that moment, the sky darkened and moved, the earth trembled, the whole world turned dark. Graves split open. Onlookers struck their breasts and wailed in remorseful agony. Heaven and earth moaned over Jesus' tragic death. Many of them said, "This man is indeed the Son of God." Who else could have brought forth such an astounding change on the whole earth?" In fear they covered their heads and faces and dispersed. Remaining beneath the Cross were the Blessed Mother, John, Mary Magdalene, and some other holy women weeping in unspeakable compassion for the death of Jesus, their Lord and Savior.

One of the soldiers came and broke the legs of the two crucified thieves in order to speed up their deaths. To make sure that Jesus was indeed dead, he thrust his lance through His ribs into His Holy Heart, and out flowed the last drops of His precious blood.

Jesus, may Your passion and death strengthen me and never let me betray You.

We adore You, O Christ, and we praise You;

Because by Your Holy Cross, You have redeemed the world.

The Thirteenth Station:

The Burial of the Holy Body

A man by the name of Joseph of Arimathea, together with Nicodemus (both were disciples in secret), petitioned Pilate and they received the body of Jesus. They brought along tools and took Jesus' sacred body and placed it at the bosom of His Blessed Mother. Conforming to the Jewish custom, they anointed the body with perfumed oils then wrapped it in burial cloth. They placed the body in a newly hewn tomb prepared for Joseph of Arimathea himself, then they rolled a big rock against its entrance. Because it was the day of preparation for the Sabbath, the Blessed Mother and the holy people helping in the burial needed to complete the ceremony quickly. Then they descended the mountain in great sadness and returned to the city.

Now the chief priests sent guards to keep watch over the tomb, in order to stop Jesus from fulfilling His prophecy of rising from the dead on the third day. The poor fools' plan was defeated. No one even attempted to steal Jesus' body in the night while the soldiers were guarding the tomb. But at the predicted time, Jesus was gloriously raised from the dead. Thus the guards who were sent there to prevent the resurrection became witnesses to the resurrection.

We adore You, O Christ, and we praise You;

Because by Your Holy Cross, You have redeemed the world.

The Fourteenth Station:

Mourning the Death of Jesus

The sacred Body of Jesus was now laid to rest in a stone tomb. We ought to reflect on His life. He spent over thirty years glorifying God and teaching us His divine way. He endured agonizing pain, insufferable humiliation during the crucifixion. Now, all this was over and the price paid for the redemption of all mankind and for all generations. He paid for the sins of mankind; He manifested the glory of God; He set the example to exhort mankind to put aside their own desires; and He instituted sacraments to give us the Grace to do good and to avoid evils. If only mankind would follow Jesus' teaching and make good use of the sacraments, everyone could be assured of the Kingdom of God. O Victory! Victory! Triumph and glory to our Lord Jesus Christ, Alleluia!

We adore You, O Christ, and we praise You;

Because by Your holy Cross, You have redeemed the world.

Meditation on the Crucifixion of Jesus

Our Lord Jesus is on the Cross. His whole body is covered with wounds, His hands and feet are nailed to the Cross, His head is crowned with thorns, for His drink, only vinegar and bitter gall. Although He suffered so much, He knows that many will remain indifferent. This mental anguish is even more painful than His physical torment.

God suffered so much for me. Why am I not willing to give up some worldly pleasure and accept some suffering in this life? I know well that Jesus suffered in reparation for my sins and yet I still go against His will and commit sin. How can I reject His grace and increase His sorrow?

Jesus accepted suffering inflicted by every kind of person. The apostles betrayed Him, the Jews made accusations against Him, the Gentiles cursed Him, high priests, officials, soldiers and people all determined to kill Him. Because Jesus suffered in order to save all classes of people, so He accepted sufferings caused by all kinds of people, including all of us. Are we not increasing His suffering by our lack of faith, committing sin and not loving His Sacred Heart?

Where was our Blessed Mother at that time? She was weeping beside the Cross, watching Her Son suffer. This was not just the human love between mother and son. She united her love of Jesus with her love for all mankind, offering it in sacrifice to God the Father for the salvation of the whole world. Our Lady is indeed the Mother of our salvation.

Each and every one of us should imitate Our Blessed Lady, contemplating Jesus on the Cross. We should offer our sufferings in reparation for our sins and those of others, asking for mercy and forgiveness and not fail to respond to the graces Jesus obtained for us through His Passion.

Meditation on the Burial of Jesus:

With His death and burial a pessimistic, shortsighted person may have questioned: What came out of Jesus' thirty years of preaching throughout Judea? What result is remaining now? Those who were converted by miracles have dispersed out of disappointment and for fear of the angry and threatening crowds. Peter, the leader among the twelve apostles, had a strong spirit but his flesh was weak. Three times he rejected his master due to fear of suffering an ignominious death; Judas betrayed his master for money, later fell into despair and committed suicide; the rest of the apostles had all but vanished; Jesus himself had died and was buried, dashing the grand hope of reviving the Kingdom of Israel and spreading the Gospel of salvation. All hope dashed; all seemed finished. . . .

O people of little faith, have you forgotten that the Messiah was to suffer first before He would be glorified? Followers of Christ similarly must bear their Cross before experiencing joy, submitting to the will of God, accepting temporary difficulties and setbacks before attaining total and everlasting victory and happiness.

Consider this: Suppose the Messiah was to be born to royalty with boundless wealth. He would employ worldly power to achieve success in glorifying God and redeeming mankind without much effort or worries! But the children of Adam and Eve, living in this valley of tears and enduring hunger and cold, would blame this Messiah for not living up to what He preached, generous to Himself but mean to mankind without Himself experiencing their hardship. How could such a descendant of royalty assume the honor of the Messiah according to the prophecies?

Consider again: Suppose that when Jesus was being arrested by the temple soldiers at the Garden of Gethsemane, God the Father had sent twelve legions of angels to rescue Him from their grip; or suppose Jesus came down on His own from the Cross to prove that He was indeed the Son of God. . . .our redemption then would have been achieved through the working of miracles. But, in reality, it was not to be so:

1. Redemption would not have been accomplished since it was not in accordance with God's plan; 2. When the Church eventually spread to Rome, its faithful would witness the destruction of churches and holy sites, and the cruel killing of the apostles and early Christians. His followers questioned: why did God the Father rescue only His Divine Son, and ignored the injustice done to His sons' faithful children? As to the arrests: If God really existed would He not unlock the prison gates and iron cuffs of the disciples and Christians to silence all ridicule? How would these questions be answered?

Therefore, since God the Father did not rescue His dying Son, permitting rather the completion of the redemptive sacrifice, would God have saved the Christians from temporary sufferings that would deprive them of the martyr's crown of glory?

Let us meditate deeply on the lessons Jesus gave to the two disciples on their way to Emmaus: Christ's followers must not be consumed with self-pity whenever their faith is being tested. Sink not to the level of a stray dog without any sense of belonging. On the contrary, rejoice in the glory of being able to share in the suffering of our Messiah.

Appendix 14

Cardinal Kung's Meditations on the Seven Last Words of Christ. [247]

First. "My God, why have you forsaken me?"

The Lamb of God, silent unto death! Never moaned even under immense suffering, being whipped or crucified, bearing unimaginable cruelty. And yet, why did He cry to His heavenly Father, "My God, my God, why have you forsaken me?" This is similar to His remarks to the apostles when He prayed at Gethsemane, "My soul is sorrowful even unto death." This is the manifestation of the immeasurable deep sorrow and pain in His soul, a million times more so than His physical pain.

When we sin, we commit a despicable act of turning against God and submitting ourselves to material desires. We deserve to be forsaken in vengeance by all creatures of heaven and earth. In the state of sin, a person feels that his happiness of the past has vanished in a flash and he sinks into a state of bitterness with self-hatred. The greater his sin, the deeper his anguish. Having nowhere to hide and having no courage to live in disgrace, a sinner may wish to seek an end to his dishonored existence. Such is the mental punishment and vengeance of sins. For one Person to bear the pain and vengeance of the sins committed by millions & trillions of people, the suffering of Jesus was indeed beyond imagination!

Jesus, our Savior came to pay the debts and atone for the sins of mankind from all ages. The most righteous Father in heaven wanted His holy son to fully experience the mental anguish and the punishment that ought to be borne by countless sinners -- so as to equate the price of mankind's sins. The Sacred Heart of Jesus bore the pain for our sins. For this, Jesus felt the pain and anguish of being forsaken by His Father. This is the cause of the sorrowful cry of the Lamb of God who takes away the sins of the world.

Man may be able to empathize and imagine the torturous pain suffered by Jesus, such as His flesh being flailed by the whips or His hands and feet being pierced by nails, but how can man ever fully comprehend the enormously deep sorrow in Jesus heart? Let us now try, with empathy, to meditate on the enormity of Christ's suffering.

---

[247] Cardinal Kung Foundation. Bishop Kung composed these meditations after he was paroled after more than 30 years in prison on July 3, 1985, while he was still under house arrest by the Chinese government, under the watchful eyes of the Patriotic Association, the government version of the Catholic Church.

Second. "Father, forgive them, for they know not what they do"

Didn't the omniscient Christ know all about the hatred of his accusers and the soldiers? Didn't Christ see their pride & obstinacy, blind even to the miracle of the resurrection of Lazarus? They plotted to kill Lazarus to destroy the evidence of the miracle. They were deaf to the welcome cry of truth, "Jesus, Son of God, our Messiah!" Instead, they accused Jesus of the crime of blasphemy and condemned Him to be crucified.

No, No, Jesus knew well of the vicious intent and relentless evil of his accusers. Jesus' pleading to His Father for forgiveness only shows that He returned hatred with kindness, did not bear grudges or vengeful intent; instead, He defended sinners and absolved the debts caused by the sins of His enemies.

O Jesus, the first to bestow mercy and forgiveness! I implore you to grant me the grace to sincerely forgive those who tried to defile my image, destroy my name and endanger my life. Let me wholeheartedly forgive my enemies who conspire and sin against me.

Third. "Woman, behold, your son....Behold, your mother."

John, so very blessed! In a twinkle of an eye, he rose from being the son of Zebedee to become the adopted son of the Virgin Mary and the brother of Jesus.

Jesus used John to represent all mankind, making sure that men would not be poor helpless orphans in this valley of tears. Instead, similar to the position of John the apostle, men were suddenly elevated into the position of being the adopted sons of Blessed Mother and the brothers of Jesus.

John would not leave the Blessed Mother, closely following Jesus while He carried the cross up the hill, until John stood at the foot of the cross at the top of the hill. Thus John was rewarded with the blessing of being able to bid farewell to the King of kings.

Holy Mary, merciful Mother of God, we implore you to protect us just as you care for all who belong to you. Let us never desert you, nor depart from your Son, Jesus.

Fourth. "This day you will be with me in Paradise."

Deaf to the ugly ridicule and curses of the mob, but sensitive to the sinners' pleas and repentant prayers is the usual practice of our merciful Jesus towards sinners. Thus Jesus was silent to the accusations that He claimed to be King, that He encouraged people not to pay taxes to Caesar, to rebel against the ruler of Rome, and the priests challenged Jesus to descend from the cross as a proof that He was the Son of God. To all these wild accusations and challenges, Jesus was as silent and submissive as a lamb. However, as soon as he heard the repentant plea of one of the thieves crucified with Him, begging to be remembered in His heaven, Jesus immediately granted his request, promising that he would be with Him in paradise that day.

The way that Jesus was quick in listening to prayers and generous in bestowing grace leaves me touched beyond words. O, Jesus, with total reliance on you, I pray that I may be blessed with the humility to pray frequently, not to be arrogant or despairing, so that one day I may be able to enter the kingdom of God with you.

Fifth. "I thirst."

Jesus' whole body was covered with wounds and He was bleeding profusely; this loss of blood was the source of His thirst. But Jesus was not referring just to His physical thirst, but to the thirst for the completion of His Father's work-- to save mankind and to redeem the world. He thirsts for saving more souls to enable all mankind to enjoy eternal happiness in heaven; He thirsts for mankind to keep His commandments, to receive sacramental grace and thus complete the work of redemption for the glory of God.

Sixth. "Father, into your hands I commend my spirit.

This is an example of the most comforting and effective prayer that the merciful Jesus has given us to use at the critical and painful hours of our death.

Most Holy Cross, we worship you and we venerate you! You are the support to sinners at their final hours, the comfort to the sick, the frightened and worried, and the means to total indulgence. O most beautiful Holy Cross, I hold you and I kiss you, I'll never let you leave my heart. Jesus, I firmly believe in you! I eagerly look towards you! Jesus, I fervently love you! I place my soul in your hands! Lead me safely across the ocean of this world; let me safely pass through my critical final hours and ascend to the heavenly kingdom.

Seventh. "It is finished."

The coming of the Messiah as foretold by the prophets and ancient fathers for several thousand years was fulfilled. The work to redeem mankind was accomplished to the full through immense sufferings; the debt for the sins of mankind was repaid; the verdict of Original Sin was removed and cleansed with blood; humanity has been restored to filial sonship as children of God which was originally intended by the Creator; the mission given by His Heavenly Father had been brilliantly accomplished. By his holy example and grace, Jesus helped mankind to do good and avoid evil; He proclaimed the ways to practice virtue and attain sacramental grace. He has clearly spelled out the conditions to steadily walk the way towards heaven. By abiding and practicing His teaching, everyone can enjoy eternal happiness.

Appendix 15

The First Public Sermon preached by Bishop Ignatius Kung after his release, given on the 33rd anniversary of the arrests of Catholics in Shanghai, Saint Joseph Medical Center, Stamford, Connecticut, September 8, 1988. [248]

My Brothers and Sisters in Christ:

Today is September 8, the Feast of our Holy Mother's Birth. We specially bear in our hearts the spirit of thanksgiving and the quest for greater mercy in offering up this special Mass. Thirty-three years ago to this day, was the time when over thirty priests, several dozens of seminarians and sisters and several hundred children of the faith belonging to the Shanghai Diocese were arrested and taken into custody. It commemorates the beginning of our silent and suffering Church laboring in the travail of every type and kind of hardship. During these months and years of bitter pain, how many religious superiors and sons and daughters of Christ, have remained loyal and true. They have borne heroically their cross, they have been sent to prison, forced to do manual labor; some have had to leave their homes and their families, abandon their wives and their children, and furthermore they have been confronted with unemployment or expulsion from school. And what is more, some have sacrificed their precious lives. And all for what? They are not confused, nor are they foolish, and all this in order to obey the teaching of Jesus Christ: never abandon the Good Lord, always preserve their pristine faith, always maintain the priceless dignity of being His sons by adoption, never to become rebels against their Holy Mother, the Church, possessed of the determination to die in the defense of the Church.

Today, all of you seated in front of me, all brothers and sisters in Christ, have been able to guard our faith intact. Loyal to Christ and his Church, loyal to the Pontiff, because of the signal grace which God has bestowed upon us to remain loyal, courageous, and intrepid. And so we should utter with one voice praise to the Good Lord and offer up our gratitude to Him.

Our second cause for thanksgiving is the fact that during these thirty-three years, many of those in prison, labor camps, or other such places, have drunk their cup of suffering to the very dregs, but they have remained faithful and loyal, so that all those religious superiors and Catholic laymen who have been willing to sacrifice their lives for God, they are truly our models of perfect behavior, for they

---

[248] "September 8th " Editorial Board, *Blessings of the Divine Bounty of "September 8th"*, Taipei 1999, p. 129.

can even measure up to the Church of the catacombs, and their witness to the truth of their faith in the early stages of the Church. "The blood of the martyrs is the seed of the Church". Today they wear the laurels of victory, and they intercede for us in Heaven, for they pray that the Church in China can spread their faith as swiftly as possible.

And more especially we wish to pray for all our dearly beloved religious superiors and brothers and sisters in the faith who have withstood for thirty-three years and more the trials and tribulations of loneliness and poverty and who continue to withstand even until this day, all the temptations of suffering for their faith. We pray for their continued perseverance against all odds, uncomplaining and without anxiety, for they believe that it is a privilege and honor to walk the bitter path in the companionship of Christ or to be called upon at any time to testify for their faith in God. We shall not forget them, the entire Church cannot forget them, and our love for them will continue to strengthen them and confirm them in the faith, and to remain constant in their love for God and man. "Blessed are those who are persecuted in the cause of uprightness: the Kingdom of Heaven is theirs" [*Matthew* 5:10].

Furthermore, we still wish to pray for those who have lost their way, or who have fallen by the wayside under serious pressure, and more especially to pray for those who wish to run the Church under total self-autonomy and independence, and for their criminal behavior in consecrating bishops on their own. We pray that they may not cling stubbornly to separation and cleavage, and may return soon to the One, Holy, Catholic, and Apostolic Church, to become again members of one flock under the guardianship of one shepherd.

Finally, we have not yet completed our journey; may all our energies in spreading the Gospel be strengthened and enhanced. Let us pray earnestly to the patron mother of the Shanghai Diocese, our Holy Mother of Mount Sher, protector of the faithful, that she may bestow upon us the same mind and spirit, so that the great design of the Good Lord may be gloriously accomplished on our national soil for generations and generations to come. Amen.

Appendix 16

Cardinal Kung's sermon for Catholics in China, offered in the Church of the Queen of the Angels and Queen of the Martyrs, Rome, Italy, June 30, 1991.[249]

Dear Fathers, Sisters and Catholics of Shanghai, Soochow and Nanking Dioceses, all the dear Chinese Catholics and all the beloved Catholics present here,

I am very happy that today I am in Rome, the Holy City, and that I can celebrate Mass in this Church of the Queen of the Angels and Queen of Martyrs. Today is Sunday and the Mass is that of the thirteenth Sunday of the year. But today is also June 30th, the feast of the First Martyrs of the See of Rome. The Church wants us today in this Mass to commemorate all the martyrs of the first three centuries of the Church's history. Jesus Christ redeemed us by His Passion and Death. The Church He founded was destined to be a suffering Church. Jesus repeatedly and solemnly said to His disciples, "Whoever wants to follow Me, must take up his cross daily and follow me." Again he said, "No disciple is greater than his master. As they treated Me, so they will treat you."

Jesus Christ built His Church on Saint Peter, the Rock. The gates of hell cannot prevail against it. This rock is nothing else but our strong faith in Jesus Christ, our great love for Jesus Christ, a love which will lead us not to hesitate to shed our blood and accept execution. Yesterday, we celebrated the great feast of the martyrdom of Saints Peter and Paul. Today, we celebrate the first martyrs of the first three centuries of the Church. But we must not make the mistake of thinking that the persecution of the Church was an event of past history. No! Never! The Church, from the time of its foundation by Jesus Christ, throughout these two thousand years up to the present time, has always grown and developed amidst persecution. Persecutions began and ended but they never ceased to be a mark of the Church's life.

So we must not be surprised when persecution comes because it is a normal event for the Church to suffer persecution. Once, when Pope Pius XII received a group of seminarians in audience, he asked them how many special signs distinguished the true Church of God? They answered immediately without further thinking, "it is One, Holy, Catholic and Apostolic". The Pope said, "There is a fifth sign" [by which he meant persecution]. The seminarian did not know how to answer. So, if the Church enjoyed peace all the time without any persecution, it would be very abnormal. It would be a reason for us to worry and examine

---

[249] Cardinal Kung Foundation Archives.

ourselves lest anything was going wrong. Perhaps we were not living as faithful disciples of Christ? As persecutions must be expected, it comes as a special sign of the Church and we should not try to make compromises or concessions of any kind in order to bring the persecution to an end quickly. We ourselves cannot take the initiative to create or arouse persecution. But if it comes to us one day, not only should we accept it readily from the hand of God but we should even rejoice and be glad. As the Acts of the Apostles records, ". . . after they were beaten, the Apostles left the Council, full of joy that God had considered them worthy to suffer disgrace for the name of Jesus" [*Acts* 1:41].

During the past 40 years, the Church in China has suffered severe persecution. We have been able to stand in the front line of the Church. This is our glory. We should be glad and rejoice. As the Shanghai Catholic youths said, "We are greatly honored to have been born and lived at this important time, able to bear witness to Christ." Christ sees that we are worthy of this honor and wants us to participate more closely in His work of redemption. As Saint Paul said and as our Holy Father repeated today during the *Angelus* message, "We should fill up in ourselves what is lacking in the Passion of Christ". What a great glory it is for us that we can co-operate with Christ in carrying out His work of redeeming the world.

Also, we should not be frightened when persecution comes, because it is not by our own strength that we conquer the world but by the strength of the glorified Christ who has risen from the dead. He said, "Do not fear, for I have conquered the world". In Russia, during the time of Stalin, one of the Communists attacked the Church mercilessly in a speech he made to the Catholics. When he finished, an old man stood up and said, "The Lord is truly risen! Alleluia!" After saying this, he sat down peacefully. This was the shortest but most powerful reply that could have been made. Jesus has died and risen, He has redeemed the world. We live and die with Him. Our suffering and death will bring forth the fruit of redemption. Jesus said, "If the grain of wheat does not fall into the ground and die, it remains a single grain. But if it dies, it bears abundant fruit" [*Jn.*12: 24]. During the severe persecutions in the Primitive Church, it was said that "The blood of the martyrs is the seed of the Church".

You have come with me to Rome to accompany me to receive the honor of being a Cardinal. The day before yesterday, during the ceremony when the Holy Father gave the red hat to the new Cardinals, he said, "I am deeply moved as I give my greetings to the Churches which have paid the great price of suffering for their faith, to the priests, religious and Catholics. Today, several of the new Cardinals come from those places". From these words, we know that the Holy Father wants to honor through me, the Church in China, to praise its indomitable spirit shown through so much suffering. Yesterday, in the Hall of Pope Paul VI and today in Saint Peter's Square, all the Catholics who had come from many different parts of the world, praised, supported and encouraged in their faith, our suffering Church in China. We should make continued efforts, deepen our love for our holy faith and strive continually to be faithful to the Church.

During the ceremony when the Holy Father gave the red hat, he used the ancient words, "Receive the Red Hat. . . , you must be faithful, steadfast, indomitable, even to the shedding of blood". The Holy Father repeatedly emphasized, "Even to the shedding of blood". From the day when I was officially proclaimed Cardinal, I will make every effort to be faithful to the teachings of the Church, disregarding any sacrifices. Before, I was in prison for 30 years for my faith and it can be said that I only suffered half a martyrdom. I have not yet come to the point of shedding my blood. Now that I wear the Red Hat and have heard what the Holy Father expects from all the Cardinals, although I am old, I must be more vigorous, make more effort, that I may be faithful to Christ, to His Church, to His Vicar on earth unto death, even to the shedding of blood and execution. Please pray for me. Pray for the suffering Church in China!

Appendix 17

Ignatius Cardinal Kung's sermon at the Mass of Possession of his Titular Church, Saint Sixtus II, Rome, Italy, July 1, 1991. [250]

Dear Brother Bishops, Fathers, Sisters and all the Faithful,

There is a special, unique and intimate relationship between every Cardinal and the Bishop of Rome—the Pope. Every Cardinal becomes a "parish priest of Rome" and he has a church of his own although it is only nominal, or his "titular" church. After the Holy Father gave me the red hat of the Cardinal on June 28th, he assigned me to be the parish priest of the Church of Saint Sixtus II. I felt it was a great honor. It has a profound meaning for me that the Pope has assigned me to be honorary parish priest of the Church of Saint Sixtus II, the church of a Pope and martyr.

Saint Sixtus II was Pope during the years 257-259, and suffered martyrdom for the Lord, being buried in Saint Callistus Cemetery. It is said that when he was arrested and was being taken to be executed, he met his deacon, Saint Lawrence, who was waiting for him at the beginning of the Appian Way. Saint Lawrence said to the Pope, "Oh, Father! Why do you go to be executed alone without bringing me with you?" The Pope answered, "Soon you also will be arrested and the martyrdom you will suffer will be greater than mine". And we all know that Saint Lawrence was roasted to death. Later, the bones of Saint Sixtus II and several other popes and bishops were buried in the first little chapel on the left side of this church and there was an old monument in memory of them. We can still see even now the ancient church of the fifth century though it has been repaired during the past fifteen centuries.

Saint Dominic lived here for a period of time and performed at least four important miracles here. He brought three persons back to life. Angels came here to distribute bread in the refectory. The Dominican Sisters here still take their meals in this same refectory. I have become the honorary parish priest of this church so I feel it is a great honor.

With profound significance in his choice, the Pope assigned me to be the honorary parish priest of this church. The Holy Father wants us to understand that the Church has suffered persecution from the very beginning. This was also the main idea of my sermon to the Chinese Catholics to whom I spoke yesterday. The

---

[250] Cardinal Kung Foundation.

Appian Way was one of the chief roads of ancient Rome. Saint Peter, Saint Paul and many other martyrs or confessors traveled along it and left their footprints on that road. Some of them, like Pope Saint Sixtus II left the traces of their chains fastened on their feet. The Roman Church in the third century and the Church in China in the twentieth century are separated by eighteen centuries and are thousands of miles apart, but at the same time, they both have a deeply intimate relationship. Both of them constitute the Church of Christ. Christ founded only one Church on earth, the Church built on Saint Peter, the Rock. In both places, the Church was destined to be persecuted.

It is my deep hope that now when I have come to Rome to receive the honor of being a Cardinal still deeper bonds will be forged with the See of Peter. As I was nominated to be the honorary parish priest of Saint Sixtus II, thus drawing even closer, the bonds uniting us with the See of Rome, we pray to be faithful unto death, as the Holy Father said, "We do not hesitate to shed our blood. The blood may be shed, the head may be cut off but our union with the Pope can never be broken". This is my last word to you. May God bless you!

10369599R00117

Printed in Great Britain
by Amazon